Affective Mapping

Affective Mapping

MELANCHOLIA AND THE POLITICS
OF MODERNISM

JONATHAN FLATLEY

HARVARD UNIVERSITY PRESS

Cambridge, Massachusetts, and London, England   2008

Library of Congress Cataloging-in-Publication Data

Flatley, Jonathan.
    Affective mapping : melancholia and the politics of modernism / Jonathan Flatley.
        p. cm.
    Includes bibliographical references and index.
    ISBN-13: 978-0-674-03078-7 (alk. paper)
    1. American literature—19th century—History and criticism. 2. American
literature—20th century—History and criticism. 3. Melancholy in literature.
4. James, Henry, 1843–1916. Turn of the screw. 5. Du Bois, W. E. B. (William
Edward Burghardt), 1868–1963. Souls of Black folk. 6. Platonov, Andrei Platonovich,
1899–1951. Chevengur. 7. Melancholy—Social aspects. 8. Modernism (Literature)
I. Title.
    PS214.F57 2008
    810.9'353—dc22   2007052771

Contents

Affective Mapping

Introduction

Melancholize

They get their knowledge by books, I mine by
melancholizing.

—ROBERT BURTON, *ANATOMY OF MELANCHOLY*

The writing of this book originated in my desire to explain something
that seemed simultaneously self-evident and poorly understood. That is:
not all melancholias are depressing. More precisely, if by melancholia
we mean an emotional attachment to something or someone lost, such
dwelling on loss need not produce depression, that combination of in-
communicable sorrow and isolating grief that results in the loss of interest in other persons, one's own actions, and often life itself. In fact, some
melancholias are the opposite of depressing, functioning as the very
mechanism through which one may be interested in the world. This
book is about these non- or antidepressive melancholias.

Even as understandings of melancholia have changed, the basic clus-
ter of symptoms (sadness, grief, fear, affective withdrawal, loss of interest) it describes has remained relatively consistent.[1] Likewise, whether
melancholia has been seen to stem from physiological imbalances (too
much black bile or *melaina-kole*), astrological misfortune (born under
the sign of Saturn), failures of faith (the sin of *acedia* or sloth), or unmourned losses, also persistent has been a sense that there may be a
valuable aspect of this condition.[2] Within the discourse of melancholia
we find a dialectic between emotional withdrawal and its apparent opposite, the most intense or exceptional devotion of affective energy.
Thus, for example, the Aristotelian *Problemata* asks: "Why do all men
of extraordinary ability in the field of philosophy or politics or literature or the arts prove to be melancholics?"[3] Or, moving to the seventeenth century, in his *Anatomy of Melancholy*, Robert Burton affirms

the knowledge that might be produced by the creative contemplation uniquely facilitated by melancholy states: "They get their knowledge by books, I mine by melancholizing."[4] The word Burton uses here, *melancholize,* long since out of use, suggests that melancholy might not just be a mood state into which one falls, or which descends on one like bad weather. Instead, melancholizing is something one *does:* longing for lost loves, brooding over absent objects and changed environments, reflecting on unmet desires, and lingering on events from the past. It is a practice that might, in fact, produce its own kind of knowledge.

This book is concerned with a particular mode of modernist melancholizing. My analysis centers on three distinct texts: Henry James's *Turn of the Screw* (1898), W. E. B. Du Bois's *Souls of Black Folk* (1903), and Andrei Platonov's *Chevengur* (1928).[5] What melancholizing produces for James, Du Bois, and Platonov is the knowledge of the historical origins of their melancholias, and thus at the same time of the others with whom these melancholias might be shared. This knowledge, an "affective map," this book argues, is what, for them and for their readers, makes possible the conversion of a depressive melancholia into a way to be interested in the world.

Several things distinguish late nineteenth- and early twentieth-century understandings of melancholia from earlier ones. Most significant is the connection made around that time between depressive melancholia and the problem of *loss,* a connection crystallized in Freud's now famous argument first outlined in his 1917 essay "Mourning and Melancholia."[6] Briefly, Freud argued there that the mood state long associated with melancholia was caused by the failure to mourn a loss. Instead of mourning, which Freud saw as a kind of libidinal decathection from the lost object, the melancholic internalizes the lost object into his or her very subjectivity as a way of refusing to let the loss go. (I examine the twists and turns, revisions and contradictions of Freud's theory in Chapter 1.) In laying out this paradigm, I argue, Freud is not so much correcting or improving (as he supposed) our view of melancholia as giving us in his theory of melancholia an allegory for the experience of modernity, an experience (as I will discuss) that is constitutively linked to loss.[7] In this, Freud is responding to the same problem as James, Du Bois, and Platonov: he seeks to find an aesthetic practice that could change one relation to loss into another, which in his case is the practice of psychoanalysis itself.

Where Freud was concerned to develop a universal theory of melancholy that would enable analysts to help patients arrive at individual

cures, Walter Benjamin saw melancholia as a definitely historical problem related to the experience of modernity. In this view melancholia is
no longer a personal problem requiring cure or catharsis, but is evidence of the historicity of one's subjectivity, indeed the very substance
of that historicity. In his connection of melancholia to the historical experience of modernity, Benjamin helps me to outline the conception of
melancholia implicit to the practices of James, Du Bois, and Platonov.
For these authors, insofar as the losses at the source of individual
melancholias are seen to be generated by historical processes such as
white supremacy (Du Bois), the mass cultural reification of the literary
sphere combined with the reification of identity accompanying the invention of homosexuality (James), or the upheaval generated by war
and revolution (Platonov), melancholia comes to define the locus of the
"psychic life of power" (to borrow an evocative phrase from Judith
Butler), the place where modernity touches down in our lives in the
most intimate of ways.[8] As such, melancholia forms the site in which
the social origins of our emotional lives can be mapped out and from
which we can see the other persons who share our losses and are subject
to the same social forces. We might say that the melancholic concern
with loss creates the mediating structure that enables a slogan—"The
personal is political"—to become a historical-aesthetic methodology.
This methodology's questions are: Whence these losses to which I have
become attached? What social structures, discourses, institutions,
processes have been at work in taking something valuable away from
me? With whom do I share these losses or losses like them? What are
the historical processes in which this moment of loss participates—in
other words: how long has my misery been in preparation? These are
the questions, *Affective Mapping* argues, that must find their way into
the heart of an aesthetic practice if it is, in Walter Benjamin's words, to
"arm one" instead of "causing sorrow."[9]

In writing about this distinctly modern antidepressive melancholia, I
aim to contribute to the project Nietzsche called for when he lamented
in *The Gay Science* that we lack a history of the passions: "All kinds of
individual passions have to be thought through and pursued through
different ages, peoples, great and small individuals . . . so far all that has
given color to existence, still lacks a history."[10] Nietzsche wonders how
we can understand things such as friendship or marriage, punishment
or asceticism without an examination of the function of affect in these
formations. Although he did not, he might have spoken as well of the
specific experiences of modernization—urbanization, industrialization,

colonialization and imperialism, modern warfare, the invention of "race," the advent of the modern commodity and mass culture, the emergence of modern discourses of gender and sexuality, and the pathologization of homosexuality. How can we understand the nature and the impact of such historical processes without some sense of how they work on and through affect? It is not hard to see (whether we are thinking, for instance, of *Les Fleurs du Mal, Ulysses, Mrs. Dalloway,* "The Waste Land," *The Weary Blues, Nightwood,* or *The Trial*) that many modernist attempts to find a way to represent the experiences of modernity have done so by being especially attentive to the affective—as distinct from the cognitive or the corporeal for example—components of modern experience. Indeed, behind the extraordinary level of aesthetic experimentation that we sometimes call "modernism" we can see the desire to find a way to map out and get a grasp on the new affective terrain of modernity. In doing so, such modernisms have been concerned not only with the affective impact of modernization but also with the ways the social forces of modernity work *through* emotions, the ways we become the subjects that we are by the structuring of our affective attachments.

+

"Affective mapping" is the name I am giving to the aesthetic technology—in the older, more basic sense of a *techne*—that represents the historicity of one's affective experience. In mapping out one's affective life and its historicity, a political problem (such as racism or revolution) that may have been previously invisible, opaque, difficult, abstract, and above all depressing may be transformed into one that is interesting, that solicits and rewards one's attention. This transformation can take place, I argue, not only because the affective map gives one a new sense of one's relationship to broad historical forces but also inasmuch as it shows one how one's situation is experienced collectively by a community, a heretofore unarticulated community of melancholics. Of course, this does not mean that collective consciousness *necessarily* follows—the functioning of the strands of collective affective attachment is a complicated topic in itself—but I do argue that the desire for that consciousness is always implicit in the writing of an affective map, and it lies nascent there for the motivated reader to take up.

I propose that we understand the task of turning one's melancholia into a mode of vital connection with the world as changing one's "mood." By "mood" I mean Heidegger's *Stimmung*, which has also been translated as "attunement."[11] One's *Stimmung*, for Heidegger, is one's primary way of being in the world, "the 'presupposition' for, and 'medium' of thinking and acting" (FCM, 68). That is, one's *Stimmung* is one's way of having certain things in that world matter to one; it is the atmosphere in which intentions are formed, projects pursued, and particular affects can attach to particular objects. Ontologically, Heidegger insists, *Stimmung* "is a primordial kind of Being for Dasein, in which Dasein is disclosed to itself *prior* to all cognition and volition and *beyond* their range of disclosure" (BT, 175). For *Dasein* (literally "being there," Heidegger's word for "a being," in the sense of a human being who necessarily finds itself in some "there"), everything about one's being-in-the-world is filtered through and founded on one's mood. And because we never find ourselves nowhere, because we always already find ourselves somewhere specific, we are never not in a mood; to be in the world is to be in a mood. We find ourselves in moods that have already been inhabited by others, that have already been shaped or put into circulation, and that are already there around us. As Charles Guignon puts it, "as we grow up in the social order into which we are thrown, we also become masters of a determinate range of possible moods that are 'accepted' in our world."[12] I will say more about *Stimmung* shortly (in the Glossary), but the point to make here is that depression is the *Stimmung* in which the world and the people in it seem incapable of sustaining one's interest or desire. And as anyone who has been depressed knows, one cannot simply *decide* to see the world differently. Changing one's *Stimmung* is not simply a matter of will or decision. Rather, one must invoke or awaken a "counter-mood," a task for which aesthetic activities of various kinds have long been a resource.

The kind of aesthetic practice I am concerned with here, however, is quite particular in its relation to melancholic moods. It is neither cathartic, compensatory, nor redemptive—probably the most commonly encountered ideas about the uses of aesthetics in relation to melancholia. In such views, art may be seen to transcend the exigencies of everyday life in the realm of beauty, or to relieve repressed emotions through a cathartic release. (In fact, as Herbert Marcuse argued in his essay "The Affirmative Character of Culture," this compensatory mode may be seen historically as the dominant Western mode of aesthetic experience in general.) This is a tradition that perhaps peaked in the Romantic period and which still produced powerful results within what is sometimes called "high modernism."[13] To this day it is probably the dominant discourse about the relationship between melancholia and aesthetics.[14]

The publication of Charles Baudelaire's *Fleurs du Mal* in 1857 represents a turning point in the history of the relationship between melancholia and aesthetics. With Baudelaire, we see the emergence of a decidedly antitherapeutic melancholic poetry. Its aim is not to make you "feel better" or to redeem damaged experiences but to redirect your attention to those very experiences. One leaves Baudelaire's poetry not relieved of grief but aggrieved, clearer about what the losses at the origin of one's grief might be and what or whom may to be to blame for them. At the same time, however, as in "A Une Passante," for example, we are shown how one's losses might be a secret source of connection, interest, and perhaps even pleasure. Baudelaire's could be called a splenetic modernism, for it is his task to transform *ennui,* that "monstre delicat" that renders the world incapable of sustaining emotional involvement, into *spleen:* a state in which one is exceedingly aware of, angry about, and interested in the losses one has suffered. For Baudelaire, it would seem, feeling those losses, losses that in Baudelaire as much as in Freud have penetrated into the very structure of subjectivity, is the only way to be attuned to the unavoidably melancholic nature of modern life.[15]

Walter Benjamin wrote that the "decisive ferment" that allows the transformation from *ennui* into *spleen* is "self-estrangement," and I make a similar claim about the antidepressive effects of the affective map.[16] I take Benjamin to mean self-estrangement first of all in the sense of being able to treat oneself as an object, so that one is able to subject one's emotional life to analysis, reflection, and direction. One must be self-consciously alienated from one's emotional life for it to become historical datum. But I also read estrangement in the sense of the Russian formalist *ostraneniye* or Brechtian "alienation effect": making strange or defamiliarizing. My own emotional life must appear unfamiliar, not-mine, at least for a moment, if I am to see its relation to a historical context. The idea is to allow one's emotions to lose their invisibility and necessity and become instead contingent, surprising, relative. Thus, for example, by way of the experience of loss, Baudelaire identifies alternately with widow and ragpicker, lesbian and drunk. Through poetic identification with this surprising and apparently diverse set of characters, Baudelaire defamiliarizes the experience of loss, lack, and alienation they all share, allegorizing for him and for us elements of the melancholic nature of his own life and of modern experience more generally.

What I am calling an affective map is essentially a mobile machine of self-estrangement. James, Du Bois, and Platonov not only give a narrative or representation of a particular structure of feeling, they seek to produce a particular kind of affective experience in their readers, and at the same time to narrate this very experience. In other words, the affective map narrates the production of its own reader. Thus, for example, in *The Turn of the Screw,* Henry James solicits a kind of epistemological interest from his readers by leaving the reality of the ghosts and the sanity of the governess textually indeterminable. The reader must guess or "read into" (in James's words) the text to come to any kind of "knowledge" about the ghosts or the governess. At the same time, the story narrates just such an epistemological interest on the part of the governess herself, who is reading into the behavior of the children to try to get at the truth of their intercourse with the ghosts. This will to knowledge on the part of the governess rhymes with the reader's own, and reproduces the eponymous phenomenon described by Foucault in relation to the knowledge of sexual identity. In a direct allegorical gesture, this pursuit ends in the death of Miles. In this way, James provides a nugget of affective experience for the reader, one with direct historical resonance and relevance, and then also tells the reader something about that experience within the narrative itself. In essence, the reader has an affective experience within the space of the text, one that repeats or recalls earlier, other experiences, and then is estranged from that experience, and by way of that estrangement told or taught something about it. This is the moment of affective mapping.

I mean "mapping" here, I should emphasize, in a slightly unexpected manner. That is, the affective map is not a stable representation of a more or less unchanging landscape; it is a map less in the sense that it establishes a territory than that it is about providing a feeling of orientation and facilitating mobility. I mean the term to suggest something essentially revisable; when it works, it is a technology for the representation to oneself of one's own historically conditioned and changing affective life. In this sense, it is a map in the sense proposed by Gilles Deleuze and Felix Guattari in *A Thousand Plateaus,* when they distinguish the rhizomatic map from the tracing: the rhizome is open, connectable in multiple directions, related to the real in an experimental fashion. (I discuss all of this in more detail in Chapter 2.) The revisable, rhizomatic affective map not only gives us a view of a terrain shared with others in the present but also traces the paths, resting places, dead ends, and detours we might share with those who came before us.

For better or worse, this book follows a fairly standard organizing principle: in the first part I explain and contextualize the book's key concepts and its methodology, and in the second part I make use of these concepts in readings of a range of texts. Of course, the book was not written in this order; I only figured out what concepts were important and what method I was using by way of these readings, and I hope that some of the tension and conversation between the more abstract thinking about concepts and methodology and the readings of particular texts remains legible.

Before anything else, I explain some key terms—mood, structure of feeling, affect, emotion—in a kind of glossary. Then, in a long first chapter, I briefly sketch out the relationship between melancholia and modernity, and the place of modernism therein, and lay out the concepts and arguments from Freud and Benjamin that will be useful for the rest of the book. I examine Freud's theory of melancholia in relation to the long history of theories of melancholia, proposing that we see psychoanalysis as itself a modernist aesthetic practice. My sense of the distinction between a depressive, depoliticized melancholia and a non-depressing, politicizing melancholia probably owes more to Walter Benjamin's "On the Concept of History" than to any other text. In this first chapter I read this text, with others by Benjamin, to elaborate my approach to this distinction and also to lay out the reading of Benjamin's take on melancholia, which will remain axiomatic for the rest of the book.

In Chapter 2, I elaborate this notion of the affective map, drawing on the use of this term and of cognitive mapping in environmental psychology and urban planning—the context from which Fredric Jameson adopted the concept of cognitive mapping, bringing it into the sphere of literary theory. Then, borrowing from Adorno's ideas about the "aesthetic shudder," I explain a bit more carefully than earlier what I mean by affective mapping.

From here I move to the primary literary texts. These texts are by no means the only ones I might have written about; Djuna Barnes and Nella Larsen, for example, are other figures I considered. But, besides the fact that James, Du Bois, and Platonov are all authors in my fields of specialization, I have also chosen them strategically as authors who may in one way or another be representative, foundational, or paradigmatic. Henry James is, of course, central to the Anglo-American tradition. And because one of the earliest texts of psychoanalytic literary criticism, "The Ambiguity of Henry James," by Edmund Wilson, focused on this story, and Shoshana Felman's rereading of Wilson's reading has been an important essay in the establishment of a new, more sophisticated, Lacanian deconstructive criticism, *The Turn of the Screw* in particular is a classic text of psychoanalytic criticism. It is thus an ideal site to engage with and historicize psychoanalytic thought. Du Bois's *Souls of Black Folk* is foundational for African American letters as aesthetic theory, literary performance, and political, sociological, and psychological analysis, as is well known and much remarked. And Platonov, although very poorly known outside of the Russian reading public (in part because of the difficulty of translating his work, due to its experimental character), is widely acknowledged within that public to be one of (if not *the*) most important Russian writers of the twentieth century.[17] *Chevengur* is his only full-length novel (although he did write several short novels or "tales"). Of the three, Chapter 3 is the shortest, as I wanted to provide a quickly graspable example of the mode of reading I am proposing. A final note on the chapters: knowing how most people read books (or at least how I do), I have tried to write the chapters so that they can usefully be read without reading the chapters that precede them. This means that, occasionally, I repeat myself regarding some point or other from Benjamin, Freud, or Heidegger so that the reader need not go back to an earlier section in order to make sense of whatever local argument I am making about the text at hand.

This is a comparative book. Even though Henry James read *The Souls of Black Folk,* and Du Bois studied with Henry's brother William and would later become interested in Freud and the Soviet Union and Marxism, and Platonov had recently read Freud when he wrote *Chevengur,* this is not a book about influence, about the social or institutional formations of modernism, or about sites of transnational contact or communication.[18] I am not making any claim about actual contact or influence between or among these authors.

That is to say, I am interested only in their shared approach to aesthetic activity as a response to the losses generated by the experience of modernity. I hope through the juxtaposition of these different figures to suggest that they are all responding to distinct but nonetheless parallel experiences of modernization. While it is outside of this book's scope to *prove* such a case, I want to propose that the problem with loss, with the loss that cannot be mourned, is common to the experience of modernity in general. The point is not that modernity is experienced everywhere in the same way but that the experiences *are* similar, and that melancholia is one site where we can perceive more finely the particularities as well as the similarities among the different experiences of modernity.

Glossary

Affect, Emotion, Mood *(Stimmung)*, Structure of Feeling

The vocabulary of affect can be confusing, in part because there are many terms—*affect, emotion, feeling, passion, mood*—and a long history of debate not only about which terms are the right ones and how to distinguish between them, but about what they mean in the first place. And while there is a great deal of excellent recent work on affect in several disciplines (including literary studies, history, philosophy, psychology, psychiatry, sociology, cognitive science, and neurobiology),[1] this does not mean that a general consensus, or even a common conversation, has emerged. While providing a map of the terrain opened up by this new work is a task beyond the scope of this book, I hope it will be helpful at least to gloss the terms this book uses and give a sense of the theoretical traditions to which I am most indebted.[2] There are four such terms: *affect, emotion, mood* (or *Stimmung*), and *structure of feeling*. What I aim to provide here is nothing so ambitious as a "theory of affect" but, rather, the understanding of these terms that I will take as axiomatic for the rest of the book. Because this part of the book endeavors to summarize a body of material for the reader who is not familiar with it, readers more acquainted with recent work on affect may wish to skip sections they find covering material they already know.

Affect and Emotion

In the long history of work on affect and emotion, sometimes the two terms are taken to be synonymous, other times a sharp difference is asserted, and in both cases the meaning of the terms is and has been highly variable. In everyday usage, while the words are often interchangeable, there are significant connotative differences. Where *emotion* suggests something that happens inside and tends toward outward expression, *affect* indicates something relational and transformative.[3] One *has* emotions; one is affected *by* people or things. Although a strong conceptual distinction between affect and emotion is not central to this book's argument, I exercise a preference for *affect* as the more useful term and precise concept in part because it is the relational more than the expressive I am interested in. For the most part, however, it seems least confusing to follow everyday usage of the two terms (that is, more or less synonymous but with the aforementioned connotative differences) and to be explicit about it when I think a difference between them needs to be emphasized.

In the effort to establish a working definition of affect/emotion, Aristotle offers a useful starting place. He defines the emotions as "those feelings that so change men as to affect their judgments, and that are also attended by pain or pleasure. Such are anger, pity, fear, and the like, with their opposites."[4] In this understanding, emotions describe a moment when one's experience of the world is altered in a way that affects one's judgment of that world. Together, the emotions constitute one of our basic ways of establishing value, of assessing or judging our world, often prior to cognition or will. In many ways, Silvan Tomkins, whose theory of the affects I more or less follow, is elaborating this Aristotelian understanding when he writes: "It is our theory of value that for human subjects value is any object of human affect. Whatever one is excited by, enjoys, fears, hates, is ashamed of, is contemptuous of, or is distressed by is an object of value, positive or negative" (SIS, 68).[5]

Tomkins argued for treating the affects as a kind of irreducible "motivation system" or "assembly," one that inevitably interacts with but is nonetheless distinct from the drives, from strictly physiological factors, from perception, and from elements of "cognition" such as belief, thought, and choice. Like visual perception or the reasoning mind, the affects have an internal logic—a systematicity—all their own.

In attributing centrality and specificity to the affects, Tomkins seeks to displace the psychoanalytic emphasis on the drives or instincts as the primary sources of human motivation. Freud, who never really developed a coherent account of the affects, often treated them as the quantitative energy stemming from the drives, a kind of undifferentiated intensity that is given form and content by the ideas or objects to which they were attached. (See Chapter 1 for more on Freud and affect.) On the whole, however, Freud was not really interested in affect as a thing in itself, attributing basic human motivation and evaluation instead to the libido (or, depending on the period of his career one is considering, other instincts such as the death drive). And although he does offer very interesting considerations of the "emotional tie" (also discussed later), even here his account suffers from lack of explanation of the specific affects that may comprise this tie.

For Tomkins, one of the key differences separating the affects from the drives was their degree of freedom in object and duration; for example, one can be terrified of anything, for any amount of time, but can only breathe air, and cannot do without it for very long. Affects are not necessarily attached to any one object, indeed can attach to any object, and are free to modify each other and to change one's experience of the drives as well. Tomkins notes, for example, that "the panic of one who experiences the suffocation of interruption of his vital air supply has nothing to do with the anoxic drive signal per se," but is the result of the amplifying effects of fear.[6] Similarly, the sexual drive could just as easily be diminished by shame, anxiety, or boredom as increased by excitement.

It is, of course, not just Freud to whom Tomkins is responding. In some ways his emphasis on the specific "feeling" of affects, as well as their rootedness in physiological phenomena—facial behavior above all—recalls the famous theory proposed by William James, who held that emotions were essentially the "feeling" of a bodily change or state. James writes: "My thesis . . . is that the bodily changes follow directly the PERCEPTION of the exciting fact, and that our feeling of the same changes as they occur IS the emotion."[7] Thus, for example (and counterintuitively), weeping did not follow on sadness, but the reverse: sadness *was* the feeling of weeping, happiness was the feeling of smiling, and so forth. In this view, one cannot have an emotion without the corresponding bodily change—the surge of adrenaline, hair on end, rush of blood to the face—and one's qualitative experience of that change is the emotion itself. While Tomkins does pick up on the connection between affects and facial/bodily movements in exploring the particularity of each affect, unlike James, Tomkins would always insist on the autonomy of affect, the extent to which the affects could not be understood exclusively in terms of this bodily response.

During Tomkins's career, the Jamesian theory was challenged most forcefully by what had come to be called a "cognitive" view of emotion. In the 1960s, the work of Stanley Schachter and Jerome Singer signaled a shift toward this perspective.[8] Schachter and Singer conducted a series of studies in which they injected subjects with adrenaline in different contexts, finding that the emotion the subjects "experienced" depended on the interpretation or label they imposed on the physiological change. They hypothesized that an emotion is a relatively undifferentiated physiological arousal combined with a cognitive interpretation of it. To simplify and generalize, this view, which has been extensively developed not only in cognitive psychology but also in Anglo-American philosophy, is interested in the ways emotions get their "content" from the ideas, beliefs, thoughts, expectations, or other "cognitive" aspects of consciousness that modify corporeal affects. Part of the motivation behind this argument appears to be a desire to defend emotions as rational, not simply "dumb" or undifferentiated physiological phenomena.[9] Tomkins, although he was no less insistent (than defenders of a cognitive theory of emotion) on the internal complexity of affect, always maintained that the affects had their own specificity. Thus, he was an early and energetic critic of the cognitive position, writing that "surely no one who has experienced joy at one time and rage at another time would suppose that radically different feelings were the same except for different 'interpretations' placed on similar 'arousals.'"[10] Affects, in Tomkins's view, are not productively examined in terms of a body-mind dichotomy; they occur neither in mind nor body but in an assemblage, network, or system that is not comprehensible in terms of its corporeal or cognitive component parts.[11]

Recent research on the brain, as described by Joseph Le Doux and Antonio Damasio, supports Tomkins's case for the specificity of affect from another angle. Le Doux, for example, argues for "emotion and cognition . . . as separate but interacting mental functions mediated by separate but interacting brain systems."[12] That affect systems can operate independently from at least some elements of cognition such as object perception and recognition and reasoning is evinced by examinations of a range of brain-damaged patients who lose capacity in an area of the brain that limits their capacity for emotional processing without any effect on their cognitive faculties. Their research also suggests that many affective responses take place automatically, before reasoning, deliberation, or other cognitive functions can begin.[13]

Some recent research also seems to confirm Tomkins's view that there are basic, more or less universal affects that are linked to corresponding facial expressions and other autonomic bodily responses.[14] The case for innate emotions had been made earlier by Darwin, and has been bolstered more recently by the crosscultural research on facial recognition by Paul Ekman and Carrol Izard.[15] Although Ekman set out to prove that affects were in fact culturally constructed, he found that basic facial expressions, and understandings of the situations likely to produce such expressions, were surprisingly consistent across cultural contexts.[16] What was variable, he found, were "display rules": the norms and habits through which people manage their emotional expressions. In other words, while everyone may know what a smile is, or recognize the look of disgust, people can still learn to suppress or modify these facial responses.

Even more culturally variable than display rules are the ways affects combine with their objects. If certain affects are basic, what are not at all basic are the ways our affects are educated as to which objects are right for which affects in which situations (i.e., one should be ashamed of this, but angry about that, disgusted by this other thing, but only if other people are present, and so on). Thus, to claim that there are some basic affects does not mean that people's experience of these affects is not variable, just that there are elements of invariable, autonomic affective response that we all share. Consequently, an insistence on the irreducibility or universality of certain affects does not necessarily contradict an anthropological or sociological emphasis on the constructedness and diversity of emotions and emotional expression.[17]

In arguing that affects operate according to their own specific logic Tomkins borrowed from cybernetics and systems theory. Put simply, systems theory replaces the model of a whole made out of parts with a model in which systems interact with environments. The basic principle of the system is the distinction between an inside (the system) and an outside (the environment) and the establishment of a "feedback mechanism" or "feedback loop" that takes in (input) the results of an act (output) in order to modify the initial act.[18] The thermostat, for example, is the mechanism by which a heating/cooling system regulates itself, by testing the results of its acts (the turning on or off of the furnace) and takes it back in as information to determine what to do next (the turning on or off of the furnace). The thermostat, like any feedback mechanism, is monologic; it does its work by seeing everything else—the "environment"—only on the terms relevant to the system; nothing about the world matters to the thermostat except the temperature.

Thus, like all systems, affects reduce "infinite to finite information loads" through a kind of functional simplification.[19] As many theorists of affect have noted, affects serve the valuable function of focusing our attention on something very specific—such as a danger, a loss, or the presence or absence of a smile on the face of an interlocutor.[20] Each affect is a very particular filter: some stuff gets in and gets tested by a feedback mechanism, and other stuff is irrelevant. In a real sense, when one is experiencing shame, a different world is being perceived than when one is joyful or fearful.

Because the reason for the system's coming into being is precisely to cope with an environment, all systems are always interacting with other ones. By definition, although the system is totalizing and monologic in its own space, it is never singular. Deleuze and Guattari, using the rhetoric of the machine to explain this systemic logic, write that "one machine is always coupled with another . . . a connection with another machine is always established, along a transverse path."[21] Affects are always amplifying, dampening, or otherwise modifying some other affect, or drive, or perception, or thought process, or act or behavior, resulting in a well-nigh infinite number of combinations between different affective microsystems and their feedback mechanisms in interaction with their environments.

In contrast to affects, then, we might distinguish emotions as the result of the inevitable interaction of affects with thoughts, ideas, beliefs, habits, instincts, and other affects. If affects are not reducible, emotions are, and it is emotions that vary from context to context, person to person.[22] Thus, for example, if we posited joy and interest as basic affects, we might say then that love is an emotion, inasmuch as it includes joy and interest, along with certain ideas about what love is, what a love relationship should look like over a period of time, whom one should or should not feel love toward, expectations or hopes of reciprocity, and so forth. Likewise, shame would be an affect and guilt an emotion, inasmuch as guilt implies the acceptance of or belief in some kind of moral code that has been broken, whereas shame is the momentary reaction to the interruption of an emotional relation. That is, I am not claiming that the attitudes we have about our affects do not affect our experience of that affect, only that the affect itself has an irreducible systematicity that must be taken into account in any analysis of it.

✦

Strictly speaking, affects (unlike moods, for example) are always experienced in relation to an object or objects. Indeed, affects need objects to come into being. They are in this sense intentional. However, the objects that affects can take are limitless, including other affects, ideas, and imaginary or implicit objects. There is no kind of object that has not at one time or another been linked to one or another of the affects, and thought, of course, greatly expands this range of objects: "Although affects which are activated by drives and by special releasers have a limited range of objects, the linkage of affects to objects through thinking enormously extends the range of the objects of positive and negative feeling" (SIS, 54).

Part of what is interesting about the intentional aspect of affects is that they produce a kind of subject-object confusion. Between an affect and its object there is what Tomkins calls a "somewhat fluid relationship." That is, it is often difficult to tell whether the affect originates in the object or the affect produces the object.[23] Am I interested in this because it is interesting or because I have interest that needs to go somewhere? Here, as I will discuss shortly, mood is an important concept as well, as a kind of state of readiness for some affects and not others (i.e., in an irritable mood some things are annoying that otherwise may not be).

This "somewhat fluid relationship" can make it difficult to tell where in fact the affect happens, or whether the subject-object distinction holds up at the moment of being-affected. This was one of the reasons Walter Benjamin was interested in affectively charged, emotionally rich experience (one of the significant aspects for him of experience in the *Erfahrung* as opposed to *Erlebnis* sense).[24] In this passage from "One Way Street," Benjamin speculates that love does not exist in one's head (or one's heart, for that matter) but in the specific materiality of the object of love.

> He who loves is attached not only to the "faults" of the beloved, not only to the whims and weaknesses of a woman. Wrinkles in the face, moles, shabby clothes, and a lopsided walk bind him more lastingly and relentlessly than any beauty. This has long been known. And why? If the theory is correct that feeling is not located in the head, that we sentiently experience a window, a cloud, a tree, not in our brains but rather in the place where we see it, then we are, in looking at our beloved, too, outside ourselves. But in a torment of tension and ravishment. Our feeling, dazzled, flutters like a flock of birds in the woman's radiance. And as birds seek refuge in the leafy recesses of a tree, feelings escape into the shaded wrinkles, the awkward movements and inconspicuous blemishes of the body we love, where they can lie low in safety. And no passer by would guess that it is just here, in what is defective and censurable, that the fleeting darts of adoration nestle.[25]

If sensory feeling *(Empfindung)*, Benjamin hypothesizes, is not experienced in the brain, but in the materiality of the place, then affect travels along the material paths of sensation to find a dwelling place. And here, it is as if beauty is too abstract and generalized; because it produces an overall effect that "dazzles" one, it cannot provide a nestling place for the "fleeting darts of adoration." Thus, Benjamin's feelings locate themselves in the more material and particular wrinkles and lopsided walks. For Benjamin, experiences of affective attachment are interesting because they put us—precisely at those moments when we care most, when we feel the value of something—"outside of ourselves." In a similar way, Proust found that crucial experiences from his childhood were locked in tea-soaked madeleine, because in a sense the experience is located in that madeleine. Powerful emotional experiences—quite different from more cognitively mediated ones—connect us with, even transport us *into* the materiality of the world around us. In fact, Benjamin contended that because affects come into being through attachment, and because they actually occur in the materiality of the world, affective experience can provide us with a link—unmediated by concepts—to that material world.[26] This has far-reaching implications not only for Benjamin's analysis of aesthetic experience but also for his historical practice, and the hopes he placed in the possibility of political transformation, as I will discuss.

By way of contrast, we might briefly examine the theory of the emotions offered in Sartre's book *The Emotions: Outline of a Theory.* There, Sartre holds that emotions are a form of consciousness that arises in relation to thwarted will.[27] We have an emotion, he writes, when "the paths traced out become too difficult, or when we see no path, we can no longer live in so urgent and difficult a world. All the ways are barred. However, we must act. So we try to change the world, that is, to live as if the connection between things and their potentialities were not ruled by deterministic processes, but by magic."[28] Emotion is a magical transformation of the world whereby we trick ourselves into thinking that the world is other than it is, rather than accept that our will is thwarted. It is a sour grapes theory of emotion—we want some grapes, we can't reach them, so instead we become disgusted by their sourness. And in a sense, a real transformation does take place—except it is our own body that is transformed rather than the world: our body actually experiences that disgust.[29] Because emotions thereby act not on the *world* but on the *body*, they represent (in a prefiguring of bad faith) an escapist, ineffective, corrupted form of consciousness.[30]

Clearly Benjamin is quite far from Sartre. Where Benjamin sees emotion as the chief characteristic of experience in its "strict sense" (i.e., *Erfahrung*), for Sartre emotion is a kind of false, ineffective experience. And whereas emotion for Benjamin is a mechanism of attachment to the material world, for Sartre it is precisely the entry into a completely imaginary world. Nothing, as it were, could be *less* political for Sartre, since emotions are the barrier to effective action in the world.

In sum, I take as axiomatic, then, the following: affects are irreducible, in the sense that they operate according to their own systemic logic; they involve a transformation of one's way of being in the world, in a way that determines what matters to one; affects require objects, and, in the moment of attaching to an object or happening in the object, also take one's being outside of one's subjectivity.

Mood *(Stimmung)*

This book argues that there is a set of aesthetic practices concerned with the transformation of one mood, or *Stimmung* (e.g., depression), into another (a mode of vital connection with the world). Following Heidegger, I take "mood" to refer to a kind of affective atmosphere, as I remarked earlier, in which intentions are formed, projects pursued, and particular affects can attach to particular objects.[31] If I am anxious, for instance, things in the world are more likely to appear as fearful; only when I am curious can new objects present themselves to me as interesting. Whether I am enthusiastic, eager, confident, irritable, despairing, jubilant, indifferent, excited, or nervous—in any one of these moods different objects will come into my emotional view, different memories will come to mind, and some tasks will seem possible or attractive while others will not present themselves at all. In a real way, our mood creates the world in which we exist at any given moment. In this sense it is objectless: we don't have a mood about any one thing in particular but, rather, about everything in general. Furthermore, even or especially when a mood seems to be isolating in effect (as in depression) it is always a plural phenomenon; we all only have access to the moods that we find around us, the moods into which we have been educated, and the moods that have been shaped or determined by the concrete historical context in which we coexist.[32]

As a concept, mood provides a way to articulate the shaping and structuring effect of historical context on our affective attachments. In fact, extrapolating from Heidegger, we can say that it is on the level of mood that historical forces most directly intervene in our affective lives and through mood that these forces may become apparent to us. Like-wise, it is through the changing of mood that we are most able to exert agency on our own singular and collective affective lives; and it is by way of mood that we can find or create the opportunity for collective political projects.

Heidegger's case for the foundational quality of *Stimmung* is directly related to his broader project. Part of Heidegger's argument about human 'being' is that we always find ourselves somewhere, in a given 'there' (thus *Dasein*, being-there). That is, we find ourselves in a particular world or historical context that, as Charles Guignon puts it, "provides us with a determinate range of possible roles and self-determinations."[33] Thus, for example, in a society where the class divisions are feudal, the possi-bility of a proletarian consciousness does not present itself. We are all thrust not just into specific historical contexts but are placed in a given position therein. Du Bois finds himself in a white supremacist world in which he is "black," Henry James in a world where the kind of writing he had been doing loses, with some suddenness, its public. In this sense we are "thrown" or "delivered over" into a world in which we must fig-ure out somehow how to live. Of this, Heidegger writes, "This charac-teristic of Dasein's Being—this 'that it is'—is veiled in its 'whence' and 'whither', yet disclosed in itself all the more unveiledly; we call this the 'thrownness' [*Geworfenheit*] of this entity into its 'there' . . . The ex-pression 'thrownness' is meant to suggest the *facticity of its being deliv-ered over*" (BT, 174). We do not know how we got to the "there" in which we find ourselves, nor where we are going; what we can appre-hend is the "there-ness" of our "there," the situation we find ourselves in, in its given-ness, and the unavoidability of always finding ourselves somewhere.

This thrownness is disclosed to us, Heidegger asserts, through our "sense of the situation," "disposition," or "situatedness" (all possible translations of *Befindlichkeit*, which everyone agrees is translated incor-rectly as "state-of-mind" by Macquarrie and Robinson).[34] The form that this "sense of the situation" takes is always a *Stimmung*: "what we indicate ontologically by the term 'state of mind' [*Befindlichkeit*] is on-tically the most familiar and everyday sort of thing; our mood [*die Stim-mung*], our Being-attuned [*das Gestimmtsein*]" (BT, 172).

Put more simply, we might say that "moods [*Stimmungen*] are the fundamental ways in which we *find* ourselves *disposed* in such and such a way. Moods are the *how* according to which one is in such and such a way" (FCM, 67). On the level of *Stimmung*, as Michel Haar writes, "the world presents itself as what touches us, concerns us, affects us."[35] And only when we are touched, when we feel what matters to us, can we appreciate the extent to which we have been thrown into a world that is the way that it is and not some other way. This is because otherwise we could not *care* about the world and the possibilities that inhere there; it is only through mood that we engage purposively with the world.

For Heidegger, then, moods are not transitory or fleeting elements of everyday life, but are foundational and primordial. They have a power of disclosure "*prior* to cognition and volition." Heidegger emphasizes that "moods are not *side-effects*, but are something which in advance determine our being with one another. It seems as though a mood is in each case already there, so to speak, like an atmosphere in which we first immerse ourselves in each case and which then attunes us through and through" (FCM, 67). (Here, it should be noted, we see especially the way the German *Stimmung* is closely related to "tune" and "attunement.") To be in a mood is to "be attuned," an attunement that is the foundation or starting place for everything else, the "presupposition" for our "thinking, doing, and acting," (FCM, 67) the medium in which these things happen. One is never not-attuned; one is always in one mood or another. The world never presents itself to us as some kind of value-less set of facts or perceptions—things always appear to us as mattering or not mattering in some way.

It is by way of mood that we attribute value to something. And since value for Heidegger, as for Tomkins, is a question of affective attachment, this is another way of saying that it is only possible to be affected when things have been set in advance by a certain mode of attunement. In fact, "nothing like an affect would come about," Heidegger insists, unless being-in-the world "had not already submitted itself to having entities within-the-world 'matter' to it in a way which its moods have outlined in advance" (BT, 177). For example, he continues, "only something which is in the state of mind of fearing (or fearlessness) can discover that what is environmentally ready-to-hand is threatening. *Dasein*'s openness to the world is constituted existentially by the attunement [*Gestimmheit*] of a state-of-mind" (BT, 176).

Even though it is only by way of moods that we know *how we are* in relation to the situation we are in, this, however, does not mean that we are necessarily *aware* of our moods. In fact, we are often ignorant of the determinative effect our moods have on the world we see and how we relate to it. It is usually when moods are suddenly disrupted or when a mood is particularly dramatic or intense that we notice it as such. More often we make our judgments about the world as if they were rational, sensible, not determined by something as subjective as mood: some particular colleague offends one because he or she is insensitive or rude, not because one is anxious or irritable; one likes the film because it was a good film, not because one was in a good mood following an especially stimulating dinner with friends, and so forth. Indeed, acknowledging that our assessment of the world comes to us by way of our mood, within the context of a mood, would make it possible for others to easily dismiss our judgments, since moods are seen as merely personal, transitory, irrational—they interfere with impartial judgment. But it is just such a way of thinking that Heidegger argues against, noting that in fact it is "precisely *those* attunements [*Stimmungen*] to which we pay no heed at all, the attunements we least observe, those attunements which attune us in such a way that we feel as though there is no attunement there at all, as though we were not attuned in any way at all—those attunements are the most powerful" (FCM, 68).

Inasmuch as moods are an atmosphere, a kind of weather, they are not "psychological," located in some interior space we can reach by way of introspection or self-examination.[36] Moods are not in us; we are in them; they go through us. ("It is *not* at all '*inside*' in some interiority, only to appear in the flash of an eye; but for this reason, *it is not at all outside either*" [FCM, 66].) They "assail us." And in this sense mood is also total, or totalizing. Moods do not shed light on some one thing in particular, but on a whole environment: "*Stimmung* imposes itself on everything" (66). Any orientation toward anything specific requires a presumed view of the total picture, a presumption that is usually invisible to us—that is just the way the world *is*. "*The mood has already disclosed, in every case, Being in the world as a whole, and makes it possible first of all to direct oneself toward something*" (BT, 176). Thus, for example, Baudelaire can write of l'Ennui "swallowing the earth in a yawn"; boredom transforms the entire world at a single stroke. This mood of boredom, Baudelaire knows, is not just his; it is shared by his audience, his "semblables."[37] And it is by way of this shared mood that Baudelaire seeks to reach his audience. *Stimmung* is a collective, public phenomenon, something inevitably shared. Moods constitute the "*way in which we are together*" (FCM, 66).

The knowledge we gain by way of *Stimmung* is authentic in the sense that it tells us what is collectively possible at that moment; it tells us what our shared situation is and what may be done within this situation. That this is historical, specific or situated knowledge makes it no less useful in a practical sense. This is why Aristotle, Heidegger notes, devoted himself to understanding the logic of affectivity in *The Rhetoric.* Publics, audiences, collectivities have moods, and indeed can make moods for themselves, and it is these moods that orators and politicians must orient themselves toward. In this sense, Heidegger calls Aristotle's *Rhetoric,* which is concerned with affectivity precisely as a matter of public and political concern, "the first systematic hermeneutic of the everydayness of Being with one another" (BT, 178).

Thus, in general terms, as Baudelaire writes of the boredom enveloping his readers, we might speak of a particular *Stimmung* in Seattle at the 1999 World Trade Organization (WTO) meeting that allowed the antiglobalization activists to join up with the labor unions, a mood that was shifted at a crucial moment by police violence and mass arrests.[38] Or we might talk about the way an audience was attuned to a Detroit Tigers baseball game in 1967, the kinds of emotional energies that were collectively available because of the rebellion (or so-called riots) that had recently occurred in Detroit, or indeed of the *Stimmung* that allowed for the rebellion to get going in the first place, or the mood following the rebellion, in which workers who had been fired on and/or arrested organized the League of Black Revolutionary Workers.[39] In each instance, certain objects in the world come into view in a particular way, certain persons (or social formations) appear as friends and others as enemies, and some kinds of actions present themselves that might otherwise not even come into view. But we may speak of and seek to analyze in each case the *Stimmung* that made some events possible and others not. Any kind of political project must have the "making and using" of mood as part and parcel of the project; for, no matter how clever or correct the critique or achievable the project, collective action is impossible if people are not, so to speak, *in the mood.*

Heidegger insists that we should not just give ourselves over to moods. On the contrary we must do our best to exert agency in relation to them, singularly and collectively. But since mood is prior to will and cognition, this has to be done tactically, in a mediated fashion. One cannot just decide to change one's mood. "When we master a mood," Heidegger writes, "we do so by way of a counter-mood; we are never free of moods" (BT, 136). One must come to know what kinds of practices, situations, or encounters (such as seeing friends, going to a concert, settling down to write, attending a political rally, making a trip) are capable of producing a counter-mood. Speaking collectively, the understanding necessary for the rousing and guiding of moods is always a specific historical one. Thus, for example, because what could affect mood among enslaved African Americans in the 1830s was not the same thing that could affect mood among middle-class African Americans in 1900, Frederick Douglass had an understanding of the affective value and force of the sorrow songs that was quite different from that of W. E. B Du Bois.

Heidegger writes that Aristotle's orator "must understand the possibilities of moods in order to rouse them and guide them aright" (BT, 178). Similarly, any aesthetic practice, if it is to reach an audience, must be able to attune itself with that audience's mood. All three of the writers I address in this book are fundamentally concerned with this question of mood, not only in the sense that they seek to transform a depressing melancholia into a mood that promotes interest and attachment but also to the extent that this shift in mood can be accomplished only if a text already resonates with an audience's *Stimmung*. In order to affect his "fastidious" readers, Henry James had to first catch them, which he does by creating an object of affective attachment within the story that is visible and attractive within his public's mode of attunement. Only once caught does the audience find itself in another world, that of the novel—which turns out to be another *there*. The disjuncture between one *there* and another allows James (and Du Bois and Platonov) to show one, as reader, one's own mood, estranging one from oneself and one's mood, so the mood—and what it makes possible, what it precludes, and by what historical forces is it kept tuned—as such can become apparent. And this catching sight of ourselves in the *Stimmung* we are in is, in itself, the evocation of another *Stimmung*, one in which *Stimmung* and those with whom we share it have become themselves objects of interest and attachment.

Structure of Feeling

Insofar as the term "structure of feeling" describes the ways social forces shape or structure our affective lives, it is in some ways similar to *Stimmung*. Its emphases, however, are different, and thus, so are its uses. The term was coined, as is well known, by Raymond Williams, and is now sometimes used in senses broader than those he described in his relatively brief treatment of the term.[40]

Williams conceived of the term, however, in a very specific sense. He initially describes the term as useful not only because it enables us to talk about the sociality of affect, but because it enables us to describe those structures that mediate between the social and the personal that are more ephemeral and transitory than set ideologies or institutions. The problem with most forms of social analysis, Williams notes, is that the "habitual past tense" that such analysis falls into creates a set of "finished products"; it fixes the social forms in which we participate. What this inevitably misses is the lived, affective and very unfixed, half-articulated way that most of us experience our lives most of the time. For this more ephemeral, nascent thing—specific qualitative changes in the ways people experience their lives, the ways they think and feel about the world, that have not yet hardened into ideologies—Williams proposes the term "structure of feeling." The task, Williams writes, is to think in a manner whereby

> specific qualitative changes are not assumed to be epiphenomena of changed institutions, formations and beliefs, or merely secondary evidence of changed social and economic relations between and within classes. At the same time they are from the beginning taken as social experience, rather than as personal experience or as the merely superficial or incidental small change of society . . . they are social in the sense that . . . although they are emergent or pre-emergent, they do not have to await definition, classification or rationalization before they exert palpable pressures and set effective limits on experience and on action.

Here, Williams is defending the social significance of small, local moments of "practical consciousness." He emphasizes how important and yet how difficult it is to appreciate the pressures exerted by forces that feel and seem quite personal but that we know are social, but social in a way that is not reducible to a fixed institution or discourse. While Williams's use of the term "structure of feeling" was intended to describe the nascent or ephemeral, the phrase has lost something of this meaning as it has traveled into more everyday intellectual speech. My sense is that it is this next part of the definition that has really stuck. On the choice of the term "structures of feeling" to describe this moment, Williams explains:

> The term is difficult, but 'feeling' is chosen to emphasize a distinction from more formal concepts of 'world-view' or 'ideology.' . . . [W]e are concerned with meanings and values as they are actively lived and felt, and relations between these and formal or systematic beliefs are in practice

variable (including historically variable). . . . We are talking about characteristic elements of impulses or restraint and tone; specifically affective elements of consciousness and relationships: not feeling against thought, but
thought as felt and feeling as thought: practical consciousness of a present
kind, in a living and interrelating continuity. We are then defining these elements as a structure: as a set, with specific internal relations, at once inter-
locking and in tension.[41]

Williams wants to find a way to speak about how "meanings and values are actually lived and felt." And they are lived and felt in ways that
are variable over time. But, even if they are involved in the flow of time
and if they are local and difficult to articulate in set terms, they nonetheless have "specific internal relations." When certain objects produce a
certain set of affects in certain contexts for certain groups of people—
that is a structure of feeling. And sometimes structures of feeling are
personal and idiosyncratic, but more often they are not: a social group
of which the subject is a member shares them. Thus we can talk about
particular working-class structures of feeling, or masculine ones, or
Russian ones. Generational style, class tastes, shifts in linguistic usage—
these are the elements of "practical consciousness" that Williams wants
to be able to describe.

When I use the phrase "structure of feeling" I mean it in this more
widely applicable sense: "specifically affective elements of consciousness and relationships," elements that function "as a set, with specific
internal relations." For Williams, "structure of feeling" was still a supplementary term that emphasized the fleeting and nascent quality of
structures of feeling that could or might later harden into ideologies. I
do not think it should be a supplementary term, and I will argue that
structures of feeling can be ephemeral but also just as durable and force-
ful as ideologies, perhaps even more so. I think that structure of feeling
should emerge, as it has begun to, as a full-fledged parallel to ideology.
If the function of an ideology is to narrate our relation to a social order
so as to make our daily experience of that order meaningful and man-
ageable, then *structure of feeling* would be the term to describe the mediating structure—one just as socially produced as ideology—that
facilitates and shapes our affective attachment to different objects in the
social order.

Although Williams and Heidegger are coming from different theoretical traditions, I do not think that *Stimmung* and structure of feeling are
incompatible concepts; their points of emphasis are just different.
Where *Stimmung* as a concept focuses attention on what kinds of af-

fects and actions are possible within an overall environment, structures of feeling are more discrete, less total, and they orient one toward a specific social class or context. For example, depression is a mood, not a structure of feeling; however, we might describe the particular depression of the Russian peasant in the steppe in the 1920s as a structure of feeling, or the depression of the residents of a decimated New Orleans after Katrina as a structure of feeling. Or, to return to an earlier example, we might talk about the structures of feeling created by the civil rights movement and the Black Panthers, structures of feeling that were mobilized within the *Stimmung* that allowed the 1967 rebellion against the police in Detroit to happen. And although mood will be the more useful concept for me in this book, it is the Marxist tradition in which Williams participated to which I bring my interest in attunement and affectivity. That is, this book is less concerned with being-in-the-world or a reassessment of our understanding of Being than with the way aesthetic practices respond to and represent concrete historical situations, and I hope to suggest the suitability of Heidegger's concept of *Stimmung* for this project. My aim, besides my desire to argue for the importance of an antidepressive, political, and politicizing melancholia, and the local arguments the book pursues about the particular practices I am concerned with, is to make a case for the importance of mood and affect to a Marxist concern with the representability of history—"what hurts," in Jameson's memorable phrase—and the possibility for our collective participation in and transformation of our own history as it unfolds.[42]

CHAPTER ONE

Modernism and Melancholia

Modernity and Loss

> We are all of us celebrating some funeral.
>
> —CHARLES BAUDELAIRE,
> "ON THE HEROISM OF MODERN LIFE"

It is not difficult to see how modernity—in its meanings as a particular experience of time and as a set of concrete transformations of the material world of everyday life—is related to the experience of loss. The very origin of the word "modernity," from *modernus,* meaning "now" or "of today" (as opposed to "of yesterday") implies a problematic sense of anteriority, the sense that the past is lost and gone.[1] This was a new time-consciousness, one not oriented toward repeating cycles or the promises of divine eternity, but a temporality that was linear, sequential, irreversible, and measurable in discrete units, what would become clock time.

Perhaps since the word's first usage, around the time of the collapse of the Roman Empire, and at least since the *Querelle des Anciens et Modernes,* modernity signified an epochal shift, the sense that we live in a historical moment that in its totality is somehow categorically different from the periods that preceded it. Later, the word was used also to characterize the subjective experience of such a difference: the feeling that one's own experience of the present is contingent, fugitive, and fleeting, that the passage of time itself means that the world around one is forever eluding one's grasp, producing, as in Baudelaire, an endless accumulation of losses. ("J'ai plus de souvenirs que si j'avais mille ans.") In either the subjective or epochal, collective sense, modernity and loss would seem to be inextricably linked: to be "modern" is to be separated from the past. In fact, it may be that modernity signals nothing more or less than the impulse to declare the difference of a present moment in respect to the moments that preceded it, to perceive the specificity and difference of one's own historical moment.[2]

We can read a troubled relation to the past, for example, even in one of the earliest figures for expressing a modern time consciousness, that "we moderns" were "dwarves standing on the shoulders of giants."[3] The metaphor implies that we moderns are better—more knowledgeable—only because we can stand on the shoulders of the now dead giants who preceded us. It suggests that even as we are able to see farther and better, it makes us feel smaller. This ambivalence is amplified by the figure's funereal character: we modern subjects owe our "progress" to the dead bodies stacked beneath us on which we stand. We are haunted by the dead even as we are lifted up by them.

As we know, over a period of centuries, regularized clock time organized daily existence in new and various ways. It changed human conceptions of the world and of space itself: a portable clock was the crucial invention that allowed for the measurement of longitude (as detailed in the popular book and TV miniseries *Longitude*) and hence for travel across the oceans and the mapping of the world and colonial development.[4] Standardized clock time also has transformed how people have experienced their bodies and their daily emotional lives, inasmuch as the clock was used (and perhaps invented in order) to measure the workday. This process reached a culmination in the early twentieth century with Fredrick Taylor's time-and-motion studies and with the advent and broad institutionalization of the Fordist assembly line.[5] "The time is past," as Paul Valery remarked, "in which time did not matter."[6]

But it was not only changes in the nature and experience of temporality that altered the quality and scope of loss. The whole conglomerate of transformations that took place and continue to take place under the rubric of "modernization" all bring their own losses (and it is primarily, though not exclusively, these changes with which James, Du Bois, and Platonov are concerned). Industrialization changed the nature of work, not only making it quite simply brutalizing and dangerous, especially in the early stages, but also creating a new situation in which workers were isolated from each other and from the work process as a whole, substituting the abstraction of value known as "wages" for a sense of value based on human contact or recognition. Moreover, industrialization required peasants to become workers, who in turn needed to become more mobile, and so eroded the traditional community and extended family.[7] The destruction of what is now called simply "the environment" by industrial processes has been lamented at least since the Romantic poets. "All that is solid melts into air" in terms of belief systems as well, as the increasing social and cultural authority of science combined with the secularism of the market greatly diminish the ability of religion to organize and give meaning to everyday life.[8] New technologies of movement and transportation made locality less and less important. The train, for example, was experienced as a radical and upsetting break in the experience of space-time.[9] As is well known, beginning in the eighteenth century and accelerating into the twentieth, massive emigrations of people looking for work, escaping from famine, often moving from the colony to the metropole, meant that more and more people experienced life as exiles, permanent foreigners. Urbanization, in Georg Simmel's famous argument, increased the shocks the human sensorium was required to absorb—not only automobiles and advertising but also the sheer volume of human faces one sees in a given day—meaning that people became less and less open to the world around them because the everyday life world was more and more something from which one had to shield oneself.[10] New discourses of racial and sexual identity became technologies of identification and administration by the modern state in hospitals, prisons, schools, and elsewhere.[11] The acquisition of an identity that excluded one from the "normal" brought with it the loss of state-provided rights and/or privileges and a sense of *being* lost, of being left out of the human community more generally. Along such lines, Franz Fanon, for example, described the experience of racial identification as one in which his body was returned to him "sprawled out, distorted, recolored, clad in mourning."[12] Technologies of war and destruction have continued to become more and more powerful, so that each new war, from the American Civil War up through World War II, was experienced as a shocking revelation at the human capacity to destroy other humans as well as a massive experience of local and personal loss. Think of all the people struck by grief for the 20 million Soviet citizens who died during World War II. And of course the Nazi Holocaust itself engendered a sense of loss so great that it seems to defy the very possibility of mourning.[13]

One could continue. I have here by no means exhausted the ways modernization has been experienced as loss. I want here only to point out that we have, even at first glance, more than sufficient evidence to suggest that one of the central problems of modernity is the attempt to grapple with these losses, with the fact of a new scale, scope, and quality of loss itself. It is in such a context that Freud's theory of melancholy, composed as the horrors of World War I were beginning to become apparent, begins to look like a symptomatically modern text.[14]

However, modernity has also signified on a quite different register as well, a more optimistic, utopian, even revolutionary one. That is, modernity has been understood not only as an experience of temporality and a set of social transformations but also as a project.[15] In this sense modernity was something to achieve: "Il faut être absolument moderne." Such a modernity-as-project is closely linked to the set of ideas and conversations that came to be called the Enlightenment: the promise of endless human perfectibility, progress, democracy and universal equality, self-determination, better living through the advances of reason in the realms of medicine, technology, economy, and elsewhere—in short, progress and reason, progress through reason.[16] The utopian element of the project of modernity has played an important role in most of the transformative political projects of the twentieth century from the Bolshevik Revolution to the civil rights movement in the United States. More recently, this element has supplied the rhetoric for both the massive state-supported efforts toward the globalization of capital (sometimes simply called "modernization") as well as the organized opposition to globalization as it has so far taken shape (by way of appeals to universal human rights, to the right to self-determination, or to rational discussion of the global common good as opposed to the "free market"). That is to say, "modernity" has no necessary ideological content, especially recently, and has instead been a site of regular contestation.

Yet precisely the utopian promises of modernity put the modern subject in a precariously depressive position. This is because the promises of modernity are never fulfilled. At any given moment, the preoccupation with the ways the world has *not* met the promises of modernity renders the world apparently lackluster, stale, and profitless even if (or precisely because) the possibility of transformation always seems to lurk on the horizon. There is the danger that a kind of depressive "learned helplessness" is the eventual lesson awaiting the enthusiasts of the project of modernity.[17] Worse still, it seems that the greater the hopes placed in science, or technology, or international cooperation, the more dramatic the failures have been, with the thoroughly modern, bureaucratically organized and administered Holocaust as exhibit number one. Silvan Tomkins has suggested that this kind of a situation, one between "Heaven and Hell on earth," between great hope and catastrophic disappointment, is the paradigmatic "depressive script."[18]

I propose that this insecure position between the promises of modernity and the realities of modernization is the place of modernism itself. "Modernism," in this sense, would refer not to any one thing in particular, but to the wide range of practices that attempt in one way or another to respond to the gap between the social realities of modernization and the promises of the project of modernity. We find such practices not only in the literature and arts, but in law or international relations (the League of Nations), economics (Keynes), language (Esperanto), technology (electrification, cinema), and so forth. This means that the situation of modernism is one in which modernization is felt to be incomplete, still in progress, and thus potentially redirected. It also means that the promises of modernity are still felt to be relevant, vital, and achievable.

Thus, it should be clear, I do not here view modernism as a specific set of formal gestures (difficulty, nonrepresentation, etc.) or even a particular representational problem, nor as the aesthetic response to a determining historical factor (such as industrialization, urbanization, the rise of mass culture, or the expansion of capital). Instead I propose to think about modernism as the symbolic space in which what counts as modernity, what modernity is or should be, and for whom, is contested, debated, reevaluated, or otherwise articulated.[19] In relation to any given modernism, in any given social subsystem, one should be able to ask what the relevant aspects of modernization are; what promises of modernity are felt to be still fulfillable; and how this given modernism is or is not motivated by the project of somehow bridging the gap. This means that all of the modernisms share an awareness of a gap between the promises and the social processes of modernity. Within the aesthetic modernisms, this awareness implies a position taken on what the relevant social processes and promises are and a shared sense that art *can* and *should* do something about this gap.

Melancholia's History

> I write of melancholy, by being busy to avoid
> melancholy.
>
> —ROBERT BURTON, *ANATOMY OF MELANCHOLY*

The discourse of melancholy has a long history, originating, as we know, in the humoral theories of ancient Greece. While there have been several paradigm shifts in this history, as Klibansky, Saxl, and Panofsky have noted in *Saturn and Melancholy,* new understandings or theories have not displaced each other so much as accumulated on top of or adjacent to each other, producing a situation in which contradictory theories and approaches have coexisted at any given moment.[20] Despite this somewhat convoluted and contested definitional scene, there is a remarkable consistency in descriptions of a basic affective experience from the time of the Hippocratic writings through Augustine, William Langland, Shakespeare, Marsilio Ficino, Robert Burton, and Goethe right up to very recent writing on antidepressives and the *Diagnostic and Statistical Manual of Mental Disorders (DSM).* Even as the specific forms of melancholia have varied, what Galen, court physician to Marcus Aurelius, wrote in the second century holds true for much of melancholia's history: "Although each melancholic person acts quite differently from the others, all of them exhibit fear or despondency."[21] Other symptoms regularly referred to include feelings of hopelessness, an inability to experience pleasure or to sustain interest, self-loathing, guilt and shame, a tendency toward suicide, and a range of physical difficulties such as sleep disturbance, flatulence, and coldness in the hands and feet.

If there is some consistency in descriptions of a certain experience, quite variable have been understandings of its origins, just what type of condition it is, how it relates to other forms of human experience, what its value might be, and how we might cure it, if indeed cure is seen to be necessary. While I am focused here on one particular moment in this history, one in which melancholia is oriented around the problem of loss, it is useful to look briefly at the broader history, not only to appreciate the specificity of the modernist moment's focus but also to see the long-standing association between melancholia and aesthetic practices whose value is directly related to their origin in melancholy.

In the humoral understanding of melancholia, *melaina-kole* referred to black bile, a normal substance in the body, of which, reasonably enough, there could be temporary and/or chronic excesses, resulting in melancholic illnesses. This schema not only was the earliest but also has been the longest surviving understanding, retaining currency in one form or another from Hippocrates until the nineteenth century.[22] (And it is echoed by recent physiological theories of depression in which the regulation of neurotransmitters such as serotonin and norepenephrine play a key role.) In brief, the humoral system posited that there were four basic humors: black bile, yellow bile, blood, and phlegm. Each humor corresponded not only with a body part and a combination of elemental qualities but also with the seasons, as follows.

Blood: the heart, warm and moist, spring
Yellow bile: the liver, warm and dry, summer
Black bile: the spleen, cold and dry, autumn
Phlegm: the brain, cold and moist, winter

The humoral theory was part of a whole cosmology in which one's individual health and mood were linked to transpersonal forces such as the season and the elements. As Klibansky et al. write, "[t]hese humours corresponded, it was held, to the cosmic elements and to the division of time; they controlled the whole existence and behavior of mankind, and, according to the manner in which they were combined, determined the character of the individual."[23] Health was a question of proper balance between the different humors, "that state in which these constituent substances are in the correct proportion to each other, both in strength and quantity, and are well mixed. Pain occurs when one of the substances presents either a deficiency or an excess, or is separated in the body and not mixed with the others."[24] Various cures, from changes in diet, purgatives, and bleeding to labor and the avoidance of solitariness were prescribed over the years in order to restore the proper balance.

Melancholia could thus refer to two things within the humoral paradigm. One was a temporary excess of black bile, a condition or illness that could be cured by restoring balance. The other was a "normal abnormality," a chronic imbalance in the humors in which black bile was dominant over the other humors in a kind of natural and permanent way, resulting in a particular temperament. Klibansky and colleagues write: "The natural melancholic, however, even when perfectly well, possessed a quite special 'ethos', which, however it chose to manifest itself, made him fundamentally and permanently different from 'ordinary' man; he was, as it were, normally abnormal."[25] Here, the melancholic was one of the four humoral temperaments, along with the sanguine, the choleric, and the phlegmatic. Depending on one's temperament, one was more or less inclined toward different imbalances and diseases. In the different seasons, for example, one or other of the humors could be more dominant, which might produce temporary imbalances or changes in everyone but would affect people of different temperaments differently. If one was choleric, for example, then one tended to be dry already, and thus a very hot and dry summer would have a more harmful effect than it would on the phlegmatic, whose cold and moist nature would be balanced by the summer's heat and dryness.

The distinction between the melancholic as a type (whom we would today call the depressive) and melancholia as a disease or mood created the space for the connection between melancholia and genius to emerge. If one was clearly disabled when suffering from melancholia at its most severe, the temperamental melancholic could have a moderate amount of black bile, enough to create a susceptibility to melancholic illness, but also enough to encourage a certain, somewhat mysterious capacity for great achievement. It was this temperamental melancholia that was linked to "men of extraordinary ability" in the Aristotelian *Problems*. (Klibansky et al. make the case that melancholia is linked to greatness and creativity in this Aristotelian text by way of an incorporation of the Platonic notion of creative frenzy or mania, a frenzy facilitated by the right, moderate amount of black bile.[26] Beyond this, however, the explanation of the relationship between melancholia and various forms of intellectual achievement remained vague.)

In contrast, within the medieval Christian worldview the sense of dejection and withdrawal of interest that had characterized melancholia became a sin. And not just any sin, but potentially the most offensive of sins, as it indicated a rejection of the glory and presence of God, a failure to see God's presence in the world. This idea appears to have originated in the early Christian Egyptian desert monks who were, due to their isolated mode of living, particularly subject to such a mood, which John Cassian described as a "weariness or distress of heart . . . akin to dejection"[27] and which was called "acedia."[28] Cassian wrote that acedia was a particular danger among the solitary monks, producing "dislike of the place, disgust with the cell, and disdain in the company of his brethren," as well as making one "lazy and sluggish about all manner of work."[29] The notion of a disease of the black bile did not disappear during this period so much as the sin of acedia existed alongside it as a kind of spiritual disease. Occasionally acedia was viewed as something that might motivate you to find your faith and to search for the meaning of God (William Langland's *Piers Plowman* might be read along such lines), and thus even here there appears to be the potential for a positively valued flip side to the depressive phenomenon.

The Renaissance returned to Aristotle and other Greek texts and rescued melancholics from hell, transforming them into geniuses. Marsilio Ficino is the key figure here. In 1489 he published his *Books on Life*, wherein he argued, among other things, that melancholy was the necessary temperament of thinkers and of philosophers, who are inclined to think and brood over things that are impossible and difficult and absent. Ficino also incorporated the astrological tradition of writing about Saturn into his conception, linking the melancholic to the person "born under Saturn."[30] Ficino's text was tremendously influential and signaled a subsequent interest in and positive valuation of melancholy in various forms. It appears, for example, that Dürer drew from Ficino's text the theory of melancholia that provided the iconography of his *Melencolia I*.[31] Melancholy signified as a kind of heightened self-awareness; it was seen as the mood of the poet and of thought in general, as for example in Milton's poem *Il Penseroso*, wherein melancholy's "pleasures" were celebrated. In Hamlet we find the romantic melancholic hero, who suffers a debilitating affliction, to be sure, but is all the more beguiling, complex, and attractive for it. It is his melancholy alienation and indecision that defines Hamlet as a hero and has allowed him to allegorize modern subjectivity more generally for several centuries now. At this moment melancholy even becomes a kind of fashion, a sign of glamour, a pose one might take on.[32]

Implicit if unarticulated in the idea of the temperamental melancholic who achieves greatness is the kernel of another, now almost commonsensical approach to what has been thought of as poetic or heroic melancholy. If the melancholic person knows what it is to fall, as Kristeva puts it, into "an abyss of sorrow, a non-communicable grief that at times, and often on a long term basis, lays claim upon us to the extent of losing all interest in words, actions and even life itself,"[33] then such a person may be inclined to dwell on the sources of her or his grief even when not depressed precisely in order to figure out how in the future to avoid depression. In other words, the aesthetic production of the melancholic may be an attempt precisely to combat depression, not, as one might assume, by way of an escape into aesthetic pleasures but precisely by directing her or his attention toward melancholy itself. As Robert

Burton puts it in his *Anatomy of Melancholy*, "I write of melancholy, by being busy to avoid melancholy."[34] Kristeva similarly writes that "for those who are racked by melancholia, writing about it would have meaning only if writing sprang out of that very melancholia."[35]

The Anatomy not only celebrated writing about melancholy as a way to avoid it but evidently also promoted the counter-melancholic force of reading about melancholy, to judge by the testimony of readers from Samuel Johnson to Djuna Barnes. Any number of ideas about melancholy emerge in Burton's remarkably expansive book, in part because Burton seems less concerned to offer a coherent account of melancholy than to find ways to be able to keep writing about it. Thus, we find multiple, overlapping kinds of melancholy, including that universal melancholy which everyone suffers, since suffering is the basic human condition, and melancholies of the brain, the whole body, and the midsection, with various subsets of each, such as love-melancholia and religious melancholia.[36] Among the many advices, observations, theories, and cures proposed in *The Anatomy* (to which I could not hope to do justice here) is the idea that melancholy is a state of interior disorder; by analogy, one may also speak of melancholy states or nations. In his *Melancholy and Society*, Wolf Lepenies picks up on this idea to argue that Burton creates his utopia (the first in English, which takes up the first few hundred pages of *The Anatomy*) by way of a negation of this disordered melancholy. There is thus for Lepenies a dialectical and mutually constituting relationship between melancholy and utopia, one that can be traced through different historical moments, in which utopian thinking is motivated by the desire to find a remedy for melancholia.

Walter Benjamin pursues a similarly dialectical mode of argument regarding the emergence of the Renaissance version of "heroic melancholy." He writes that "[t]he deadening of the emotions, and the ebbing away of the waves of life which are the source of these emotions in the body, can increase the distance between the self and its surrounding world to the point of alienation from the body."[37] In the melancholic state, the world becomes a set of objects with no necessary function or meaning, the object world has been emptied of significance, and in this sense it has also been prepared for allegorical transformation. The melancholic state of mind, then, even as it dwells on ruins and loss, is at the same time liberated to imagine how the world might be transformed, how things might be entirely different from the way they are. In this allegorical mode of looking, "any person, any object, any relationship can mean absolutely anything else" (OGT, 186). The melancholy mind, "in its tenacious self-absorption," Benjamin writes, "embraces dead objects in its contemplation, in order to redeem them" (157). In this way, the world "is both elevated and devalued" (175). This is how Benjamin reads Dürer's *Melencolia I,* where the subject has laid aside the "utensils of active life," which have become instead objects of contemplation; the image depicts the brooding subject in the moment just prior to an allegorical awakening.

Benjamin's compelling case for a potentially disruptive imagination of radical and redemptive transformation within this melancholic mode of seeing notwithstanding, the retreat into contemplative melancholy could also serve a primarily compensatory, and thus socially affirmative, function. In his study of Elizabethan melancholy, Lawrence Babb connects the cultural fascination with melancholy to the historical world in which it arose, suggesting that "the late English renaissance was a period of progressively deepening despondency."[38] In such a context, melancholy withdrawal "offered—or seemed to offer—an avenue of retreat from a disheartening world. The melancholy man might retire within himself and find compensation for the ills of the world in sober contemplative pleasures."[39] In this way, even as melancholy retreat might preserve oppositional energies for later expenditure, the comfort it seems to have offered might also be a barrier to the collective action that would be necessary for the transformation of the conditions creating despondency in the first place. This would become a central tension in considerations of the relationship between melancholy and aesthetics.

The Renaissance interest in the relationship between melancholy and genius and the corresponding popularity of melancholy was revived in the late eighteenth and early nineteenth centuries. In British and German Romanticism, as we know, melancholy is a major theme, from Goethe's *The Sorrows of Young Werther* to Keats's "Ode on Melancholy."[40] Kant writes positively of melancholy in his *Observations on the Feeling of the Beautiful and Sublime.* At least on a thematic level, across this range of texts, melancholia is presented as a kind of mode of intensified reflection and self-consciousness, and the suffering accompanying it as a soul-ennobling force. To really appreciate beauty or experience love, one must also know melancholy. As Keats writes, "in the very temple of Delight / Veil'd Melancholy has her sovran shrine."[41]

At the same time, in what increasingly became an autonomous social and cultural sphere, melancholia was becoming medicalized; it becomes a mental illness to be studied, categorized, and treated. Slowly during the nineteenth century the humoral understanding was displaced, and in this context also the term *depression* began to supplant *melancholia*.[42] With the rise of psychiatry as a discipline, finding the physiological basis of mental illness became a priority. Probably no one contributed more to this practice than Emil Kraepelin, a contemporary of Freud, who developed his own program of clinical observation and research, producing a new system for the classification of mental illness. His influential *Textbook of Psychiatry* went through multiple editions and became a standard text. Constantly revising his clinical categories on the basis of new evidence and observations, Kraepelin made several important distinctions, but none as influential as the one between mood disorders (such as manic depression) and diseases of the cognitive faculties, such as *dementia praecox* (what we call schizophrenia today). To a great extent, contemporary psychiatry originates in the clinically based classificatory systems devised by Kraepelin.[43]

This is where Freud enters the picture, but before moving to an examination of the psychoanalytic theory of melancholia (in the next section), it is worth looking at the recent changes in our understanding of melancholia and depression, changes linked to the wide and effective use of Prozac and other SSRI antidepressants.

The accidental discovery in 1949 by an Australian doctor that Lithium treated manic depression, but not schizophrenia, appeared to confirm Kraepelin's clinical distinction with physiological evidence. More important, it awakened people to the possibility of an effective antidepressant with tolerable side effects, which in turn motivated the search for other such medications. Over the next forty years, several effective antidepressants were discovered (including imiprimine, the monoamine oxidase (MAO) inhibitors, and the trycyclics), but they all had unpleasant side effects.[44] The discovery in the 1970s of the chemical that was eventually branded as Prozac in 1987 was significant not because it treated depression any more effectively than the other drugs (it did not), but because it only affected a single chemical involved in mood regulation—serotonin. It thus lacked many of the previous drugs' side effects, and therefore became much more widely prescribed, at which point it was learned that Prozac appeared to treat a wider range of symptoms than had initially been expected, including less severe forms of depression.

As Peter Kramer reports in *Listening to Prozac,* Prozac turned out to be effective not just for people suffering major depression, but for people "whose chronic vulnerability to depressed mood has a global effect on their personality," in other words, the depressive or melancholic.[45] One subgroup of these depressives to which Kramer devotes special attention is made up of persons who are especially sensitive to loss, the "rejection-sensitive."[46] These are people who are likely to be thrown into protracted depressive moods by relatively minor slights, losses, or rejections.[47] Disagreements or awkward misunderstandings with a partner or close friend, a bad grade or review, professional rejection or conflict, minor embarrassment or romantic disappointments or rejections, instead of producing a passing pang of shame or sorrow, produce for the rejection-sensitive a longer depression.[48] On the one hand, Kramer was surprised and even occasionally amazed at the extent to which Prozac (or other SSRIs) was able to help his depressive, loss-sensitive patients, as well as how often he heard his patients proclaim that they felt more "like themselves" than before. On the other hand, he saw the possibility for a kind of social engineering by way of Prozac. What, after all, is the 'right' amount of sensitivity to loss? Does not our capitalist economy, for example, reward those who are a bit less sensitive to loss, less risk averse, more assertive, and a little bit cheerier? Who is to say that Prozac is not just creating the most socially desirable sort of person, perhaps helping people tolerate an intolerable world? Ultimately, although Kramer was interested in the way the new SSRIs have made it possible to "affect the physiology of mood through medication in stable and useful ways . . . frequently and dramatically enough to raise [a] series of existential questions,"[49] he found that his patients were *more* likely to have the confidence to be nonconformist—to leave abusive relationships or change professions, for example—when they had been able to successfully keep depressive episodes at bay. Kramer's confidence in the positive effects of antidepressive medication has only been bolstered in the years since the publication of *Listening to Prozac*, as a number of studies have shown fairly conclusively that depression causes real physiological damage, especially to the brain, and that the more one is depressed, the more one is likely to be depressed in the future.

In his more recent book *Against Depression*, Peter Kramer fashions a response to a question he found himself somewhat surprised to be asked as he unexpectedly found himself cast as an expert on depression and antidepressants. The question in its basic form was some version of "What if Van Gogh had been on Prozac? Would he still have been a great painter?" Would all the melancholy artists and authors of the past have been cured of their depressions and thus also of their creative genius? Drawing on recent studies, Kramer makes the case that depression, or at least what is called "major depression" by the *DSM*, is a disease, and an extremely debilitating and damaging one. In this sense, he insists, it cannot be seen as an aid to any kind of intellectual production.[50] He notes that recent research has shown that major depression appears not only to cause brain damage but also to increase the risk of heart disease, not to mention suicide. Kramer calls for nothing less than an end to depression, arguing we should devote ourselves to this task in the same way that we would combat any major, debilitative disease.

While Kramer makes a strong case that there is no reason to think that major depressive episodes are anything worth celebrating, the category of disease on which he insists tends to categorically isolate major depression from other, less severe depressions that may not be as damaging, and also from the depressive personality, a locus of considerable reflection in *Listening to Prozac*. Consequently, he does not really consider the "I write of melancholy so as to avoid melancholy" phenomenon, which also serves the antidepressive function he promotes, but is associated with the defense of melancholia he wishes to attack.

When I write of an "antidepressive melancholia" or "antidepressive aesthetic practice," I mean to refer to the phenomenon I have discussed, from Burton up through Kristeva, in which one turns one's attention to melancholia precisely in order to avoid falling into a depression. That is, I am interested precisely in the practices developed by the depressive, the one who knows depression, to avoid depression. Thus, although I borrow the phrase anti-depressive from the psychiatric context, I mean to add to it a different range of meanings. To be sure, there is no need to promote depression, and I am as enthusiastic a proponent of antidepressive forces of whatever nature as Kramer is. However, the antidepressive can only arise in relation to the depressive. What we would lose through the abolition of depression that Kramer calls for are all the nonmedicinal antidepressive practices, a set of practices that are quite rich and valuable to the depressed and nondepressed alike.

Freud on Melancholia and Loss: Shadow and Precipitate

> [I]t [is] possible to suppose that the character of the ego
> is a precipitate of abandoned object cathexes and that it
> contains the history of those object choices.
>
> —FREUD, THE EGO AND THE ID

Grief and loss have long been associated with melancholia.[51] The tendency of melancholics to brood over the absent and gone has been a regular theme in a range of genres since the term *melancholia* was coined. Yet theories of melancholia have only intermittently discussed loss as a possible cause. In the tenth century, for example, the Islamic physician Ishaq ibn Imran mentions the loss of loved ones or treasured possessions as potential factors in the onset of melancholia.[52] In the seventeenth century, the influential physician Felix Platter (cited, for instance, by Burton) observed that lengthy grief could lead to melancholia, an observation others would repeat.[53] Still, in these instances, the connection between melancholia and loss remained at the level of a peripheral clinical observation that was not incorporated into the theory of melancholia as such.

Thus, Freud's proposition that the failure to mourn a loss was the cause of melancholia represents a substantial departure from previous theories. His contention that melancholia was not natural or biological but was the result of the psychic processing of subjective experiences of loss stood in opposition to emergent and influential physiological theories of depression and melancholia (such as Kraepelin's and Meyer's). To be sure, Freud picked up on a literary tradition connecting loss and melancholy, as, for example, in *The Sorrows of Young Werther* and *Hamlet*, which Freud mentions in "Mourning and Melancholia." But whereas Hamlet or Goethe's Werther may have suffered from melancholias occasioned by loss, these losses were not depicted as phenomena also *interior* to subjectivity. The ghost of Hamlet's father circulates in the world; for Freud, the ghosts populate the psyche. And it is this aspect of his argument—that in melancholia an emotional tie is replaced by an internalization of the lost object—that makes the paradigm Freud proposes an apt image for modernist subjectivity more generally. That is, we find a range of other narratives and images of internalized loss in the years before and after 1900. This would include not least Baudelaire, who writes, for example, in one of his "Spleen" poems, that his brain has become "like a tomb, a corpse filled Potter's field / A pyramid where the dead lie down by scores" or, in "The Swan," of a melancholy that "never gives way" and in which "frailest memories take on the weight of rocks." In addition, as I will discuss, Du Bois's theory of double consciousness anticipates the paradigm of melancholic subjectivity rather closely. My suggestion and assumption is that more significant than a new set of ideas about melancholia is the observation and theorization of a new mode of experience, one in which difficult-to-mourn losses have become a central feature of life in a way that has fundamentally affected the nature and structure of subjectivity.

Thus, to be clear, my aim here in examining Freud's theory of melancholia is not to argue for or against his theory or to assess the many revisions and refinements of his theory from Melanie Klein to Julia Kristeva.[54] Rather, in what follows, I read Freud as offering a kind of baseline paradigm for a modernist theory of melancholia, which will serve more as a point of reference throughout the book than as a theory of melancholia to use. In this, my project is very different from, for example, Kristeva's, which seeks to establish a theory of melancholia that can be put to use in clinical practice and in readings of aesthetic practices.[55]

✦

The initial insight of "Mourning and Melancholia" concerns an association Freud made as early as 1895, when he noted that "the affect corresponding to melancholia is that of mourning—that is, longing for something lost." The correspondence of affect led him to hypothesize that melancholia also "must be a question of a loss—a loss in instinctual life."[56] This idea had been picked up and developed by Freud's colleague Karl Abraham, who proposed by way of clinical evidence that indeed melancholia and mourning displayed the same affect and that in melancholia, mourning had been for some reason prolonged or blocked.[57] Freud continues this line of inquiry in his essay, setting himself the task of distinguishing between melancholic and nonmelancholic losses.

He begins with what he presumes to be already easily understood—mourning itself. Mourning, Freud writes, "is regularly the reaction to the loss of a loved person, or to the loss of some abstraction which has taken the place of one, such as one's country, liberty, an ideal, and so on" (MM, 243). In such situations, we expect the temporary condition Freud calls "the normal affect of mourning": the experience of a "painful frame of mind," a loss of interest in the outside world, in other people, in activity, and in love. The withdrawal we see in mourning, Freud proposes, is due to the energy demanded by what he calls the "work of mourning." On the loss of an object, Freud explains, "reality testing has shown that the love object no longer exists, and it proceeds to demand that all libido be withdrawn from its attachments to that object" (244). This is difficult, since "it is a matter of general observation that people never willingly abandon a libidinal position, not even, indeed, when a substitute is already beckoning to them" (244). Thus, although "normally respect for reality gains the day," mourning remains a slow, painful, difficult process.

If libidinal attachment in Freud's view is something like a set of sticky strings attaching us to the object, then mourning involves the laborious process of disattaching and carefully repairing "each one of the memories and expectations in which the libido is bound to the object" so that the strands of attachment can be used again. As this work of disattachment is carried out, "the existence of the lost object is psychically prolonged" (245). In this task of meeting reality's "demands," however, the work of detachment requires a temporary hallucination (a "hallucinatory wishful psychosis"). We must, in essence, pretend that the object is still "there" in some sense in order to disattach from it. When the work of mourning is done, presence and reality have won the day, and the mourner can move on to make other libidinal attachments.

The term *libido* here and throughout the essay, it should be noted, bears a great deal of explanatory weight for a term that remains frustratingly vague throughout Freud. At its most basic, Freud uses *libido* to refer to the energy, the raw stuff of the sexual instinct as it is directed toward objects and translated into the mental (as opposed to the bodily) sphere. In *Group Psychology* he writes that "libido is an expression taken from the theory of the emotions. We call by that name the energy, regarded as a quantitative magnitude . . . of those instincts which have to do with all that may be comprised under the word 'love.' "[58] So in one sense, Freud uses *libido* to mean the instinctual energy constituting love. Yet the introduction of the idea of "love" here, and his proposition that the "emotional tie" (a term with its own interesting career in Freud, on which more shortly) may be a neutral equivalent to what he calls a "love relationship,"[59] suggests that Freud may also mean something more qualitatively distinct and perhaps more internally differentiated than a quantitative magnitude of instinctual energy. At least this would seem to be the case in "Mourning and Melancholia," where, as we will see, the key aspect of the libidinal attachment for Freud is not so much "love" as such but the negative feelings (e.g., "hate") that sometimes accompany love. These negative feelings, we presume, cannot be reduced to or accurately described as libido, unless *libido* is expanded to mean any kind of affective attachment to an object. In any event, here, as throughout Freud, we perceive the lack in Freud's work of a theory of the affects (on which more later). My own approach to this problem, like that of many of Freud's critics, is to import a more nuanced understanding of affect where it is helpful.

That said, in "Mourning and Melancholia," Freud observes that the more persistent state of melancholia shares the characteristics of mourning but is more confusing to the observer, because the instigating loss is often unclear, even or especially to the melancholic herself or himself. Therefore, in his effort to make sense of melancholia, Freud places a great deal of weight on the one unique feature of melancholia, its self-critical, self-deriding aspect. "The distinguishing mental features of melancholia," Freud writes, "are a profoundly painful dejection, cessation of interest in the outside world, loss of the capacity to love, inhibition of all activity, and a lowering of the self-regarding feelings to a degree that finds utterance in self-reproaches and self-revilings, and culminates in a delusional expectation of punishment" (MM, 244). He adds, "in mourning it is the world which has become poor and empty; in melancholia it is the ego itself" (246).

Freud sees at the source of this devaluing of the ego an internal splitting: "one part of the ego sets itself over against the other, judges it critically, and, as it were, takes it as its object" (MM, 247). In the key move of the essay, Freud argues that the criticism of the self is really a criticism of the lost object that has been transferred to the ego: "reproaches against a loved object which have been shifted away from it on to the patient's own ego." Freud explains the logic of the process in the following way.

> An object choice, an attachment of the libido to a particular person, had at one time existed; then, owing to a real slight or disappointment coming from this loved person, the object-relationship was shattered. The result was not the normal one of withdrawal of the libido from this object and a displacement of it on to a new one, but something different, for whose coming-about various conditions seem to be necessary. The object cathexis proved to have little power of resistance and was brought to an end. But the free libido was not displaced on to another object; it was withdrawn into the ego. (249)

The cathexis that *had* been attached to the object is disattached (as in mourning), but instead of being redirected to a supplemental internal hallucination and then, once the work of mourning has been completed, being made available for new attachments, it attaches to the ego itself. (This internalized libido, Freud observes, produces an attachment that bears a resemblance to an early narcissistic stage of object-cathexes, where the child takes her or himself as a libidinal object; he hypothesizes that the melancholic identification may be a regression to this earlier form of attachment.) By way of this redirected, internalized libido the ego is identified with the lost object.

> There [withdrawn into the ego], however, it [the libido] was not employed in any unspecified way, but served to establish an *identification* of the ego

with the abandoned object. Thus the shadow of the object fell upon the ego, and the latter could henceforth be judged by a special agency, as though it were an object, the forsaken object. In this way an object-loss was transformed into an ego-loss and the conflict between the ego and the loved person into a cleavage between the critical activity of the ego and the ego as altered by identification. (249)

Even as Freud presents the process as if it is crystal clear, interesting tensions begin to build within his account, especially concerning the logic of identification. That is, on the on hand, Freud writes of an identification of the ego with the object, as if the *object* were directly transferred from outside to inside. On the other, he appears to prioritize the withdrawal of the *libido* itself, suggesting that it is the emotional tie, or the energy that comprised that tie—and not the object as such—that has been imported. "By taking flight into the ego love escapes extinction" (257).[60] Once inside the psyche, this introjected libido needs to find somewhere to direct itself. In order to do this, it splits the ego from within, as it were, projecting out from the ego a new "critical agency" that can be the subject of the emotion, the object of which will be the ego. (Later, this critical agency will be named the *ego-ideal* and then the *super-ego*.)

Freud underscores the mediated economy of this process with his metaphorical elaboration of it: "the shadow of the object falls upon the ego."[61] By "shadow" here he seems to mean the libidinal attachment, or more nearly its negative aspects: the complaints about the object have been redirected toward the ego. But the metaphor of the shadow substantially complicates the picture, for it implies not that the object has been *identified* with the ego but that it has gotten between the ego and the light. What Freud is here calling an "identification" is a kind of shadow play in which a certain portion of the ego has been marked in the *shape* of the lost object as darker than the rest. If the shadow itself is the libido, then the libido, like a light, projects the form of the object onto the ego. This means that it is not really the object that is interiorized but the libido, which had been attached to it; it is the libido (or affect) that moves, that is transferred, not the object. Moreover, the ego does not so much *become* the object as it comes to *look* like it, at least in its basic outline.

Terminologically, therefore, calling the process "identification" is misleading, inasmuch as its result is not an exact copy (the identity indicated by the term *identification*), but an imperfect one, carried out through a process of negation mediated by the texture and shape—the aesthetic, as it were—of the emotional tie. It is closer in its mode of representation to the stencil, the stamp, or the photo-graph, a writing with light.[62] For this reason, I think the connotations of Freud's term *introjection,* a neologism he borrows from Sandor Ferenczi (and alternates with *identification* and *incorporation*), more subtly gives a sense of this mediated process. Coined in relation to *projection,* it means literally "to throw in." Inasmuch as introjection is an interior projection—the psyche as Plato's cave—it can convey the sense of the object casting a shadow that then shapes or imprints the ego.

So this introjected emotional tie, to reiterate, introduces a particular relationality into the ego, producing a "cleavage" (as Freud writes) in which one part of the ego (the "critical agency") "rages" against the other. The source of this critical raging, Freud proposes, is an ambivalence present in the emotional tie. While Freud would acknowledge that most emotional ties are ambivalent in one way or another, he writes that "the loss of a love object is an excellent opportunity for the ambivalence in love-relationships to make itself effective and come into the open" (MM, 250–251). Ambivalence is especially likely to be present in those losses stemming not from a death but from the more subtle, socially overwritten, and difficult-to-discern losses of everyday emotional life: "situations of being slighted, neglected or disappointed, which can import opposed feelings of love and hate into the relationship or reinforce an already existing ambivalence" (251). In these situations, in addition to the loss suffered, one may be angry at the refuser, or ashamed, or contemptuous; any number of complicating, negative affects—summed up by Freud under the rubric of "hatred"—may enter into the picture here. "If love for the object—a love which cannot be given up though the object itself is given up—takes refuge in narcissistic identification, then the hate comes into operation on this substitutive object, abusing it, debasing it, making it suffer and deriving sadistic satisfaction from its suffering" (251).

Why, we might still wonder, cannot these ambivalent ties be mourned? What particular difficulty does the ambivalent tie present? Freud has established that if there is melancholia, then there must have been an ambivalent tie, but he does not determine if or why some ambivalent ties might produce melancholia and others not. It is possible, for example, that the melancholic tends to make ambivalent object-cathexes in general, constitutionally. Another solution he suggests, without quite arguing it, is that ambivalence poses a problem for mourning because such ties are likely to be or to become unconscious at the moment of loss.

The losses that stem from slights and rejections may often involve or produce emotions that the person losing may repress for one reason or another. In the case of death, Freud might have mentioned the prohibition on criticism of the recently deceased, itself ample motivation for a repression of the negative components of an emotional tie. Hamlet, for example, we might suggest, falls prey to a melancholic indecision because his emotional tie to his father was ambivalent to begin with, complicated by multiple, contradictory affects and desires: he may have been envious of his father, in a classic Oedipal scenario, in competition for his mother's affections, or he may have been angry that his father allowed himself to be duped, and/or ashamed of him for the same reasons. With the addition of the usual prohibition on criticism of the dead, the normal process of mourning is blocked. In such situations, it is far more likely that the result will be melancholic, an introjection of the emotional tie; without another place to go, this emotional tie directs itself back toward the ego.

How then do melancholias come to an end, Freud wonders. For he notes that a melancholia, like mourning, sometimes just lifts. He conjectures that there may to the work of mourning be an analogous "work of melancholia." "Just as mourning impels the ego to give up the object by declaring the object to be dead and offering the ego the inducement of continuing to live so does each single struggle of ambivalence loosen the fixation of the libido to the object by disparaging it, denigrating it and even as it were killing it" (MM, 257). The raging against the ego-as-object has the effect of devaluing the object. Freud suggests that this may encourage an unconscious abandonment of the object; the love would no longer feel the need to preserve itself, and could be dissolved. Or perhaps the internal conflict has the effect of loosening the hold of the object, of altering the nature of the emotional tie. The emotional tie, once introjected, would then be available for a slow alteration that may eventually allow for something like mourning. While Freud himself appears not entirely persuaded by his own idea about how the work of melancholia works, he is more certain that there is some kind of potentially productive labor going on within the economy of melancholia. In this way, Freud leaves open the possibility for a conception of an active, transformative, ultimately antidepressive melancholia.

In *The Ego and the Id*, Freud returns to the problem of melancholia and offers a substantial revision. While he does not quite propose an outright antidepressive melancholia, he does fairly radically rethink his earlier opposition between mourning and melancholia, hypothesizing instead that *all* losses require some kind of identification or introjection.[63] The simpler view of the work of mourning as a difficult but relatively straightforward process of disattachment and repair appears to no longer be tenable. There is no nonmelancholic loss, no mourning that leaves the ego unchanged. Indeed, he goes even further to argue that the very character of the ego is *formed* by its lost objects.

> When it happens that a person has to give up a sexual object, there quite often ensues an alteration of his ego which can only be described as a setting up of the object inside the ego, as it occurs in melancholia; the exact nature of this substitution is as yet unknown to us. It may be that by this introjection, which is a kind of regression to the mechanism of the oral phase, the ego makes it easier for the object to be given up or renders that process possible. It may be that this identification is the sole condition under which the id can give up its objects. At any rate the process, especially in the early phases of development, is a very frequent one, and it makes it possible to suppose that the character of the ego is a precipitate of abandoned object cathexes and that it contains the history of those object-choices.[64]

Here Freud proposes that all losses of sexual objects are dealt with melancholically though the establishment of the object inside the ego. How this melancholic internalization exactly works he is not sure, as his reference to the process, even in this short passage, as an "alteration," an "introjection," and an "identification" suggests. Perhaps, he suggests, regression to the oral phase makes it easier to give up an object; perhaps it is a kind of iron law of the id that it only gives up objects if the ego identifies with them. (He notes that in identifying with the object, the ego is, in effect, forcing itself on the id as a love-object: " 'Look you can love me too—I am so like the object.' ")[65] Then, in a rather remarkable leap, Freud suggests that the "character of the ego" is constituted by these losses as a kind of "precipitate of abandoned object cathexes." This means, furthermore, that the ego thus contains, like an archive or archeological site, "the history of those object choices." In essence, he is suggesting, our losses become us. Thus, Freud is not only revising his ideas about how the process of melancholic internalization works, he is placing the melancholic mechanism at the very origin of subject formation.

As in "Mourning and Melancholia," Freud turns to figurative language at a key moment to fill in or cover over a moment of obscurity. Just as "the shadow of the object" suggests a complexly mediated process, so too does "precipitate," although it is a figure taken from an entirely different rhetorical register. As we know, a precipitate is the result of a chemical process whereby the mixture of two solutions causes a new solid substance to be created, which appears to fall out of the solution. Typically, the precipitate is formed by some part of each of the solutions disattaching from their original compound and coming together to form a third compound. That is, a precipitate contains some part of each of the solutions that have been combined, but does not resemble either of them: indeed it is another *kind* of thing. If one presumes here that the two solutions are the id and the object, then the ego then is this third, entirely different substance that emerges. The metaphor recalls the notion of Hegelian sublation, that moment in the movement of the dialectic when a contradiction is resolved and the two terms are at once canceled out and preserved or incorporated into a third term. In contrast to "Mourning and Melancholia," where love preserves itself by refusing to be sublated and then imprints the ego in the image of the object, here there is a full-fledged transformation of the object-attachment.

In sum, then, what we have are two different melancholias, two different ways to internalize a lost object. In one, the depressive one, the ambivalent emotions are internalized without changing, where they then create an internal and antagonistic split; Freud does not abandon this model, and in fact returns to the metaphor of the shadow of the object again later in summarizing his views on melancholia. In the other, the lost object itself is transformed into the "character" of the ego. What Freud leaves behind is the idea of an achievable mourning, if mourning means somehow disattaching from the object without somehow taking in part of the object as part of oneself.

Transference; or, Affects in Psychoanalysis

> We would like to have at our disposal a satisfactory
> theory of affects, but that is not the case.
>
> —ANDRE GREEN

Affect occupies a central but undertheorized place in psychoanalysis.[66] Especially at the beginning of his career (through the 1890s), understanding and working with affects and the emotional tie composed a central element of Freud's project as he understood it. Later, however, with the invention of what Freud saw as "psychoanalysis proper," with the discovery of the unconscious and repression, and with the increasing emphasis on the centrality of the instincts and especially the sexual instinct (or "drive") in the formation of human subjectivity, affect and emotion tended to be conceptually and rhetorically obscured in Freud's work.[67] Indeed, Freud was less than sanguine about what he came to see as the confusing nature of the emotional tie, and seemed to spend much of his career distracting himself from it, trying to find ways to limit and contain the past-present and self-other confusions that emotional relationality invoked. Nevertheless, as is often the case with Freud, he accomplished quite a bit of conceptual work regarding that which he hoped to manage or contain (think, for example, of femininity).

The story of affect as a concept in Freud's work can be usefully understood in relation to his attempts to theorize melancholia. As just shown, Freud argues in his writings on melancholia that "if one has lost a love object, the most obvious reaction is to identify oneself with it, to replace it from within, as it were, by identification."[68] This "replacement from within" preserves the tie, allowing the affective attachment to live on. This introjection of and preoccupation with this loss can become a problem (as Freud argues in "Mourning and Melancholia") inasmuch as it leaves us living in the past, unable to create new emotional ties. (The problem is even worse, and especially depressing, if, as we know, we had an ambivalent relation to the object—so that we incorporate this ambivalence as well, which when introjected becomes ambivalence about the self.) On the other hand, as Freud came increasingly to understand, there may be no other way to deal with loss other than through the "work" of melancholia.

Although Freud alternately uses the complex metaphors of the shadow and precipitate to describe the melancholic process, when we see it from the point of view of his analysis of the emotional tie, we may understand the work involved therein to be largely mimetic: the lost object is a model that, in one mediated way or another, some part of the "self" imitates. At times, Freud suggests not only that this mimetic, "identificatory" process is the way we respond to losses, one that may be constitutive of the ego (or super-ego, depending) but moreover that it may be the paradigmatic form of the emotional tie itself. In *Group Psychology and the Analysis of the Ego*, one of Freud's most sustained analyses of such ties and of affect more generally, he asserts that "identification is known to psychoanalysis as the earliest expression of an emotional tie with another person"[69] Not only, then, are emotional ties originarily identificatory, but the suggestion is that identity itself is generated out of this initial moment of identification and affectivity, rather than the other way around. Identification comes before identity.[70]

What Freud leaves unresolved, however, is the relationship of this first emotional tie to loss. In other words, if (1) identifications come after losses, and (2) identification is our first form of an emotional tie, then might we conclude that this first emotional tie comes after a loss? Or is there an emotional tie *before* loss that is somehow different from those identification-emotional-ties that come after losses? Is there a *non*melancholic identification, a nonmelancholic form of emotional attachment? At times Freud suggests that there is a primary nonmelancholic, identificatory, emotional tie, that as infants we "naturally" form an identificatory, mimetic affective attachment to our first caretakers. Then, as we become aware of them as subjects in their own right, as subjects who can be absent, and (to simplify greatly) as we suffer through the twists and turns of the Oedipal scenario, we lose our parents as objects and then mime and incorporate them anew and again. But the nature and precise mechanism of this "earliest emotional tie" and of our first experiences of loss was never resolved within Freud's work itself and has, since Freud, been a topic of substantial and productive controversy. In Judith Butler's reading, for example, our primary caretakers are our foundational objects of mimesis because inevitably they are also the first objects we lose.[71] Our sense of identity is generated out of this experience of loss: "the self only becomes a self on the condition that it has suffered a separation."[72]

In such a view, one that Derrida also suggests in various places, neither relationality nor the miming of something could be said to happen either before or after the awareness of its loss.[73] The emotional tie requires the ability for melancholic introjection; it is only because we can melancholically imitate an object that we are able to emotionally engage with objects in the world. In order to be able to cope with the absence of our first caretaker—on whom, after all, our life literally depends—and to recognize that person when she or he returns, we imitate this first other in order to preserve something of him or her "in" our "self" (*as* our initial self). This is not simply a process of taking an image of the other inside us, because, at this moment, the distinction between the self and other is not yet in place; our first way of preserving the other in his or her absence is to model ourselves after that person. We are all miming what we lack, in a melancholic process that creates the very possibility of relationality. The "self" is at once the instrument and creation of this imitative incorporation provoked by a primary experience of absence.

✦

In *The Studies on Hysteria,* Freud and Breuer theorize that hysteria is caused by affects that have not been "abreacted," or disattached, from their ideas or memories. For Freud and Breuer (in this text), an affect is a quota of energy (not unlike what Freud elsewhere called the libido), a quantifiable "intensity" that by nature seeks release. Laplanche and Pontalis write that this release usually consists of a reaction to the event that provoked the affect and that "such a reaction may be composed of voluntary or involuntary responses, and may range in nature from tears to acts of revenge."[74] In the hysterical case, the nonabreacted affect is "strangulated," embedded like an "internal foreign body" within the psyche. This results in what, borrowing from Charcot, Freud and Breuer call "reminiscences"—the unexpected repetition, escape, or conversion of these affects in sometimes bizarre and often disabling ways and places. Strange pains, linguistic disturbances, nervous tics, and seemingly unmotivated emotional reactions are the hysterical symptoms.

Freud and Breuer found that while it is best if the affect is abreacted at the moment of the event, the strangulated affect will persist unchanged by the passage of time and can be disattached much later. Somewhat to their surprise, Freud and Breuer discovered that it was often possible for patients to gain access to this affect and abreact it if, under a hypnotic trance, they were led to reexperience the past traumatic experience and put it into speech. Freud and Breuer wrote:

> [W]e found, to our great surprise at first, that *each individual hysterical symptom immediately and permanently disappeared when we had succeeded in bringing clearly to light the memory of the event by which it was provoked and in arousing its accompanying affect, and when the patient had described that event in the greatest possible detail and had put the affect into words.* Recollection without affect almost invariably produces no result. The psychical process which originally took place must be repeated as vividly as possible; it must be brought back to its *status nascendi* and then given verbal utterance.[75]

Being brought back to the traumatic moment under hypnosis produced the first "talking cures," but only so long as the recollection was accompanied by affect—the affect, Freud and Breuer supposed, that had been occasioned by the initial event and had lived on unchanged. Thus, at the moment of the cure there seem to be—although Freud and Breuer do not appear to notice the tension—two kinds of memory at work: a mimetic, repetitive kind of memory and a conscious, narrative, diegetic one. The event must be consciously recollected and narrated (bringing it "clearly to light," describing it in "the greatest possible detail").[76] But, as they note, this recollection alone is insufficient. There must also be a repetition or return to the original "psychical process"—in its "state of being born."

Significantly, Freud and Breuer here suggest that the affect as such is incapable of representation; it cannot qua affect become an object of memory. It can only repeat its appearance, but in paradoxical form; it appears *again* but as if for the *first time: in status nascendi.* The therapeutic moment is like a time machine that brings us back to the moment of the birth of the affect. That is, for the affect, there has been no passage of time, hence the moment of therapeutic abreaction is not, strictly speaking, a repetition.

In any event, Breuer and Freud found that for the relief of the symptoms to be effected, both ways of accessing past experience (recollection *and* this strange kind of repetition) seemed to need to be employed and conjoined: "recollection without affect almost invariably produces no result." While the phenomenon itself was not difficult to observe, it proved quite resistant to theorization.

One problem was the lack of conceptual clarity concerning the nature and status of the "talk" in the "talking cure." Although Freud and Breuer were confident in asserting that it is the affect-filled speaking of the traumatic event that effects the cure, it remained a matter of some doubt—and Freud especially felt a need to adjudicate the matter, a need that increased over time—as to whether the curative element of the speech was its element of narrative recollection or of mimetic reenactment. At times Freud and Breuer suggest that reenactment alone could be curative. Bringing the psychic process back to its *status nascendi* is, as Borch-Jacobsen notes, "neither telling a story nor representing a past event *as past*."[77] It is a reliving, a reenactment of the event as if it were present and real. That Freud and Breuer use the term "catharsis" to describe the nature of the talking cure unmistakably references Aristotle's "imitation of an action" and in doing so suggests that it is the emotionally purgative effects of mimetic rather than narrative representation that cure.[78]

However, Freud and Breuer also assert that the cure is effected insofar as the speech produced by the analysand "brings to an end the operative force of the idea which was not abreacted in the first instance, by allowing its strangulated affect to find a way out through speech; and it subjects it to associative correction by introducing it into normal consciousness."[79] Here, they suggest that it is precisely by bringing the affect into the realm of the conscious, cognitive mind that it can be "worn down" through the effects of linguistic chains of association, by being transferred from one idea to another. It is as if bringing affects into language allows them to age (and to thereby prevent them from repeating themselves *in status nascendi ad infinitum*) by putting them into sequential time. Although in the *Studies* this ambiguity did not seem to bother Freud and Breuer (since they were happily distracted by the efficacy of the "talking cure"), later Freud would become convinced that the affect-filled speech of repetition was ultimately supplemental, a dangerous battlefield that must be confronted on the way toward the associative, narrative, curative force of recollection (but more about this later).

Another (related) problem raised in the *Studies* concerns the status and function of the analyst himself. Although Freud and Breuer knew that their hypnotic presence was crucial to the cure, Freud was a bit uncomfortable with the intimacy involved in the role and his and Breuer's lack of insight into what it actually was about the presence of the analyst that allowed the analysand to reenact a past experience. The hypnotic method, which involved a light touch on the forehead and a suggestion—"You feel sleepy," "You will remember," and so on—is basically an imitative identification between analyst and analysand. It is by taking on the analyst's words as one's own, by allowing the analyst to speak for one and through one, that the hypnosis is effected. As Borch-Jacobsen points out, "the basic phenomenon of hypnotic 'verbalization' was that the 'subjects,' far from *speaking to* another, let themselves be *spoken by* another, while miming the other."[80] Here we find what is surely one of Freud's most interesting discoveries: in order to repeat or mime a powerful emotional event from the past, it seems that it is necessary also at the same time to have a mimetic relation to someone in the present. In other words, the mimetic repetition of a past emotion is enabled by the imitation of the analyst, as if it is a question of jump-starting what Walter Benjamin called the "mimetic faculty," or as if mimesis itself occurs in an entirely distinct temporal register. The help the analyst provides suggests that perhaps what was missing in the earlier moment was the mimetic presence of someone else who could give one a feeling for the reality of the affect, as if one cannot experience an affect without being able to imagine someone else also experiencing it; as if affects are somehow essentially collective.[81]

The moment of imitation turned out to be a problem for Freud, in part because it affected *him* as well. That is, not only do affects seem to be invoked by imitation and hence to be themselves imitative but also they promote imitation (which was why Plato argued that plays and poetry, relying as they often do on mimesis, should be banned in the ideal republic). In *Group Psychology and the Analysis of the Ego,* Freud observed that "something exists in us which, when we become aware of the signs of an emotion in someone else, tends to make us fall into the same emotion."[82] Emotions are inherently contagious. The dilemma for Freud is that in making himself available for identification and imitation in order to allow the patient to repeat past emotions, he "could not avoid participating in what the hysteric was telling him," as Lacan noted.[83] So, soon after the *Studies,* Freud abandoned hypnosis, even though he would occasionally return to it, for example, as "proof"— inasmuch as it was a thing that happened—of the unconscious.[84] Freud saw his task as fortifying himself against the analyst's tendency to fall into the emotion of the analysand. But what if, we might ask, this "falling into" the emotion of the other *was* the cure?

✦

Freud's desire to avoid the confusions of hypnosis led him to adopt the method of "free association" as his main analytic technique. In principle, this involved no identifying with or imitation of the analyst and thus no affective contagion from analysand to analyst either. Freud would be strictly a reader, an interpreter of the messages bubbling up from the unconscious through the free associations.[85] However, he found that in the transference the mystery of the emotional tie reappears: "In every analytic treatment there arises, without the physician's agency, an intense emotional relationship between the patient and the analyst which is not to be accounted for by the actual situation."[86] Freud would find that this emotional relationship in the scene of analysis is in effect the transference of an emotion on the part of the analysand from a past relationship onto the therapeutic relationship. Once again, reenactment prevails over narration: "the patient remembers nothing of what is forgotten or repressed, but he expresses it in action. He reproduces it not in his memory, but in his behavior; he repeats it, without of course knowing that he repeats."[87]

Although the transferential repetition distracts the analysand from remembering and recounting and is therefore a kind of barrier or stalling tactic ("resistance"), it is, in Freud's view, also the potential key to the cure, since it brings the lost and buried emotions into the scene of analysis. In Freud's view, this makes the scene of transference a kind of battlefield.

> The unconscious feelings strive to avoid the recognition which the cure demands; they seek instead for reproduction, with all the power of hallucination and the inappreciation of time characteristic of the unconscious. The patient ascribes, just as in dreams, currency and reality to what results from the awakening of his unconscious feelings; he seeks to discharge his emotions, regardless of the reality of the situation. The physician requires of him that he shall fit these emotions into their place in the treatment and in his life history, subject them to rational consideration, and appraise them at their true psychical value. This struggle between physician and patient, between intellect and instinct, between recognition and the striving for discharge, is fought out almost entirely over the transference manifestations.[88]

In the transference, the patient repeats the past instead of remembering it. This repetition of what Freud calls here "unconscious feelings" is "hallucinatory" and does not "appreciate time." The problem, as well as the main interest of the scene, is that the patient thinks that these hallucinations are real: a piece of dream life in the waking world. As Freud sees it here, the cure clearly requires that the unrecognized emotions be put into a rational context and subjected to narrative form and sequential ordering. Yet the underlying problem he is grappling with remains the same as before: the cure can only be effected if a past emotion is repeated (mimed) in the present (and then contained), which appears to require the still problematic mimetic emotional tie between analyst and analysand. In other words, although he thought he had left the moment of identification that characterized hypnosis behind, it turned out that he could not prevent it from returning.[89] The rhetoric with which Freud represents the transferential moment—on the one side, hallucinatory unconscious feelings, instinct, discharge; on the other intellect, recognition, and *cure*—seems designed more to dramatize the difficulty of the moment than to explain how it works.

Freud saw his analytic task as the renarrativization and re-presentation of the transferred emotions. (The goal: "fit these emotions into their place in the treatment and in his life history, subject them to rational consideration, and appraise them at their true psychical value.") The transference then appears as a kind of necessary but dangerous detour or supplement. Except the "dangerous supplement" here reverses that of Derrida's Rousseau; here it is not writing and absence that supplements speech and presence. Rather, emotional presence is the dangerous detour on the way to a narrative representation of the past; the transference of affect is necessary, in fact unavoidable, but dangerous.[90] Freud writes: "It is undeniable that the subjugation of the transference-manifestations provides the greatest difficulties for the psychoanalyst; but it must not be forgotten that they, and they only, render the invaluable service of making the patient's buried and forgotten love-emotions actual and manifest: for in the last resort no one can be slain *in absentia* or *in effigie*."[91] The analyst must play the role of that (dead and gone) addressee in order to raise the dead emotions. These emotions, as he notes, are *actually* present—they are not *in effigie*—and they are actually present because they are conjured through the person of the analyst. This actual ghost from the past must be slain; the time is out of joint, and it is Freud's job to set it right. Stranger still, the analyst must alternately be the person who will be slain—the instantiation of the dead-and-gone addressee, to whom the emotions are in some sense "really" addressed—and then the slayer who provides the narrative resources of intellect and recognition. For Freud, the negotiation of these two positions came to constitute the analyst's main task in the therapy.

The confused structure of address in transference produces a reading problem for the analyst. It is not always possible to discern what role you as analyst are playing for the analysand at any given moment: when are you slayer and when slain? Transferential speech may *appear* to be addressed to the analyst, but in reality it is addressed to a ghostly presence from the past. In this sense it may—even or especially when it seems quite narrative and descriptive—be designed to elicit a particular affective response from the analyst; that is, the "remembering" done in therapy might be alibis for the creation or continuation of the emotional tie with the analyst. The analyst's task, as Freud sees it, is to read the hidden emotional demand and thus the buried memory being reenacted—an especially tricky task, since the diegetic memory of the past is in fact what the analyst *wants* from the analysand. The production of the speech that the patient knows the analyst wants was just one way that speech designed to elicit an emotional response from the analyst often succeeded: this came to be called the "counter-transference."

Even as Freud's understanding of what happened in the space of analysis became more sophisticated, his sense of the logic of the cure did not advance much beyond what he and Breuer figured out in the *Studies*. The basic phenomenon remained the same: "the psychical process which originally took place must be repeated as vividly as possible; it must be brought back to its *status nascendi* and then given verbal utterance." The affect must come into being, and it must be put into language.

Once he had discarded the notion that the cure was "cathartic," he was left mainly with the notion that therapy allowed one finally to leave the past behind, to stop repeating the same old emotions over and over again, or at least to know that one is repeating them instead of repeating them unwittingly. This notion, which has become something like therapeutic common sense, might be rendered as follows: the transference is what allows therapy to become a laboratory in which we get to see our affects in all their messiness play themselves out on a relatively neutral, contained, and autonomous field. During that process, we learn to recognize certain patterns, tendencies of our emotional life. We learn to recognize where an emotion is coming from—what it is repeating and hence can recognize it when it appears and so can dampen its effects. The process allows us to get some distance and perspective on our emotions, to defamiliarize them and to take them both more and less seriously as a result. We can remember, for example: "Oh this emotion, this emotion is not really about my boyfriend or girlfriend or colleague or whoever, it's about someone else from my past. This is a pattern for me." Indeed, that moment of recognition is a powerful and necessary one, since it allows one to see one's affective life in a broader context, and thus to make it newly strange so that it can become the object of analysis and action.

✦

When he does write about affectivity explicitly, as in his "Papers on Metapsychology" (1915), Freud's rhetoric is different from that of his writings on the practice of therapy itself. Usually, as in the *Studies on Hysteria,* he conceives of affect as sheer quantity; it manifests as intensity. Thus, affects resist representation, not only by the psyche itself, but by the psychoanalytic theorist as well. Furthermore, because they are not ideas, and because they cannot be represented, affects cannot, strictly speaking, be repressed. This means that the term "unconscious feelings" that Freud sometimes used (as in "the patient ascribes, just as in dreams, currency and reality to what results from the awakening of his unconscious feelings; he seeks to discharge his emotions, regardless of the reality of the situation") was—according to Freud's own theory—at best an imprecise one, and at worst incorrect and misleading. He wrote: "It is surely of the essence of an emotion that we should be aware of it, i.e., that it should become known to consciousness. Thus the possibility of the attribute of unconsciousness would be completely excluded as far as emotions, feelings, and affect are concerned."[92] Rather, it is the idea to which an affect has become attached that is unconscious. While affects may attach to unconscious ideas and in this sense be "unconscious feelings," they do not like to sit still in the unconscious; they always search for a way out. However, Freud has a difficult time generalizing about their paths as they try to make their way out—what we might call their vicissitudes. As Lacan put it: "Freud emphasizes that it is not the affect that is repressed. The affect . . . goes off somewhere else, as best it can."[93]

Despite this lack of clarity about the logic that affects follow in their movements in Freud's writings, we can nonetheless discern several things about what affects *do* do in Freud. If he *had* written about the vicissitudes of the affects, he might have observed the following.

First, affects operate according to their own temporality, a temporality that is neither linear nor homogeneous. Hence, for example, they reappear *in status nascendi*. While in linear, clock time, affects seem to be *repeating*, in that the same affect can occur over and over again (in symptoms, or dreams, or in the transference itself), this is not strictly speaking a repetition, since they appear each time as if they are being born *for the first time*; they appear always as a becoming.

Second, affects attach (to just about any kind of object—people, things, ideas, desires, thoughts), and they transfer (from one object to another, from one idea to another, and from one person to another, from the past to the present). In *The Interpretation of Dreams*, Freud hints that transference and attachment might describe the vicissitudes of affect more generally. There, *transference* refers not to the transference of an unconscious feeling from the past onto the person of the analyst but the general process whereby the unconscious manages to communicate with consciousness. "An unconscious idea is as such quite incapable of entering the preconscious . . . it can only exercise any effect there by establishing a connection with an idea which already belongs to the preconscious, by transferring its intensity onto it and getting itself "covered" by it."[94] In other words, it is not the unconscious idea itself that travels from the unconscious to the conscious but its "intensity." Transference here is a kind of communication system between the conscious and the unconscious, where "intensity" can be disattached from one (unconscious) thought and then reattached to another (preconscious) one. Freud suggests that this "intensity" may or may not alter the very nature of the preconscious thought; the intensity may retain something of the unconscious idea itself. Thus the fear or joy or shame or whatever one might feel about some inappropriate and hence repressed object can nonetheless make its way into consciousness by attaching itself to some other object. (In the case of dreams, these other objects are often taken from the residue of daily experience—people you happened to see that day, conversations you just had, the TV show you were watching before bed, etc.)

If we take this "intensity" to be what Freud would elsewhere call affect, then what we have is the suggestion that affects function like shuttles on which messages can make it from the unconscious into consciousness. These passages, as Freud would suggest elsewhere, tend to be ruled by a mimetic logic: affects transfer along paths of likeness. One's teacher reminds one a little of one's father, and so one transfers some of the feelings one had for one's father onto one's teacher. The similarity, however, can be quite slight, if the affect is trying to make its way out "as best it can": a similar color of hair, tone of voice, mode of behavior. It is by paying attention to these likenesses that Freud was able to interpret the initial source of an affect, whether in a dream or in analysis.

We might continue this line of thought to suggest that if affect travels along paths of likeness, then the analyst must be ready to be-similar, to be a like-being. In this, the analyst is something like what Christopher Bollas called "an evocative mnemic trace" of the earlier emotional tie.[95] To be affected, the other, *as* self-identical other, must be able to *not* be there. The function of analysis would then be to provide this identificatory site, the relational prop through which emotions from the past can come into being.

In this way, "falling into" the emotional world of the analysand may be necessary for the cure. Indeed, the mechanism and aesthetic of that "falling into" and the relationship thereby created may in fact constitute the cure. If this is the case, then the will to knowledge and insight that seems to be the guiding ideology of psychoanalysis may be an alibi for setting up a situation where the analyst is *required* to read into the words of the patient, to imagine what it is that the analysand is feeling—in other words, to imaginatively imitate the patient. Freud runs into problems when he treats this moment of imitative identification as a mere supplemental step toward the cure and not the point of the therapeutic practice itself, since it is the basic skill required to be emotionally involved in the world.

At its best, psychoanalysis is about learning to invoke, manage, and happily live with ghosts. This is what enables the analysand to make use of objects again, that is to say, to be interested in and to form affective attachments to objects in the world. The analysand needs to be able to see that the internal ghosts can emerge, that ghostly identification can still happen. For it is only within this spectral economy—when the other is a ghost and can therefore be confused with or identified with one's own internal ghosts—that one can be emotionally present to the present.[96]

However, for Freud, in the final analysis, therapy is curative when it is curative because it makes conscious the unconscious. The emotional tie formed in the space of analysis is useful because it encourages the analysand to accept the analyst's interpretation, an interpretation that will give the analysand a conscious, cognitive distance on his or her experience. The point, for Freud, is to mourn the losses, to get past them, to get rid of the ghosts. That moment in analysis where affects are represented (mimetically) is valuable (in a supplemental way) only insofar as it presents the necessary material, which can then be contained, narrated, and given meaning.

Even though Freud viewed as analytic failures those moments when he sometimes succumbed to the confusing pleasures of reading and being read into, it is useful to remember that he, too, took pleasure in such moments. This pleasure was likely not just the pleasure of uncovering the truth but also the pleasure associated with the intimacy of the emotional tie itself, the pleasure of affecting and being affected. One example of many would be the climactic exchange between Freud and his patient in his "Notes on a Case of Obsessional Neurosis," or the so-called case of the Rat Man. Here, the analysand is having a difficult time recounting the source of his trauma. He cannot put the memory into speech. He is trying, though, and he has gotten so far as to be able to explain that what troubles him so much is not something that actually happened to him but a story someone told him. It was a story about a particular mode of punishment that had been told to him by a man he had been with in the army. Freud, having explained to him the importance of overcoming the resistance if he was to be cured—the importance of putting into speech the traumatic story—nonetheless assures him that he (Freud) will assist him by doing his best to guess the full meaning of any hints given him. Here is the moment of revelation as Freud tells it.

> Was he perhaps thinking of impalement?—
> "No not that; . . . the criminal was tied up . . ."
> —he expressed himself so indistinctly that I could not immediately guess in what position—
> ". . . a pot was turned upside down on his buttocks . . . some *rats* were put into it . . . and they . . ."
> —he had again got up and was showing every sign of horror and resistance—
> ". . . bored their way in . . ."
> —Into his anus, I helped him out.[97]

Here, Freud seems to think that he is offering mainly the resources of cognition and narrative: the analysand is too fearful to recount the repressed memories, so Freud will help him out by offering the clinical, distanced-but-compassionate, just-the-facts voice. But in order to do this, he must identify with the analysand, imagine what he thinks the analysand *wants* to say but cannot. And so Freud says it: "into his anus." I cannot help but think that any curative effects here would be generated not from the analysand's overcoming of the resistance (piercing as Freud's analysis may be) but the pleasure that might be taken, unconscious or otherwise, in getting your analyst to play a role in your emotional-libidinal drama, indeed to put himself in your place, to identify with you, to the point that he can finish your sentences. That this finish involves an imaginary anal penetration is another turn of the screw.

While Freud may be breaking through the shield of the patient's resistance here, he is also participating in the production of the speech in analysis in a way that can have powerful emotional effects of its own. That is, the analysand is not himself solely responsible for producing the narration—it is a thoroughly collaborative effort. And while this fact caused Freud endless anxiety about the scientific status and curative powers of psychoanalysis, it may nonetheless be the very "scene-ness" of the scene of analysis, its dramatic element, that is most attractive and antidepressive about therapy for the patient.[98] It may be, in other words, that therapy is therapeutic not because it enables one to narrativize and make conscious unmourned losses but because it creates the space where one can turn a melancholic relation to one's past into an emotional tie. This space—one shaped and enacted by one's affect-filled speech—allows for the imagination of an audience, the knowledge that someone is seeing you and reading into you, and thus identifying with you, confusing his or her self with yours. Thus, it is the affective interaction and emotional tie thereby established in the space of analysis that enables us to live with the return of the ghostly, melancholic memories, to survive through them, rather than to "slay them," as Freud at times suggests it is the role of analysis to do.

Walter Benjamin: Melancholy as Method

> Historical materialism sees the work of the past as still incomplete.
>
> —WALTER BENJAMIN, "EDWARD FUCHS,
> COLLECTOR AND HISTORIAN"

It is not hard to see that the themes of melancholia and loss are central to Benjamin's thought.[99] That Benjamin himself—born, as he noted, "under the sign of Saturn"[100]—tended toward depression is well known, and the problem of melancholy recurs regularly in his work, from *The Origin of German Tragic Drama* up through his writings on Baudelaire and his reflections "On the Concept of History."[101]

For Benjamin, melancholia is not a problem to be cured; loss is not something to get over and leave behind. However, he *is* concerned to show that there is more than one way to be attached to loss—all melancholias are not the same—and that everything depends on the *how* of one's melancholic attachments. Thus, he persistently critiques a melancholia that leads to inaction and complacency, such as the one he finds in the (at the time) popular poetry of Eric Kästner. In his short 1931 review essay "Left-Wing Melancholy," Benjamin subjects Kästner to a blistering attack in which he accuses him of promoting the cynical and indulgent pleasure of a political radicalism without the possibility of any "corresponding political action."[102] In Kästner's hands, political struggle becomes an object of pleasant consumption, one with which the bourgeois public can enjoy a "negativistic quiet."[103] This "tortured stupidity," Benjamin argues, inevitably leads to "complacency and fatalism."[104]

We should not take this attack, however, to mean that Benjamin was against melancholy *tout court,* only that for him a melancholy dwelling on loss must always be connected to present political concerns. In fact, Benjamin's counterintuitive contention is that it is precisely by dwelling on loss, the past, and political failures (as opposed to images of a better future) that one may avoid a depressing and cynical relation to the present. What emerges is the picture of a politicizing, splenetic melancholy, where clinging to things from the past *enables* interest and action in the present world and is indeed the very mechanism for that interest. Where the flip side of the pathological melancholia from Aristotle to the Romantics was individual intellectual ability and creative genius, for Benjamin it is a historical-allegorical insight. Even though melancholia is a subjectively experienced phenomenon for Benjamin, its source of (potential) value is not the individual or solipsistic creative tendencies or abilities it might bring with it but the way it might allow one to gain access to the historical origins of one's suffering, and indeed to the logic of historicity itself.

Benjamin saw such a melancholy at work nowhere more emphatically than in the poetry of Baudelaire: "Melanchthon's phrase 'Melencolia illa heroica' provides the most perfect definition of Baudelaire's genius."[105] Baudelaire's melancholy is heroic in the sense that he used his own experience of loss—indeed purposefully sought out experiences of loss—as a way to research historical change. Baudelaire became what we might call a traumatophile in order to assemble, within himself, a set of historical data about a collectively experienced world as raw material for his poetic production. In so doing he also attunes himself to his audience, which, while accustomed to loss, had, in response to it, fallen into an anesthetizing *ennui.*[106] And then he can direct his transformative, poetic gaze toward his own internal collection of experience-ruins. If, in the case of baroque allegory (as Benjamin argued in *The Origin of German Tragic Drama*), the outside world became a collection of ruins to the precise extent that it was placed under a melancholic allegorical gaze, for Baudelaire it was an internal world of memories itself that was in ruins and ready for allegorical transformation. In this sense, where "the key figure in early allegory is the corpse[,] in late allegory it is the 'souvenir' [*Andenken*]" (CP, 190). We can see this internalized melancholic allegorical way of seeing at work in (among other places) the second of Baudelaire's "Spleen" poems.

J'ai plus de souvenirs que si j'avais mille ans.

Un gros meuble à tiroirs encombré de bilans,
De vers, de billets doux, de procès, de romances,
Avec de lourds cheveux roulés dans des quittances,
Cache moins de secrets que mon triste cerveau.
C'est une pyramide, un immense caveau,
Qui contient plus de morts que la fosse commune.
—Je suis un cimetière abhorré de la lune,
Où comme des remords se traînent de longs vers
Qui s'acharnent toujours sur mes morts les plus chers.
Je suis un vieux boudoir plein de roses fanées,
Où gît tout un fouillis de modes surannées,
Où les pastels plaintifs et les pâles Boucher
Seuls, respirent l'odeur d'un flacon débouché.

Rien n'égale en longueur les boiteuses journées,
Quand sous les lourds flocons des neigeuses années
L'ennui, fruit de la morne incuriosité,
Prend les proportions de l'immortalité.
—Désormais tu n'es plus, ô matière vivante!
Qu'un granit entouré d'une vague épouvante,
Assoupi dans le fond d'un Sahara brumeux;
Un vieux sphinx ignoré du monde insoucieux,
Oublié sur la carte, et dont l'humeur farouche
Ne chante qu'aux rayons du soleil qui se couche.

I have more memories than if I had lived a thousand years.

Even a bureau crammed with souvenirs,
Old bills, love letters, photographs, receipts,
Court depositions, locks of hair in plaits,
Hides fewer secrets than my brain could yield.
Its like a tomb, a corpse-filled Potter's Field,
A pyramid where the dead lie down by scores.
I am a graveyard that the moon abhors:
Like guilty qualms, the worms burrow and nest
Thickly in bodies I loved the best.
I'm a stale boudoir where old fashioned clothes
Lie scattered among wilted fern and rose,
Where only Boucher girls in pale pastels
Can breathe the uncorked scents and faded smells.

Nothing can equal those days for endlessness
When in the winter's blizzardy caress
Indifference expanding to Ennui
Takes on the feel of Immortality.
O living matter, henceforth you're no more

Than a cold stone encompassed by vague fear
And by the desert, and the mist and sun;
An ancient Sphinx ignored by everyone,
Left off the map, whose bitter irony
Is to sing as the sun sets in that dry sea.[107]

Here, the speaker's interiority, his cavern-like brain, has been stuffed with the material residue of everyday life, from bills and court documents to love letters and plaits of hair. Like Freud, who wrote of the introjected lost object, Baudelaire also writes of a subject who has cast inside himself lost objects. But in this case, the objects are the dead leftovers of human interaction, and indeed, the speaker feels, the dead themselves. Where Freud's "character of the ego" can be seen as a complex layering of precipitates, here we find a common grave, filled with the anonymous corpses of the poor, which makes a very different kind of archeological site indeed. Even though it is in his dearest dead ("mes morts les plus chers") that the worms of regret work most diligently, the *I* of the poem here suggests there is far more than abandoned love objects in his brain. Indeed, he feels as if he contains more dead than lie in the "Potter's Field," a vast tomb, or a neglected cemetery. There is in this cavernous brain an enormous but anonymous collectivity, as if the speaker has lost the entire world, the world that Boredom, in "Au Lecteur," has swallowed with a yawn—a loss that is, for Benjamin, matched by the allegorical resurrection or transformation that is its flip side.

The *I* of this poem feels as if his experience is an overwhelmingly huge catalogue of stale *souvenirs*, mute things-that-have-happened to him, which hold their odor only for the figures in a painting. In fact, he is so alienated from his memories that it is as if they belong to ancient history; he is as a pyramid or sphinx: Baudelaire's "spleen interposes centuries between the present moment and the one just lived" (CP, 166). His experiences do not affect or change him, except, perhaps, to produce regret. Apropos this situation as it is described in Baudelaire, Benjamin writes: "The *souvenir* is the complement to 'isolated experience' [*Erlebnis*]. In it is precipitated the increasing self-estrangement of human beings, whose past is inventoried as dead effects. In the nineteenth century, allegory withdrew from the world around us to settle in the inner world. The relic comes from the cadaver, the souvenir comes from the defunct experience [*Erfahrung*] which thinks of itself, euphemistically, as living [*Erlebnis*]" (CP, 183). This person who is beyond experiencing, who has been enveloped by ennui, feels like a stone, his only feeling a vague fear. Unseen, unaffected, singing to no one, he is not only emotionally alienated from the world: he has been left off the map altogether ("oublié sur la carte").

For Benjamin, this is all related to the generalized impoverishment of experience that Baudelaire saw unfolding before him. He explains this decline in the value of experience in the essay "On Some Motifs in Baudelaire" by way of a discussion of Proustian involuntary memory. In Proust's famous example, the taste of the madeleine allows him to return, with a feeling of affective immediacy, to a moment from the past that had been forgotten. This "intrusion of a forgotten past that disrupts the fictitious progress of chronological time"[108] is not an escape from the present, but (paradoxically) a more attentive return to it. In part this is because the interruption of our habitual flow through the rhythms of means-ends rationality is brought about by a material thing—a cookie, a room, a city street. Indeed, one might say that this memory-experience does not really happen *in* the subject, but outside of us in the world of things.[109] While the materiality of *mémoire involontaire* and the fact that it lies "beyond the reach of the intellect" leads Proust to be pessimistic about the possibilities of such memory experiences *in general*,[110] for Benjamin, the fact that mémoire involontaire is individual and subject to chance is a historical fact. "There is nothing inevitable," he writes, "about the dependence on chance in this matter. A person's inner concerns are not by nature of an inescapably private character. They attain this character only after the likelihood decreases that one's external concerns will be assimilated to one's experience" (MB, 315). The speaker of Baudelaire's second "Spleen" poem is the very paradigm of the person who cannot assimilate his world by way of experience.

We can see that there is nothing inevitable about this situation, Benjamin asserts, by recalling, for example, that in the past, rituals, traditions, and festivals could work like collective, planned tastes of the madeleine, allowing one reliable access to experience and memory. "Where there is experience [*Erfahrung*] in the strict sense of the word, certain contents of the individual past combine in the memory with material from the collective past. Rituals, with their ceremonies and their festivals . . . kept producing the amalgamation of these two elements of memory over and over again. They triggered recollection at certain times and remained available to memory throughout people's lives. In this way, voluntary and involuntary recollection cease to be mutually exclusive" (MB, 316). In such a case, the affect-filled experiences of involuntary memory are no longer a matter of chance but are something for which one voluntarily plans. Tradition can work as a support for experience, inasmuch as it connects us collectively to the past, reliably providing us with an intimately felt reservoir of images from the past that exceeds our own private experience.[111]

Benjamin linked the decline in experience to modernity. A range of historical processes, such as urbanization, the commodity, new forms of technologized war, and factory work required people to shield themselves from the material world around them, to stop being emotionally open to that world and the people in it.[112] Even the simple experience of riding on a bus or railroad, which puts people "in a position of having to stare at one another for minutes or even hours on end without exchanging a word," would be overwhelming if we felt compelled to have some emotional contact with all the people we see.[113] In such circumstances, the primary function of consciousness, Benjamin argues, is to protect us from the shocks of daily life, to insulate us from disruptive emotional experiences. This prevents us from affective contact with the materiality of the world around us; we do not get outside ourselves, and so we have fewer and fewer memory-experiences stored in the objects and places of our everyday world. In part, consciousness achieves this shielding effect by riding the flow of homogeneous time, placing experience into a "rosary bead" sequence that renders events accessible to "voluntary memory" but at the same time erases its "contents." ("Its signal characteristic is that the information it gives about the past retains no trace of that past" [MB, 315].) This kind of experience is not really experience at all, but a "moment lived through," or *Erlebnis*.

In such social-historical conditions, Proust is right: we are subject to contingency and lucky tastes of the madeleine. In order to affect us, things have to break through the shield of consciousness, an experience Baudelaire actively sought, showing us the length one had to go to have an experience, and at the same time dramatizing why we usually do not. Benjamin suggests that Baudelaire's attention to the poverty of present experience focused attention on what had been lost, and thus, also, by way of these losses, on the specificity of the present moment. In this way, even as he wrote about the deadening effects of ennui, his descriptions allow the reader to see that this feeling is a product of specific historical processes, and thereby also connected to a shared situation: no person is alone in this feeling.

For Benjamin, an idealized version of *Erfahrung*—in which involuntary and voluntary memory mingle, where individual and collective experience are conjoined—remained a kind of center of gravity, not so that he could lament its passing, but so that he could remember to keep looking for the echoes of "experience in its strict form" in whatever secret places they were hiding.[114] Such was the source of his interest in a wide range of practices, including surrealist poetics, traveling to Moscow, and smoking hashish. Indeed, Benjamin saw revolution itself as a collective return to such a mode of experience, a sublation of the rituals and festivals of the past. On the subjective level, revolution would feel like Proust's involuntary memory, a surprising collective return to a past we didn't even know we had forgotten, which at the time of uprising would feel uncannily familiar. It would be brought about through a creative, melancholic relation to the images from the past, a relation he aphoristically presents in his now famous theses "On the Concept of History."

✦

> The dialectical image can be defined as the involuntary memory of redeemed humanity.
>
> —WALTER BENJAMIN, PARALIPOMENA TO
> "ON THE CONCEPT OF HISTORY"

In thesis 7 of "On the Concept of History," Benjamin makes his case by way of an explanation of the approach to history that must absolutely be avoided. Even it is generated out of the seemingly benign impulses of empathy or curiosity, the "historicist" attempt to reconstruct the past "as it was" is not only depressing but, in direct proportion to its depressiveness, politically irresponsible.

> Addressing himself to the historian who wishes to relive an era, Fustel de Coulanges recommends that he blot out everything he knows about the later course of history. There is no better way of characterizing the method which historical materialism has broken with. It is a process of empathy. Its origin is that indolence of the heart, that *acedia* which despairs of appropriating the genuine historical image as it briefly flashes up. Among medieval theologians, acedia was regarded as the root cause of sadness. Flaubert, who was familiar with it, wrote: "Peu de gens devineront combien il a fallue etre triste pur ressusciter Carthage."[115]

Historians who want to "relive an era," for Benjamin, end up involved in "a process of empathy whose origin is the "indolence of the heart," or *acedia,* that medieval version of melancholia, that sin also known as sloth, which was suffered by early Christian monks (H, 391).[116] Such a practice is, in essence, an attempt to escape into the past, to transfer one's emotions to this other time. Historicism is akin to Kästner's left-wing melancholy, in that it has no interest in the present world, trying instead to "blot it out." This is a response to acedia, in Benjamin's view, that will only intensify it, not least because it ignores rather than trans-forms the conditions that created the depressive desire to escape in the first place.[117]

The fact that this historicist practice is politically conservative exacer-bates its depressing quality. "The nature of this sadness becomes clearer if we ask: With whom does historicism actually sympathize? The answer is inevitable: with the victor. And all rulers are the heirs of prior conquerors. Hence empathizing with the victor invariably benefits the current rulers" (H, 391). For the oppressed, the medium of this empathy with the past—"culture"—is hopelessly tainted ("there is no document of culture that is not at the same time a record of barbarism"; 392) because "culture" presents itself as autonomous from its historical conditions of possibil-ity (conditions that include the ways the producers and preservers of "culture" have relied on and benefited from relations of domination). For Benjamin, "cultural treasures" can only be viewed with horror, since they amount to the spoils being held aloft in the triumphal victory parade of the class war. To continue to celebrate these cultural treasures is to step yet again on those who lie prostrate. Moreover, it is also an (un)conscious identification with the rulers of past and present; for the oppressed, nothing could be more discouraging, since one will not find there a recognition of one's suffering, but justifications for it. One must therefore view history "against the grain," from the point of view of history's losers, in an attempt to rescue from a collective past images that have the power to startle one into righteous action.

The "historicist" ignores the moments of struggle and discontinuity behind cultural documents, tending instead toward a model of histori-cal progress, where one thing happens after another in a comprehen-sible order like "beads in a rosary." That is, the historicist's practice is underwritten by "homogenous time"—exemplified in the inexorable second-by-second movement of the clock—which makes it seem as if the past is over and done with.[118] This is means-ends clock time; its mantras are: get over it, forget about the past, time marches on; progress is coming, the *future* will bring it—so just go with the flow. It breeds complacency. "Nothing has so corrupted the German working class as the notion that it was moving with the current" (H, 393).

If historicism, in giving into homogeneous time, induces acedia and complacency as it disavows relations of domination, then Benjamin's task (as "historical materialist") is to produce insight about the nature and history of oppression in a way that is capable of warding off the depression—the "feeling of resignation"—that insights about one's own oppression can produce. After all, recognizing one's oppression does not in itself make for revolutionary resistance. The historical materialist must ask: Where is the emotional reward and reinforcement, the affective center of gravity that prevents us from taking pleasure in "cultural treasures," and instead keeps us listening for "the true picture of the past" that "flits by"?

Historical materialism, Benjamin explains, is a practice of melancholic remembrance "wherein what has been comes together in a flash with with the now to form a constellation" (N, 462), a combination of surprising historico-political insight that brings with it a joltingly electric sense of emotional investment in the possibility of transformation. The constellation, or "dialectical image," avoids a developmental historical logic, disrupting, like Proust's madeleine, our sense of a progression through empty time, rendering time not empty and homogeneous, but discontinuous—interrupted. At the same time, such an image shows us the nature and source of our oppression—it shows us where to strike. In this sense, these images from the past are "used," not "interpreted."[119] This also means that the historical materialist must embrace a dual view—one toward present emotionally urgent concerns (those that "appear at a moment of danger"; H, 291) and one toward the storehouse of images of the past, from which images are "blasted" to show us "the constellation which our own era has formed with a definite earlier one."

One reason the image-constellation formed between the present and an earlier era is emotionally powerful, Benjamin argues, is that emotional investment in the present is, in *general*, generated out of remembrance. More specifically, our "image of happiness," he writes, "is indissolubly bound up with the image of redemption" (H, 389), by which he means that we are motivated most by the idea of repairing past wrongs, renewing lost friendships, proving wrong the one who had contempt for us, or winning back the affection of the one who has rejected us. "Happiness is founded on the very despair and desolation which were ours" (N, 479). The image of happiness is not abstract; it cannot be given an emotional heft by speculative wishes. Fantasies about our happiness are always (in one way or another, conscious or not) given their affective force by the extent to which they respond to a past loss.

Likewise, splenetic anger and the spirit of sacrifice are "nourished by the image of enslaved ancestors rather than by the ideal of liberated grandchildren" (H, 394). The best way to avoid being a pessimist is to "place a taboo on the future," as Benjamin claims Baudelaire did (CP, 162). The possibility of a melancholic connection to the past is enabled by the particular temporal logic of affect, the fact that, as Freud discovered, affects could live on in the unconscious unchanged, "like a foreign body," and still hold their full force many years later.[120] Affects are always ready for resurrection; the passage of "homogeneous time" is, as it were, irrelevant to them.

In thesis 2, Benjamin makes a subtle transition from a discussion of individual happiness in relation to one's own past to a consideration of our collective happiness in relation to a collective past. "Doesn't a breath of the air that pervaded earlier days caress us as well? In the voices we hear, isn't there an echo of now silent ones? Don't the women we court have sisters they no longer recognize? If so, then there is a secret agreement between past generations and the present one. Then our coming was expected on earth" (H, 390).[121] For Benjamin, it is not only that we are motivated by the abstract desire to redeem the past, but that we actually feel these emotions from the past. There is for Benjamin a definite resonance between our own personal past and a historical, collective past. The past is never solely our own anyway: "what has been forgotten . . . is never something purely individual," he remarks in another context.[122] It is as if the realm of the forgotten is not within the individual, but is some vast collective historical space, where it converses with everything else that has been forgotten. "Everything forgotten mingles with what has been forgotten of the prehistoric world, forms countless uncertain and changing compounds, yielding a constant flow of new, strange products."[123] To recover that which has been forgotten, therefore, puts one into contact with this vast archive of changing compounds and strange products.

When we feel an emotional connection with the historical losers, sensing the similarity between their situation and our own, it allows us to feel the historicity of our own subjectivity and to see how long our "present misery has been in preparation" (N, 481). This moment gives us "a high opinion of [our] own powers," in Benjamin's view, because when our own oppression can be linked up to those who have preceded us, it demonstrates the vast amount of historical time that is condensed within our own emotional lives, allowing us to feel as if our own life was "a muscle strong enough to contract the whole of historical time" (N, 479).

This muscle would contract at a moment of affective abreaction, one not accomplished in therapy but in revolution itself, where images from the past would collide with the present with explosive force.

> History is the subject of a construction whose site is not homogeneous, empty time, but time filled full by now-time [*Jetztzeit*]. Thus, to Robespierre ancient Rome was a past charged with now-time, a past which he blasted out of the continuum of history. The French Revolution viewed itself as Rome reincarnate. It cited ancient Rome exactly the way fashion cites a bygone mode of dress. Fashion has a nose for the topical, no matter where it stirs in the thickets of long ago; it is the tiger's leap into the past. Such a leap, however, takes place in an arena where the ruling class gives the commands. The same leap in the open air of history is the dialectical leap Marx understood as revolution. (H, 395)

For Benjamin, the French revolutionaries were able to engage in revolution precisely because they seized images from the past—from Rome. In making this argument, Benjamin engages in a polemic with the Marx of *The Eighteenth Brumaire*. Although it is true that for Marx the French Revolution did borrow a language from the past (and hence that is how he "understood the revolution"), Marx *worried* about these moments when people *seem* like they are revolutionizing but are borrowing from the past—it was precisely this borrowing that evidenced "the tradition of all the dead generations" weighing "like a nightmare on the brain of the living."[124] Marx suggests that we need to figure out how to mourn those losses and finally leave them in the past, to let "the dead bury their dead" in order to create a "poetry of the future."[125] The coming revolution, therefore, for Marx, would have performed its mourning already; it would not be trapped in the past any longer.[126] For Benjamin however, contra Marx, the revolutionary, say Robespierre, rescues images from the past and resurrects them by imitating them: the French Revolutionaries are "Rome incarnate"; they bring Rome back from the dead. For Benjamin, the structure of revolutionary consciousness is necessarily melancholic; and, conversely, melancholia contains within it a revolutionary kernel.

It is worth noting Benjamin's somewhat unexpected and certainly unorthodox suggestion that we can understand revolution by analogy to fashion. ("It cited ancient Rome the way fashion evokes costumes of the past.") Fashion mines the past in the same way as do Robespierre and the historical materialist. ("Fashion has a nose for the topical, no matter where it stirs in the thickets of long ago; it is a tiger's leap into the past.") In the case of fashion, that leap into the past is about selling a product, not about revolution, which is why he says "it takes place in an arena where the ruling class gives the commands." But, fashion, like the commodity, bears the same melancholy mimetic structure that we see in revolution. Hence, insofar as fashion initiates us into a melancholic historical practice and a nonhomogenous experience of temporality, it can potentially provide us with a kind of revolutionary education.[127]

This does not mean that the "tiger's leap into the past" is necessarily progressive or revolutionary. The process is essentially political, open to contestation from the left or the right. For example, the singing of spirituals or "sorrow songs" during the civil rights movement invoked the history of slavery and racism in the United States to potent effect, and the appropriation of the pink triangle by the gay and lesbian rights movement draws some of its force from its recollection of the Nazi oppression of gays and lesbians. But that temporally disjunctive evocation of the past is the same device used to sell a product—indeed one might argue that it is the master trope of the commodity fetish. And the Serbians draw on centuries old images of their conflicts with the Albanians (a church building defaced seven hundred years earlier, for instance) to put the emotional energy behind "ethnic cleansing." The point is that a melancholic relation to the past is not necessarily of one political slant. Rather, Benjamin's theory suggests that motives such as retribution and reparation are "fundamentally indifferent to the passage of time,"[128] and that there are lots of retribution-reparation feelings and images of unachieved happinesses floating around in that pile of catastrophes we call history.

CHAPTER TWO

Affective Mapping

The decisively new ferment that enters the taedium
vitae *and turns it into spleen is self-estrangement.*

—WALTER BENJAMIN, "CENTRAL PARK"

In his influential 1960 book *The Image of the City,* Kevin Lynch explored the ways residents internalize maps of their cities. These cognitive maps give one a sense of location and direction, and enable one to make decisions about where one wants to go and how to get there.[1] A later scholar helpfully defined cognitive mapping as "a process composed of a series of psychological transformations by which an individual acquires, stores, recalls and decodes information about the relative locations and attributes of the phenomena in his everyday spatial environment."[2] Lynch studied three different cities—Boston, Los Angeles, and Jersey City—and found that some cities are more "legible" to their residents than others. That is, "the ease with which [the city's] parts can be recognized and can be organized into a coherent pattern" varies from city to city.[3] In a nongrid city like Boston, with notable points of reference like the Charles River, Boston Common, and Boston Harbor, residents were quite able to assemble usable cognitive maps of the city through repetitive experience of it. Jersey City, on the other hand, organized by an incomplete grid, was found to be more undifferentiated and thus less legible. Many of its residents, Lynch found, had only fragmented or partial images of the city. Since an image of the total system in which one is located is of course a crucial element in establishing one's confidence in one's ability to live in the world—see friends, get to the hospital, buy groceries, go out to dinner, arrive at the train station on time—the lack of such an ability can produce a sense of anxiety and alienation.

In his essay "Cognitive Mapping," Fredric Jameson expanded the use of the term to suggest that just as one needs a cognitive map of city space in order to have a sense of agency there, one requires a cognitive map of social space for a sense of agency in the world more generally.[4] Such a map's function is "to enable a situational representation on the part of the individual subject to that vaster and properly unrepresentable totality which is the ensemble of society's structures as a whole."[5] In other words, in its negotiation of the gap between local subjective experience and a vision of an overall environment, the cognitive map is an apt figure for one of the functions of ideology, which is, in Althusser's now classic formulation, "the representation of the subject's imaginary relationship to his or her real conditions of existence."[6] We all need such representations, no matter how imaginary, in order to make sense and move through our everyday lives. By the same token, "the incapacity to map socially is as crippling to political experience as the analogous incapacity to map spatially is for urban experience."[7]

The difference with the social map is that where the totality of Boston is quite representable, the "totality which is the ensemble of society's structures as a whole," conversely, is not. And the socioeconomic systems we all must negotiate on a daily basis are becoming ever less representable.[8] Increasingly, Jameson argues, the distance between the structures that order everyday life and the phenomenology and datum of that life itself have become unbridgeable.[9] Cognitive mapping in this context would be an essential part of "a pedagogical political culture which seeks to endow the individual subject with some new heightened sense of its place in the global system."[10] Without such a picture insights remain partial and fragmented; we remain mired in the logic of the system as it exists.

✦

So then what is this thing I have been calling affective mapping? In the context of geography and environmental psychology, the term *affective mapping* has been used to indicate the affective aspects of the maps that guide us, in conjunction with our cognitive maps, through our spatial environment.[11] That is, we develop our sense of our environments through purposive activity in the world, and we always bring with us a range of intentions, beliefs, desires, moods, and affective attachments to this activity. Hence our spatial environments are inevitably imbued with the feelings we have about the places we are going, the things that happen to us along the way, and the people we meet, and these emotional valences, of course, affect how we create itineraries. For instance, I live in downtown Detroit, and when I am in the suburbs around Detroit, I often get the sense that some people in the suburbs who have not crossed over the city limits for years carry around with them a map on which Detroit is a large, hazily defined space, but a space clearly marked by some mixture of fear, anxiety, sorrow, and nostalgia. They avoid Detroit not because of poor urban planning or a lack of landmarks but because of the emotions they have associated with the city space of Detroit.

Thus, by way of analogy, I would suggest that social maps are also marked with various affective values. To return to the example regarding the suburban resident who avoids Detroit, this is an affective map of social space as well, in a way that parallels ideology. For in all likelihood the person from the suburbs of whom I write is white, and Detroit is largely African American, and this split is of course overwritten by a class divide, so emotions about Detroit as a space are, for these suburban residents, inevitably also emotions about class and "race" and racism. In short, it is not just ideologies or cognitive maps that shape our behavior and practices in the world but also the affects we have about the relevant social structures of our world. The term *affective map* in this sense is meant to indicate the pictures we all carry around with us on which are recorded the affective values of the various sites and situations that constitute our social worlds.

I should perhaps reemphasize here that "map" is meant in a particular, metaphorical sense, a metaphorics that I hope does not too seriously limit the concept. The affective map, like Deleuze and Guattari's rhizomatic map, is neither fixed nor stable: "The rhizome refers to a map that must be produced or constructed, is always detachable, connectable, reversable, and modifiable, with multiple entrances and exits, with its lines of flight. The tracings are what must be transferred onto the maps and not the reverse."[12] Such maps must be able to incorporate new information as one has new experiences in new environments; but this does not mean they are entirely self-invented. Rather the maps are cobbled together in processes of accretion and palimpsestic rewriting from other persons' maps, first of all those defined in infancy by one's parents, and later the maps that come to one by way of one's historical context and the social formations one lives in.

Just as the lack of a cognitive map of one's social space is crippling for effective political activity, so too is the lack of an affective map, for several reasons. Our most enduring and basic social formations—patriarchy, say, or capitalism itself—can only be enduring to the extent that they are woven into our emotional lives in the most fundamental way. Gender differences or class distinctions are not just tools we use to make *sense* of our worlds, they are things about which and in relation to which we all have a whole range of emotions, from the teenager's shame among his wealthier classmates at the shabbiness of his family's car or his parent's working-class accent to the particular anxiety of a woman alone on a city street at night. Whole sets of affects—about family, profession, sexual practices, physical appearance, eating habits, and so forth—come into being only *through* categories of class and gender. Social hierarchies surely could not work without the depression, cynicism, or despair produced among poor persons by unemployment, discrimination, or not being able to pay one's bills or, alternatively, without the joy that accompanies the purchase of a big new house or a fancy car or the pleasurable sense of achievement and entitlement the high school student feels on admission to an Ivy League university. Because our social formations work through affect, resistance to them must as well. Substitute objects of positive affective attachment must be provided where necessary, counter-moods evoked, and the emotional valence of various objects and ideas changed through processes of rearticulation and recontextualization.

And if we want to form politically agential collectives, this is most directly a question of moods, structures of feeling, and affects; anxieties must be overcome, alliances must seem not just logical but emotionally compelling. Insights about one's political oppression are unlikely to motivate resistance unless they can be made interesting and affectively rewarding. This is why Aristotle directed himself toward the affects in his *Rhetoric,* so he could figure out what situations produced which affects in whom; the politician above all must know how to make and use the moods of his audiences. In short, without an affective map, the most basic political acts—the distinction of friend from foe, danger from safety, despair-inducing from interest-enhancing experiences—become impossible; we are reduced to operating as if dumb or blind.

Our affective maps are likely to be especially in need of revision, repair, or invention at moments of rapid social change or upheaval. Just as modernity made the production of cognitive maps more difficult, it also made the assessment of one's affective surroundings more difficult, not least because of the new scale and scope of the experience of loss. Emigrating to a new country, learning a different kind of work, or losing one's parents in war are likely to render one's environment emotionally confusing. Unexpected fears, surprising disappointments, and new enjoyments must all be processed in one way or another. And then one must figure out how to negotiate the new affective terrain, to exert some agency in it.

.✦.

Here, however, I am concerned not with the creation of affective maps in general but with the ways an aesthetic practice might help with this process of affective mapping. My argument is that it does this not primarily through a realist representation of a social space in the world, but through a representation of the affective life of the reader herself or himself. Such a representation is accomplished by way of a self-estrangement that allows one to see oneself in relation to one's affective environment in its historicity, in relation to the relevant social-political anchors or landmarks in that environment, and to see the others who inhabit this landscape with one. The texts of James, Du Bois, and Platonov function as affective maps to the extent that they work as machines of *self-estrangement*. By this term, as I mentioned in the Introduction, I mean a self-distancing that allows one to see oneself as if from outside. But I also mean estrangement in the sense of defamiliarization, making one's emotional life—one's range of moods, set of structures of feeling, and collection of affective attachments—appear weird, surprising, unusual, and thus capable of a new kind of recognition, interest, and analysis.

In what follows I have tried to schematize the operation of this self-estranging machine, mostly by way of an extrapolation of certain elements of the aesthetic theories of Adorno and Benjamin, particularly regarding the logic of the moment of aesthetic experience and the role of the shudder therein, which Adorno valued so highly.[13]

The affective mapping function is achieved by means of the noncoincidence of two moments in the experience of what, following Adorno, we might call "the work of art," so long as we mean that phrase in a fairly broad sense. On the one hand, one has a perceptual and cognitive apprehension of the artwork in its otherness, which has certain effects: "As a musical composition compresses time, and as a painting folds spaces into one another, so the possibility is concretized that the world could be other than it is. Space, time, and causality are maintained, their power is not denied, but they are divested of their compulsiveness"

(AT, 138). For a moment at least, listening to a recording of Jimi Hendrix playing the "Star-Spangled Banner" or to Beethoven's late string quartets in a concert hall, reading Gertrude Stein's *Tender Buttons,* walking at Maya Lin's Vietnam War Memorial, or beholding one of Donald Judd's reflective aluminum boxes, one finds oneself in a world that does not exist, or that exists only in this space at this moment. This otherness is not liberatory in itself, but inasmuch as the relationships between space and time, for example, that we are used to in our everyday lives are altered in some way or another, we may see that the logic of the world we live in is not compulsory. Things might work differently.

On the other hand, but simultaneously, one has an affective response in this other world defined by the work. The artwork provides both the context and the objects affects need in order to come into existence. The logic is a transferential one: like psychoanalysis, the work provides a scene in which past affects can reappear as (what Freud called) new editions or as facsimiles of old ones. However, the work can only do this to the extent that the objects or moments within it recall earlier affectively charged experiences. Similarity is the key principle here; and as we know, even (or especially) in therapy, the slightest similarity will suffice if there are affects itching to find objects. One may be surprised by the affects that come out in the space of therapy, and so too with the work of art: by creating a kind of mood atmosphere with its own objects, artworks bring affects into existence in forms and in relation to objects that otherwise might not exist.

In an important sense, we never experience an affect for the first time; every affect contains within it an archive of its previous objects. Or, more exactly, there is a secret archive of objects out in the world in which our affects are residing. Like Proust with his madeleine, we do not necessarily know when or how we will encounter such objects. Benjamin recounts one such discovery in relation to a painting by Cezanne he saw during his 1927 visit to Moscow. He writes that "various very specific spots" immediately "thrust themselves" out at him. The space of the painting "opens up in corners and angles in which we believe we can localize crucial experiences of the past; there is something inexplicably familiar about these spots."[14] The painting provides a site for affects from Benjamin's past to reenter existence, and consequently for his archive of affective objects to open up, and perhaps, to become visible as such as if for the first time. By way of these affects, the world, and indeed history itself, makes its way into aesthetic experience. Affect is the shuttle on which history makes its way into the aesthetic, and it is also what brings one back from the work into the world. The affect that one has in the space of the artwork (which hovers alongside the cognitive experience as what Adorno calls a "trans-aesthetic subject") links one back to the world like a rubber band or the bungee on a bungee jumper, pulling one back from the artwork into the world, but pulling one back through a strange parabola which has altered one's view of the world and unsettled one's relation to it. To use the Heideggerian metaphor, it is as if we have been rethrown.

So, for example, here I am at a concert of the Emerson String Quartet; they are playing one of Beethoven's late string quartets. At a certain moment, some fragment of a motif being played on the viola, in the relationship it strikes with the development of the piece as a whole, surprises me, and I have that feeling of inexplicable familiarity. But it is vague; it is not as if I am somehow reminded of a *specific* experience. Nonetheless, a powerful sadness and sense of loss has latched onto that very specific viola moment in order to bring itself into being. I shudder. According to Adorno, such a shudder is generated not by the emotion evoked itself but by the transition from this emotion—experienced in this world of the quartet, that is to say, a world that bears no apparent referential relation to the world of everyday life—back to my subjectivity as I experience it in everyday life. At the moment of this return from the work, one has the sensation that one has just been temporarily dislocated from one's subjectivity. This is because one has, for a moment, had an affect in a space not defined by one's subjectivity, and then one is returned to that subjectivity, reminding one precisely of that subjectivity, and its limitedness. The return to the "self," the subjectivity as we find it in our everyday lives, and its disjuncture with the affects and the mood we have experienced *without* a self, in a nonself, is what produces, for Adorno, the shudder.[15] "Shudder, radically opposed to the conventional idea of experience [*Erlebnis*], provides no particular satisfaction for the I; it bears no similarity to desire. Rather it is a memento of the liquidation of the I, which, shaken, perceives its own limitedness and finitude" (AT, 245). Put differently, we might say that one has a shudder about the limitedness and situatedness—which is also to say the historicity—of one's affective life in toto.

Adorno suggests that the shudder is also the moment of contact with an other, with otherness as such. "The shudder in which subjectivity stirs without yet being subjectivity is the act of being touched by the other. Aesthetic comportment assimilates itself to that other rather than subordinating it" (AT, 331). The moment when one has an affective experience without being a subject, as if one exists for a moment *in* the Beethoven quartet, is one in which one loses oneself in this vague nonsubject space of the work. I am not quite sure what Adorno means by "the other" here, but I take him to be referencing a moment of apprehending the basically plural nature of one's emotional life. The work is something like a meeting place for an affective collectivity. In this sense, Adorno's "aesthetic shudder" is akin to the shudder one experiences in a large crowd experiencing a common emotion at, for example, a political protest, sporting event, or concert. "Aesthetic comportment," as Adorno puts it, is one place where one learns how to participate in a collectivity, to make contact with an other, based on a shared affective experience. While I do not think that the self-estrangement aspect of the affective mapping function necessarily or literally needs to produce a "shudder," I do think that the mechanism described here is at work in the affective maps I analyze in this book.

That said, however, in the texts I write about here, this self-estrangement is only part of the project. Each of these texts—James's *Turn of The Screw,* Du Bois's *Souls of Black Folk,* and Platonov's *Chevengur—* also have something to say *about* the very subjective experience from which a reader has been estranged. This allegorization of the experience that the aesthetic practice is itself promoting, the narration of the production of their own readers—this is the moment in which the text functions as an affective map for its readers. The effect is not unlike the moment in a therapy when the analyst says: "Hmm, well, perhaps this is about those early conflicts with your father." You have had an experience, transferring some fears or anger about your father onto the therapist, and to be sure it is strange, and you have noticed perhaps already that your emotions really are unlikely to be about the analyst as such—but then, when it is pointed out to you, it can no longer be ignored, and the analysis of the emotions in question can begin. Similarly, in *The Turn of the Screw,* for example, the first text I look at here, James narrates a kind of epistemological desire on the part of the governess, and the pleasures as well as the disastrous results of this desire; at the same time the text solicits just such a will to knowledge from the reader. Or, in a more complex process, Platonov solicits a relationship from his reader that resembles nothing so much as a melancholic friendship, at the same time that he shows how socialism might be built on just such a friendship. In other words, what I am calling an affective map here is a carefully prepared aesthetic experience, an experience that is narrated—and connected up to collective, historical processes and events—even as it is produced.

Of course, for a textual practice to work in this way, it must be able to be attuned to the moods of various readers. It is not designed to produce a uniform experience, but rather to be able to estrange one from wherever one is in relation to one's emotional world. It needs to be flexible enough to allow for readers to input different experience. In this, when it works, it is a portable map, a kind of global positioning device that tells you where you are at this particular moment, giving you a satellite view of your own life.

In sum, if an affective map is a representation of one's affective life in its historicity, then this representation works in the following way. The moment of shudder is a reaction to the simultaneous rupture and connection between the affective experience one has within the world created by the work on the one hand and the affective attachments one has within the world of everyday life on the other. In this way the shudder opens up the space of self-estrangement that is necessary to get a distance on one's affects. It also puts one into contact with others, a contact that is imaginary in one sense. But inasmuch as it is based on the shared historicity of that affective life, it is quite real.

CHAPTER THREE

Reading into Henry James

Allegories of the Will to Know
in *The Turn of the Screw*

All of these melancholies were qualified indeed by one
redeeming reflection—the sense of how little, for a
good while past . . . I had been producing. I *did* say to
myself "Produce again—produce; produce better than
ever and all will yet be well."

—HENRY JAMES TO W. D. HOWELLS, JANUARY 22, 1895

Henry James's literary career reached what was probably its nadir on
January 5, 1895, when, on the opening night of his play *Guy Domville*,
James was booed, jeered, and even assaulted with tomatoes by a literally riotous crowd.[1] This spectacular rejection left James, who in any
event tended toward depression, feeling that he had "fallen upon evil
days—every sign or symbol of one's being in the least wanted, anywhere
or by anyone, having so utterly failed."[2] Even a year after the opening
night incident, James would write: "In spite of my gain of private quiet
I have suffered very acutely by my loss of public."[3]

James's inability to capture a theatrical audience reverberated with
special emotional force because his foray into playwriting had been an
attempt to redress an earlier failure to keep the audience that had existed for his novels and stories. The process began in the late 1880s,
when the sales of his novels declined and he ceased being able to publish in the *Atlantic*. This journal, probably the most popular literary
magazine of his time, had serialized almost all of his early novels, providing James with a regular place to publish, a reliable income, and a se-
cure sense of readership.[4] However, the literary public sphere changed
rather dramatically in the late 1880s and early 1890s as a modern mass
culture originated in the United States.[5] The hegemony of the *Atlantic*
ended as picture magazines like *Ladies' Home Journal*, *McClure's*, and
others gained unprecedentedly large circulations. For the first time,
magazines made their money not on subscriptions but from advertising

revenue. Their function was to provide audiences—the bigger the better—to advertisers, and the "literature" thus had the primary function of attracting that advertising audience. This development was a major step in what Adorno and Horkheimer called the "amalgamation" of advertising and culture, and James, like many writers, had a difficult time making the adjustment. This was not only because he chafed at the need to subordinate his authorial aspirations to the aims of advertising but also because, as Meredith McGill has put it, the changes produced a rupture "between the available models of authorship and the conditions of publication they sought to describe."[6] One response to this situation was the creation of modernist and avant-garde journals for smaller, avowedly *not* general, audiences.[7] Eventually, James would move in this direction, but in 1895 he had not yet given up the hope of resisting the amalgamation with advertising while still managing to achieve the sensation produced by the "audible vibration" of a sizable reading public. Indeed, depressed by loss upon loss, he desired to feel that vibration more than ever. He hoped to write his way out of his depression, reminding himself that the key was to "produce, produce; produce better than ever and all will yet be well."[8]

Just a few days after the *Guy Domville* debacle, James heard the story that would become the basis for the production that restored his sense of readership, *The Turn of the Screw.*[9] A poor woman is hired by a wealthy and attractive bachelor to take care of his nephew and niece at a luxurious country estate. She is thoroughly charmed by the "gorgeous" children, Miles and Flora, the estate itself, and the general sense of privilege that attaches to the position. However, things almost immediately start to unravel, as Miles is kicked out of school, at which point the governess starts seeing ghosts around the estate. They are ghosts, she gradually comes to realize, of a now deceased servant and erstwhile governess, who, she learns through innuendo, seemed to have had vaguely and unspeakably improprietous, perverse relations with the children. They have come back, it is clear to the governess, to get the children, who, however, refuse to admit to their intercourse with the ghosts. The story becomes a quest for the governess to find out the secret of the ghosts' relation to the children, to get the children to confess to this relation, and thereby to purge and save them from the ghosts. First, however, the presence of the ghosts allows for a certain pleasurable intimacy with the children, because it forces her to be extra attentive and imaginative in her interactions with them, as she tries to read into the children's behavior for signs of their knowledge. Crucial to the story's effect is the fact that this is all narrated in a highly ambiguous style that makes it impossible to tell whether or not the ghosts are real or the governess is crazy. Like the governess, the reader is put in a position where s/he has to read into an unclear text. Gradually her pursuit becomes more aggressive and less rewarding. She frightens and alienates Flora, then, in the final scene, she gets Miles to utter a kind of ambiguous confession, and in the process, apparently kills him.

James meant *The Turn of the Screw* to affect audiences, and it did. The story was something of a succès de scandale, popular and controversial, not least because the (sexual) corruption of children was then, as now, a scandalous topic. No longer able to rely on familiar models of authorship to find his readers, James had created a lure for them, a scene in which audiences found it irresistible to read into the story their own emotions and fears.

"Reading Into"

> Read into my meagre and hurried words—
> well, read into them *everything*.
>
> —HENRY JAMES TO MORTON FULLERTON,
> OCTOBER 2, 1900

In 1900, Henry James sent his young friend Morton Fullerton a series of letters in which he tried to convince Fullerton, who was in Paris, to visit him in England. These letters luxuriate in a rich, sexually suggestive, and ambiguous style that *seems* as if it might be obliquely referring to quite lascivious thoughts and acts. For example, he writes:

> It isn't . . . your "handsome" telegram that makes me write . . . it is that I desire the sense of communication with you—and don't even desire it at your expense: depleting indeed though the little telegram must have been. I want *tout bonnement* to look at you and sign to you and sound to you— *show* to you, even, so far as may be: though of course, if I could *see* you also by the same stroke this would be still better . . . couldn't you, can't you . . . squeeze out three or four golden days for me? . . . I'm alone and I think of you . . . I'd meet you at Dover—I'd do anything for you.[10]

Here James makes persistent use of a lushly corporeal vocabulary (*handsome, desire, depleting, show, stroke,* and *squeeze*) and ambiguous syntax in order to suggest a sexual content that is nonetheless never clearly articulated. However, although the language is never sexually explicit, it offers little resistance to the reader who wishes to read sexual meaning there. For instance, Fullerton would have had little difficulty reading bawdy flirtation into the following sentence: "I have told you before that the imposition of hands in a certain tender way 'finishes' me." Even still, because James hovers just below a certain threshold of explicitness, readers who read salacious meanings into the text might feel a bit uncertain or even embarrassed about the prurient meanings they find there.[11] As if in response to exactly this uncertainty, at the beginning of one of his letters to Fullerton, James exhorts his reader to "read into my meagre and hurried words—well, read into them *everything*."[12] I take this to mean that James was far from unaware that readers would be inclined to imagine acts, emotions, and modes of contact that are only hinted at, and indeed that James actively desired that his readers add the touch that finishes his sentences and thoughts by reading into them. Indeed such moments of imaginative projection were so intimate as to suggest to James a kind of bodily immersion. Hence, for example, James could say to Rudyard Kipling about reading his *Kim:* "that has been the great thing, I find; that one could sink deep and deep, could sit in you up to one's neck."[13] Imagining some reader having the same feeling of sinking "deep and deep" into James would seem to be precisely the "sense of communication" he speaks of desiring in his letter to Fullerton.[14]

Ironically, achieving "the sense of communication" requires actually that one *fail* to communicate, in the usual sense of that word. There must be just enough noncomprehension to necessitate reading into the text, since it is the breakdown of clear understanding that motivates one to guess at meanings. Such speculation involves an imaginative imitation of the writer, "getting behind" (as James liked to put it) the writer so as to see the world as the writer does. As part of this mimesis, the reader must also create or project that person behind the text with whom s/he will identify. This is why Paul de Man insisted that prosopopoeia, the creation *(poiea)* of a face or person *(prosopon)*, is the master trope of reading. Strictly speaking, in de Man's view, because texts in themselves do not produce meaning, reading (in the sense of fixing a meaning) always requires first that you imagine a person having thoughts and feelings that the text itself leaves undecidable, that is, that you author-ize your reading. To produce "a reading," for de Man, always requires an extratextual intervention in a moment of specular, mimetic "mutual reflexive substitution" with the person one has pictured.[15]

This act of imagination and imposition on the part of the reader creates a moment that is peculiarly ripe for the appearance of powerful emotions. The phenomenon is analogous to the reenactments of past emotions Freud observed in the scene of analysis that he called transference. Noticing intense, seemingly unmotivated appearances of both positive and negative affects during analysis, Freud came to realize that his patients were "transferring" feelings from past objects onto the person of the analyst, substituting the analyst for the past object on the basis of some real or imagined similarity. At first this seemed to be a problem because this hallucinatory repetition of past emotions distracted the analysand from remembering and recounting and acted therefore as a kind of barrier or stalling tactic ("resistance"). Freud soon realized that the transference was the key to the cure because it was perhaps the only way these affects made it into the scene of analysis.[16]

In order to aid the perceptions of similarity that facilitated the transference, Freud recommended that analysts be relatively unemotional in therapy sessions.[17] Assisting further is the classic analytic scenario with the patient on a couch and the analyst seated behind, requiring the patient to imagine the analyst's face. While speaking, the analysand had to guess at the analyst's emotional responses: Is the analyst pleased, surprised, saddened, ashamed? With no actual face distracting one's mimetic faculties, one's imagination has more room in which to create the face that would allow those nonabreacted affects that have been buried or otherwise lost inside us to reappear. Two things happen here at the same time and seem to require each other: on the one hand the prosopopoetic imagination of the other (who can substitute for a past other) and on the other the appearance of the affect itself. Thus Benjamin's aphorism "No imagination without innervation."[18]

It hardly needs to be added here that this scene of imagination and innervation is a ghostly one. Our affects come into existence only when attached to the ghosts from our past. Emotions, we might say, never happen for the first time; like ghosts, it is in their essence to always and only *return*. It is only inasmuch as one can turn one's interlocutor into a ghost that one can have an emotional attachment to that person. To return to James and Fullerton, James is essentially urging Fullerton to use James's letters as a scene to allow his specters to appear. Reading into a text is a matter of making the dead speak, of creating a specter who can provide the sense of communication the silent text lacks. This also means that James himself must be ready to *be* a ghost—the material vehicle for someone else's buried affects—if he wishes to be the site of Fullerton's readings.

I take this detour here because it helps us to conceptualize the theory of reading and affectivity implicit in James's aesthetic practices and decisions. In desiring to affect his audience, James wanted to create the scene for a collective innervation on the part of his audience, a proliferation of transferences. On the one hand, this meant there had to be room for "reading in" on the part of the audience, a job that had been made more difficult by the replacement of "the good, the really effective and heartshaking ghost stories" with a new kind of narrative, about which James was quite pessimistic: "The new type indeed, the more modern 'psychical' case, washed clean of all queerness as by exposure to a flowing laboratory tap, and equipped with credentials vouching for this—the new type clearly promised little, for the more it was respectably certified the less it seemed of a nature to rouse the dear old sacred terror."[19] The "psychical" case, the pseudoscientific recounting of supernatural events that had achieved some popularity in the late nineteenth century,[20] gains "authority" but, in telling everything, washes it clean of all its "queerness." Where epistemological certainty is guaranteed in advance, identity-confusing imaginative imitations are precluded.

But besides providing the empty space for the perception of similarity, the scene also had to be one that was likely to resonate with those audience affects that had found insufficient abreaction, that were unresolved or mired in conflict and contradiction. This is a properly historical problem. Like Baudelaire addressing his hypocritical, bored readers, James understood that he would have to pluck the chords of a dominant structure of feeling if he were to seduce "the jaded, the disillusioned, the fastidious" into reenacting their own fears, anxieties, and losses.[21]

> What, in the last analysis, had I to give the sense of? Of their being, the haunting pair, capable, as the phrase is, of everything—that is of exerting in respect to the children, the very worst action small victims so conditioned might be conceived as subject to. What would be then on reflexion, this utmost conceivability?—a question to which the answer all admirably came. There is for such a case no eligible *absolute* of the wrong; it remains relative to fifty other elements, a matter of appreciation, speculation, imagination—these things moreover quite exactly in the light of the spectators, the critic's, the reader's experience. Only make the reader's general vision of evil intense enough, I said to myself—and that already is a charming job—and his own experience, his own imagination, his own sympathy (with the children) and horror (of their false friends) will supply him quite sufficiently with all the particulars.[22]

Affecting his audience, James understands, is a question of setting the scene for the repetition of experiences his readers already have. The "fifty other elements" that might determine and comprise that experience is the aggregate of shifting, competing, and contradictory forces that shape everyday life, what we might otherwise call "history." This means that we can see in James's trap a reverse image of his readers, and an implicit theory of the world from which these readers have been lured.

While it was the transformation of the literary public sphere and loss of audience that occasioned James's attempt to think through the historicity of his audience, once he set himself to the task, a range of historical problems entered his purview. I will focus in what follows on two related processes. The first is the generalized situation Niklas Luhmann called "autonomy without autarchy," that is, a situation in which one is continually called on to deal with problems and losses that have been generated out of one's knowable life world. This sense of suffering losses that cause us to feel lost makes us especially vulnerable to whatever institutions and discourses may come along offering to find us, to give us increased affective agency. In *The Turn of the Screw*, James is interested in the way such agency is offered by what Foucault calls "the will to know," the structure of feeling underlying the modern discourse of sexuality, a discourse on lurid display in the Oscar Wilde trials, which were happening while James was composing his tale.

✦

In the task of catching readers, the ideal case for James would be one in which his own losses and "little melancholies"—as residue of his own contact with the historical situation, and thus something others might share—would serve as the mechanism for resonating with the mood of his readers. In this instance, his loss of an audience would be redeemed, with remarkable economy, as the experience that enables him to regain one. A depressive relation to loss is transformed into one in which loss itself becomes the mechanism of interest in the world. Furthermore, to the extent that such a book is successful in affecting readers, the existence of a social collectivity that can identify with him (something about which James had his real doubts) is confirmed. And, inasmuch as depressive melancholy is precisely that condition in which interest in the world has become too difficult, in which one feels isolated and alone, the recognition of a shared situation is itself transformative.

I will argue in what follows that in *The Turn of the Screw* James is not only historicizing his own emotional life, but is providing his audience with the materials to do so as well. The analogy with transference is again useful. There, the fact that you do not "really" have those feelings about the analyst (which it is the job of the analyst to gently lead you toward) allows the emotion itself to be defamiliarized and to come into view in itself, and thereby to become an object of analysis. Freud's aim is to "fit these emotions into their place in the treatment and in his life history, subject them to rational consideration, and appraise them at their true psychical value."[23] In James's case, however, the estrangement from one's emotions is important not in order to then subject them to rational analysis so much as to allow readers to see how this emotion is a kind of historical datum, and as such is the basis for a potentially politicizing link with others. The idea is to give oneself an antidepressive sense of the historicity of one's affective life. The aesthetic practice that enables this by functioning as a mobile machine of emotional self-estrangement is what I am calling an affective map. This not only facilitates the feeling that one is part of a collectivity, that one's emotions are not one's alone, but also, ideally, gives one a sociohistorical target, something to blame for one's losses.

In *The Turn of the Screw,* James's aims are underscored in the frame he sets around the primary story. It is a nested narrative. There are three narrators: first there is an *I*, who starts off the story; then there is Douglas, who possesses the text that makes up the main narrative and the majority of the book: the governess's written narration of her own story. Here, as is often the case with framed narratives, the frame is a self-reflexive site in the text, a place where the text undoes its own identity, bringing the moment of reading inside the text. In so doing, *The Turn of the Screw* offers different models of readership, as if the text were teaching its readers how it might be read. Douglas, we learn, has received a copy of the governess's narrative upon her death, and he fetches it in order to affect and to share his own feelings about the story with an audience (including the first *I* of the narrative) gathered around a fire at an inn. Moreover, Douglas himself says he first heard the story as a kind of confirmation of affection: "I liked her extremely and am glad to this day to think she liked me too. If she hadn't she wouldn't have told me. She had never told anyone. It wasn't that she said so, but that I knew that she hadn't. I was sure, I could see."[24] Nothing is told literally, that is to say diegetically. She does not say: "I like you." Douglas has to "see" that, in other words he has to read it in. Stories, it is emphasized, are valuable and powerful because of the affections they allow to be transferred, and the relationships they thereby create, not for the knowledge one finds in them.

Lost; or, How Autonomy Can Be Depressing

> "We were as lost as a handful of passengers in a great drifting ship. Well, I was strangely at the helm!"
>
> —HENRY JAMES, *THE TURN OF THE SCREW*

The governess's story starts with her description of being hired for the job. She answers an advertisement and finds the following man: "One could easily fix his type; it never happily dies out. He was handsome and bold and pleasant, off-hand and gay and kind. He struck her, inevitably, as gallant and splendid, but what took her most of all and gave her the courage she afterwards showed was that he put the whole thing to her as a favour, an obligation he should gratefully incur" (4). As "the youngest of several daughters of a poor country parson," the governess finds in this charmer the image of a life world quite outside her realm of class experience, one of "high fashion" and "expensive habits." He explains that she is to take care of two children, a girl and a boy, with whom he has been left "by the death of his parents in India," who in turn had been left with the children when his "military brother" died two years before. The children have suffered loss upon loss—two sets of guardians. Making the situation more difficult, there is a rather stringent condition: that she never trouble him, not at all, with anything that goes on at the country estate. He gives her supreme authority to deal with the children and with the estate more broadly. Despite the strange situation, the salary is good and she is poor, and she agrees to take the position. But it is not only financial considerations that guide her: when for "a moment, disburdened, delighted, he held her hand, thanking her for the sacrifice, she already felt rewarded"(6). That she is allowed to feel as if she is performing a favor is the final charm, because it gives her a feeling of control in a class arena in which she would otherwise have little or no agency.[25]

In fact, the difficulties she encounters are structured by a situation that is paradigmatic for the modern subject: what Luhmann has called "autonomy without autarchy." By this Luhmann means the situation that arises from the division of society into different autonomous subsystems all of which have their own logic and function: civil society, law, medicine, the economy, art, and so on.[26] This "differentiation of society" systematizes the world in which we live according not to a single logic but to multiple, variable ones. To live in this world not only requires that we learn the internal logic and procedures of multiple systems but that we learn to negotiate among them as well.[27] "Functional differentiation," Luhmann writes, "leads to a condition in which the genesis of problems and the solution to problems fall asunder. Problems can no longer be solved by the system that produces them. They have to be transferred to the system that is best equipped and specialized to solve them."[28] Each subsystem has to be ready to deal with problems generated out of its sphere. Life is less and less determined by local contexts, as the local system context—whether it is the family, the city, medicine, a particular profession, the legal system, or literature itself—is always responding to problems produced somewhere else. While each system has increased "autonomy"—an ability to apply "specific rules and procedures to special problems"—it also has decreased "autarchy": less and less authority outside of its own subsystem, and less of an ability to decide *what* problems it will deal with.[29]

The governess experiences a particularly attenuated state of autonomy without autarchy, in the sense that while she can do what she wants at the estate, she has little or no power to determine what problems come her way or to change the nature of the problems she is inheriting from the past. As in the case of art and literature itself, the governess must develop "strategies to satisfy needs that originate in other realms of social interaction."[30] That these "needs" are connected to a specific historical situation is underscored not only by the class and gender inequalities that make her agreement with the bachelor uncle possible and attractive but also by the reference to colonial India as the distant, absent cause that has set in motion the whole process in which the governess finds herself. In this world, everyday life is created and determined by a set of structures that are invisible and conceptually inaccessible by way of the experiences shaped by that everyday life world.

Like a psychoanalyst, and like James himself, the governess is being called on to deal with someone else's losses, to somehow account for an emotional terrain determined by forces outside of not only her view but also her conceptual framework. What the governess lacks and what she seeks is a technique for managing this emotional terrain, a technique or system for representing to herself the problems confronting her that are generated out of her sphere. It is a needy, vulnerable position, and asking for assistance has been precluded in advance. In the governess, James has provided a precise site in which we can witness and identify with such a position, and by extension with James himself.

Faced with children whose parents and grandparents have left them orphaned, the governess must deal with a melancholia that is not her own. She not only has to respond to the children's own experience of loss—an affect eerily absent from their initial cheery presentation—but she also has to substitute for these dead-and-gone guardians. Emotions are directed at her that do not concern her. This defines a particular type of ghostly scene: when ghosts appear who seem to recognize *us*, but that we do not recognize. Jacques Derrida has suggested that this is something like a law of spectrality itself: "the spectral someone looks at us, we feel ourselves being looked at by it, outside of any synchrony, even before and beyond any look on our part, according to an absolute anteriority . . . and asymmetry, according to an absolutely unmasterable disproportion."[31] This ghost is always before us and beyond us in an absolute way: there is no hope of being present to it.

On the Use and Misuse of Ghosts for Life

> But I see ghosts everywhere.
>
> —HENRY JAMES TO FRANCIS BOOTT,
> OCTOBER 11, 1895

When the governess arrives at the estate she finds everything indescribably beautiful, marvelous, superlative in every way.[32] Hers is the reaction of a poor girl who has all of a sudden accomplished a great feat of class mobility. She encounters, for example, mirrors "in which, for the first time, I could see myself from head to foot"(7). She is bowled over at every turn. Flora, the first child she meets, she describes as "the most beautiful child I had ever seen" (7). Miles, who returns—because sent, she soon learns—from school a few pages later, is "incredibly beautiful—everything but a sort of passion of tenderness for him was swept away by his presence" (13).

Surrounded and charmed by what she perceives to be all this great beauty, and experiencing a new but fragile sense of self, the governess likes to imagine, from time to time, that the estate is *hers:* "I liked it best of all when, as the light faded—or rather, I should say as the day lingered and the last calls of the birds sounded, in a flushed sky from the old trees—I could take a turn into the grounds and enjoy, almost with a sense of property that amused and flattered me, the beauty and dignity of the place" (15). She waxes about the natural beauty of her setting and the sense of property she allows herself to enjoy. The class subject that is precluded agency in this class scene, even as it is absolutely necessary for its function, returns in the person of the governess. In a kind of perversion of the dictatorship of the proletariat, she seems to have reversed class roles by assuming the unusual authority she has been granted. But she is alone, without class allies. Moreover, while she has been put in the position of the male proprietor, guarantor of the transference of authority to the son, Miles, she lacks the social agency to manage this transfer, not only because she is a woman but also because she has had no opportunity to learn the structure of feeling of this class position and situation.

This leaves the governess feeling a bit like a ghost—not fully *there*—and she desperately wants to feel as if she is being recognized for doing a good job; she wishes her accomplishments would more "publicly appear." "It was a pleasure to reflect . . . that by my discretion, my quiet good sense and general high propriety, I was giving pleasure—if he ever thought of it!—to the person to whose pressure I had yielded. . . . I dare say I fancied myself in short a remarkable young woman and took pleasure in the faith that this would more publicly appear" (15). Because she feels unrecognized and because her "gay and kind" bachelor is constitutively absent, she must guess at the pleasure he would have if he were to see her. Like James, she suffers for her lack of a public. She has no one to read her. "It was plump, one afternoon, in the middle of my very hour: the children were tucked away and I had come out for my stroll. One of the thoughts that, as I don't in the least shrink now from noting, used to be with me in these wanderings was that it would be as charming as a charming story suddenly to meet someone" (15). Her articulation of her desire here is precise and telling in its ambiguous undecidability: it "would be as charming as a charming story suddenly to meet someone." In one reading of the phrase, the governess would be charmed as if she were *reading:* "If I were to meet someone, it would charm me in the same way that a charming story charms me." But we could with equal legitimacy understand the governess as imagining herself not *reading* the story but *in* the story, *being* read, *being* charming: meeting someone would be the kind of a (charming) thing that happens *in* a charming story. She wants to be in a story and reader of the story, reading and being read at once. This is the transitivity that is for James the essence of the "sense of communication." At this moment, a ghost appears.

> Someone would appear there at the turn of the path and would stand before me and smile and approve. I didn't ask more than that—I only asked that he should *know;* and the only way to be sure that he knew would be to see it, and the kind of light of it, in his handsome face. That was exactly present to me—by which I mean the face was—when . . . what arrested me on the spot—and with a shock much greater than any vision had allowed for—was the sense that my imagination had, in a flash, turned real. He did stand there! (15–16)

Fully consumed by her prosopopoetic reverie, the governess imagines the face of the other who would see, smile, and approve. She wants an other who would allow her to make sense of her surroundings, the face behind the uncertain text that would allow her to more confidently read it. It is the mutual reflexive substitution of the readerly situation that she wants. Like James, conjuring an audience for himself that will turn real, and like Fullerton, who erected an imagined James behind his letters in order to fantasize about what dirty things he might desire, the governess, too, sees a man seeing her.

He quickly disappears, but not before "fixing" her. He reappears soon, however, and another ghost appears, a woman. Are these ghosts "real," we wonder? Or are they projections of her imagination?

✦

With the appearance of the ghosts, the story shifts focus and begins to center around the governess's desire to uncover the secret of the ghosts. She deduces, with the help of the housekeeper, Mrs. Grose, that she has seen the ghosts of her predecessors at Bly: the previous governess, Miss Jessel, and a servant, Peter Quint. Moreover, she learns that their relationships with the children were tainted by possible sexual corruption. Quint and Jessel "took liberties." They "carried on" with each other and with the children. Quint seems to have been the more offensive figure here: the governess learns that "there had been matters in his life, strange passages and perils, secret disorders, vices more than suspected, that would have accounted for a good deal more" (28). Moreover, "for a period of several months," Quint and the boy had been perpetually together. Indeed, Miles and Quint "had been together quite as if Quint had been his tutor—and a very grand one—and Miss Jessel only for the little lady. When he had gone off with the fellow, I mean, and spent hours with him" (36). When Mrs. Grose spoke with Jessel in an effort to put a stop to it, she was told that as a servant it was none of her business.[33]

For the governess, this past that seems to be returning in the appearance of the ghosts is not exclusively fearful. In fact, it proves to be a catalyst in her relationship with the children that makes her feel much more intimately connected with them, precisely because it provides the scene for her to read into them, and in turn to feel read into. Inasmuch as "there are depths, depths!" (31) to the children's knowledge of and complicity with the ghosts, the governess must engage in a sustained effort to read into the children's behavior, moods, and speech their knowledge about the ghosts and the past they represent. This leads to a quite pleasurable feeling that she has gotten lost in the emotional world created by the children: "we lived in a cloud of music and affection and success and private theatricals" (39). Nonetheless, at each step she suspects that she has uncovered the crucial clue to justify her fear that "they know, they know, it's too monstrous" (30). But, however much she guesses, whatever she herself manages to see of the ghosts, the fact remains that "what it was least possible to get rid of was the cruel idea that, whatever I had seen, they saw more—things terrible and unguessable and that sprang from dreadful passages of intercourse in the past" (53). Of course this means that her efforts to read in and guess and pursue must become ever more intense and intimate, that they never reach quite the depth that they must. The secret intercourse the governess imagines the children to have with the ghosts creates a kind of affective intensity that would otherwise be absent; one might even say that the ghosts are a prop or alibi for the creation of that intensity.

> I don't mean that they had their tongues in their cheeks or did anything vulgar, for that was not one of their dangers: I do mean, on the other hand, that the element of the unnamed and untouched became, between us, greater than any other, and that so much avoidance couldn't have been made successful without a great deal of tacit arrangement. It was as if, at moments, we were perpetually coming into sight of subjects before which we must stop short, turning suddenly out of alleys that we perceived to be blind, closing with a little bang that made us look at each other—for like all bangs, it was something louder than we intended—the doors we had indiscreetly opened. . . . Forbidden ground was the question of the return of the dead in general and of whatever, in especial survive for memory, of the friends, the little children had lost. (51)

The goal of the game of keeping secrets is not actually to conceal knowledge so much as to employ the shared knowledge of a secret to allow for scenes of mutual reflexive glances, the prosopopoetic "reading in" that is required when a "tacit arrangement" continually forces them to "look at each other."

The governess knows that her increased and intense interest in the affective lives of her "charges" makes her relationship to them a bit queer in its own right. "I used to wonder how my little charges could help guessing that I thought strange things about them; and the circumstance that these things only made them more interesting was not by itself a direct aid to keeping them in the dark. I trembled lest they should see that they *were* so immensely more interesting" (38). Like an analyst who falls in love with his or her patient, or who is turned on or even obsessed by the details of the patient's sexual life or fantasies, the governess feels a prurient kind of interest in the children that she knows she should keep secret. But this has its affective rewards as well: it means that she can then imagine that *they* are reading into *her*. She writes: "For it occurred to me that I might occasionally excite suspicion by the little outbreaks of my sharper passion for them, so too I remember asking if I mightn't see a queerness in the traceable increase in their own demonstrations" (38).

As I have noted, the appearance of the secret of the ghosts encourages the governess to read into the children and at the same time it is the device that gets *us* to read into the story. We repeat the governess's reading in as we try to understand not only what the ghosts have done with the children, but whether in fact there are any ghosts at all. We scour the governess's narration for signs of unreliability or for signs of proof of the ghosts' existence. As Shoshana Felman has detailed, quite a critical debate raged over the reality of the ghosts.[34] In the first mode of reading, the governess was heroic and tragic, doing battle against evil ghosts and ironically, tragically, killing Miles through her efforts to save him. In the second, inaugurated by Edmund Wilson's 1934 Freudian reading, the ghosts were but inventions of the governess's hysterical imagination: the ghosts are in fact the projections of her repressed desire for the absent Master.[35] Felman reads the are-the-ghosts-real-or-is-the-governess-crazy debate as a reading effect predicted and produced by James's text itself.[36] The textual situation that demands reading in is also itself *about* reading in: the appearance of the secret of the ghosts is the mechanism for provoking not only the governess to read into the children but also us to read into the governess. As it demands that we read into it, the story comments on that demand itself.

That it is a secret, a secret charged with the sense of illicit sexuality, that solicits the governess's interpretive attention furnishes the key to understanding what the story is saying about reading in. For the sexual secret was far from a neutral topic when James wrote *The Turn of the Screw*. Indeed, at the very moment of the composition of the story, the sexual secret was playing a starring role in the trial of Oscar Wilde, which was a turning point in the creation of the personage known as "the homosexual."[37]

The structure of feeling that enabled and surrounded the Wilde trial—the "will to knowledge"—is best described in Michel Foucault's *History of Sexuality*. For Foucault, the climax of the "will to know" is reached with the invention of "the homosexual," an identifiable type who replaced the much more fluidly and obscurely defined "sodomite."[38] As Eve Sedgwick notes, "What was new . . . was the world mapping by which every given person, just as he or she was necessarily assignable to a male or female gender, was now considered necessarily assignable as well to a homo- or a hetero-sexuality, a binarized identity that was full of implications, however confusing, for even the least sexual aspects of personal existence."[39] Like it or not, an identity would be read into your person, your appearance, your behavior. This was the will to knowledge Foucault spoke of, the knowledge of one's sexual identity.[40] No person could reasonably expect to avoid this reading in, and this put intense epistemological pressures on the widest range of bodies and practices.

What Foucault called the "frozen countenance" that this will to knowledge produced received its most public personification in Oscar Wilde.[41] His trial was a clear signal that there was a new relationship between the personal and the political, a terrifying example of the intensity of juridical interest that could be marshaled around the will to read in and the closeness such a reading might become. In the Wilde trial, for example, letters like those James later wrote to Fullerton offered more than enough suggestion of improper libidinal ties and homosexual tendencies to serve as evidence of homosexuality. Moreover, the trial demonstrated that the *state* was interested in pursuing this knowledge, and the discourses of law, medicine, and education would be marshaled to this now governmental end.

✦

The new relationship the governess has created with the children (through her attentive attempts to glean the secrets hiding in their behavior) begins to self-destruct in part because in giving in to the attractions of the secret, she invites into her intimate emotional life a range of institutional discourses that precede and exceed her agency. She is no longer in the (flirtatious) realm of Fullerton-James reading in, but is courting the kind of reading in that the courts and the police were doing in relation to the person of Oscar Wilde. Hence the secrets point toward the potential demise or explosion of those emotional ties even as they allow for the adumbration of erotic tension between the governess and—at times it seems—nearly everyone else in the story. For the discourse she borrows implicitly brings with it—and not too far behind—the schools, the police, the courts, hospitals—in short, a whole range of institutions in which she is not only in unknown waters but is not even any longer at the helm.

As her efforts to uncover secrets continue to fail, the governess becomes obsessed with the central technology of the will to knowledge—the confession. Like a priest, she wishes to offer nothing less than salvation. "His clear listening face, framed in its smooth whiteness, made him for the minute as appealing as some wistful patient in a children's hospital, and I would have given, as the resemblance came to me, all I possessed on earth really to be the nurse or sister of charity who might have helped to cure him" (63). In uncharted waters, the hope of possessing (by dispossessing) Miles becomes the governess's North Star. Her mantra to Miles is "I just want you to help me save you" (65). She wants Miles to confess first of all to whatever he did that caused his expulsion from school, an imperative that is intensified when the governess realizes that Miles has stolen the letter she has written to his uncle. These confessions, it is hoped, will unfold into the disclosure of the commerce with the ghosts, as if there is really just one big secret to be confessed. And the governess asserts to Mrs. Grose, "I'll get it out of him. He'll meet me. He'll confess. If he confesses, he's saved. And if he's saved . . ." At this point Grose interjects: "Then *you* are?" The governess has found herself in a position where she imagines that her authority and agency—indeed her very sense of subjectivity—rests on her ability to extract a confession.

The final pages of the novella describe an accelerating descent into an extended pas de deux between the governess and Miles as she tries to uncover the secrets. Despite her recognition of the violent course she is pursuing and her feelings of gratitude for Miles's revealing to her the "possibilities of beautiful intercourse," she cannot help herself. She is rendered "blind with [the] victory" of getting Miles to confess to stealing the letter, and in her aggressive glee she then pushes him to tell her why he was kicked out of school. The reason, we learn, was that he "told things" to those "he liked": he is guilty of transference. Then, in the midst of a confusing exchange, like an instant allegory of the transferential "sin" Miles has just confessed, Peter Quint appears to the governess, behind Miles. And when the governess cries that she sees the "coward horror," Miles utters the magic words "Peter Quint. . . . *where?*" Miles's utterance of the name without having heard it first from the governess's mouth appears to the governess as a tremendous victory: "They are in my ears still, his supreme surrender of the name and his tribute to my devotion." Miles has, in other words, successfully read into her; he has guessed (under, of course, extreme pressure) precisely what she wanted him to say. Feeling rewarded, recognized, affirmed, and loved even, the governess now feels beyond the powers of Quint: "what does he matter, my own? What does he ever matter? I have you." In a final gesture, she "launches at the beast," and turns to calm Miles with a "There, *there.*" And then the final lines of the story:

> But he had already jerked straight round, glared again, and seen but the quiet day. With the stroke of the loss I was so proud of he uttered the cry of a creature hurled over an abyss, and the grasp with which I recovered him might have been that of catching him in his fall. I caught him yes, I held him—it may be imagined with what a passion; but at the end of the minute I began to feel what it truly was that I held. We were alone with the quiet day, and his little heart, dispossessed, had stopped. (88)

Dispossession, it turns out, was not all the governess had hoped for. Although she receives the desired confession and feels affirmed by it, the loss she was so proud of, the loss of the ghost, turns out also to be the loss of Miles himself. The will to knowledge achieves its goal—a "frozen countenance"—but it was a goal the governess did not know she was striving toward.

That the will to knowledge, meant to save and cure, turns out to be inadvertently lethal is the hard-to-miss ironic-allegorical *punctum* of the story.[42] The final movements of the story can be read as a severe cautionary against taking reading in too seriously, for when reading in gets caught up in institutional modes of the will to knowledge, the flirtatious, mimetic moments can be steamrolled by the imperative to uncover secrets and produce knowledge. James's position is clear: mimesis, possession, confusions of self and other and past and present—in a word, *ghosts*—are necessary for life.

What then to make of the *reader's* experience of the will to know while reading the story? Again it should be emphasized, the governess's will to knowledge mimes the reader's, step by step. Or the reader is encouraged at every step to mime the governess. As she reads into the children's behavior, we read into hers. The story catches us by provoking in us the will to knowledge as well. And the moment when the sanity of the governess is most in question and when we hope that Miles's confession will tell us what is really going on—precisely at this moment, the very act of reading in is dramatized in the story as a violent, harmful process. The story strongly—and very critically—allegorizes the very experience it promotes, drawing the reader into the circle of complicity.

This critique of the readerly experience the story solicits is what enables it to function as an affective map for its readers. That is, this critique allows James's reader to acquire a representation of how one got into the emotional situation one is in and also how it might be possible to get out. For in the person of the governess, James shows us how one might become affectively invested in a will to knowledge, and at the same time he gets the reader interested in doing so as well. The will to knowledge is attractive first of all because it allows for a reading in— like the one James encourages Fullerton to engage in and like the one the governess indulges in with the children, even as she senses it might be somewhat inappropriate. The attraction becomes more pointed, even urgent, when she finds herself in the situation Luhmann called autonomy without autarchy. That is, one's lack of authority in determining the problems one faces—particularly attenuated in the case of the governess, who has inherited problems (and losses) beyond her ken— can become a problem when one is, as she is, all the same "at the helm." The governess's simultaneous lack of agency and responsibility for the children leaves her searching for ways to steer, possible sources of authority or "autarchy" for making her way in uncharted waters. The feeling of knowledge and power, even salvation, promised by the hidden (sexual) secret proves irresistible. Meanwhile, the vaguely sexual intimations and the unclear mental state of the governess increase the reader's will to knowledge as well.

In catching the readers in this way the story creates a nugget of affective experience for them, one that draws on and repeats their earlier experiences, and then tells them something about those experiences. It tells them: do not trust the will to knowledge; it does not deliver what it promises. James maps out the affective territory created by the new discourse of sexual identities. He shows us whence the emotional attraction of reading into the secrets lingering especially around children's bodies and behaviors, and what happens when one gets caught up in the desire to find and fix a truth there.

James also provides us a map for finding pleasures within the new regime. That is, the existence of a new will to knowledge, of a new proliferation of secrets everywhere, can in fact allow for and indeed provide cover for a flirtatious reading in. This is a mode we see in his letters to Fullerton, and in the renewed pleasure the governess takes in the children's company once she imagines a secret to be hiding there. Likewise, James's prose itself opens up an aesthetic space for reading into someone else. But this is a reading in that does not need to—indeed, that needs not to—turn into a will to actually find knowledge there. Knowledge is not the cure but is the alibi that allows hallucinatory, ghostly relationality to come into being. Ghostly relationality is itself the cure. For James, we might even say that it is only as ghosts (when we are possessed by an emotion from our past) and with ghosts (the people who are stand-ins for lost objects from our past) that one can be affectively attached to the world and the people around us. He sees ghosts everywhere.

CHAPTER FOUR

"What a Mourning"

Propaganda and Loss in
W. E. B. Du Bois's *Souls of Black Folk*

My career as a scientist was to be swallowed up in my
role as a master of propaganda.

—W. E. B. DU BOIS, *DUSK OF DAWN*

What a mourning, when the stars begin to fall.

—SORROW SONG

This book has so far argued for the usefulness of the term "affective
mapping" to name a particular set of aesthetic strategies that allow one
to perceive the historicity of one's affective experience, especially experiences of difficult, potentially depressing loss.[1] By historicity here, I
mean first of all the specificity of a particular historical moment. The affective map represents subjective emotional life as the precipitate
formed by the intersection of a set of social processes and institutions,
and as such shared by other persons who are subject to the same forces.
I also mean historicity in the sense suggested by W. E. B. Du Bois when
he wrote of the value of seeing one's suffering in relation to "a long historical development and not [as] a transient occurrence."[2] Connecting
one's emotional life to historical processes in this way allows us to see
"how long our misery has been in preparation," as Walter Benjamin put
it, and thus to see our lives as the site and potential culmination of a
long historical struggle. Each act of resistance or even survival thereby
acquires a new gravity, since one feels as if one is not combating an occasional or accidental enemy but rather is fighting against an entire history of oppression. Moreover, seeing the "long historical development"
allows you to understand that you are engaged in a struggle not by
yourself but with and in the name of others—from the past and the
present—who share this history with you. Thus, as I argued earlier in
the book, the (revisable, rhizomatic) affective map not only gives us a
view of a terrain shared with others in the present, but also traces the

paths, resting places, dead ends, and detours we might share with those who came before us.

The disclosure of the historicity of subjective emotional life always beckons toward a potentially political effect. Through the articulation of a subjective experience of loss with a collective one, the affective map facilitates the transformation of a depressive disengagement into an (at least splenetic and at best actually hopeful) interest in the social and political histories and processes that lie at the origins of one's losses. In this way, it opens up the space for what I have been calling an antidepressive melancholia. However, as I suggested in Chapter 4, the political potential of the affective map can lie nascent and unrealized in the aesthetic practice, waiting for an audience to take it up.[3] The affective map must be met by the right circumstances for it to have actual galvanizing, transformative, collectively experienced effects.

Such circumstances met W. E. B. Du Bois's *Souls of Black Folk*. Although its overt address was to a "white" audience, its impact on African American thought and culture is well known; James Weldon Johnson wrote, for instance, that this book "had a greater effect upon and within the Negro race in America than any other single book published since *Uncle Tom's Cabin*."[4] This book of "sketches and essays" seems to have provided for many African American readers what one critic described as the "special exhilarating feeling any reader gets when an author names things that the reader has felt very deeply but could not articulate."[5] Du Bois articulated African American feelings not only in the sense of putting them into language but also in the connective sense stressed by Stuart Hall.[6] He created a constellation of relations, linking the critical-historical analysis of social, economic, and political structures with phenomenologically rich and highly personal accounts of the emotional effects of being a black person in the white-supremacist United States, allowing his readers to recognize their own subjectivities as examples of broader social formations, and thus to see their commonality with others in the same situation.

Du Bois wrote, for instance, of the state-sanctioned murderous violence against black persons, the absence of equal protection under the law, the denial of voting rights and lack of access to education, the virtual slavery of economic peonage, the naturalized public disdain and discouragement expressed toward and about the achievements and existence of black persons, and the enforcement of social inferiority and stigma, as, for example, in the Jim Crow laws. These elements of white supremacy that characterized the American South (which Du Bois referred to as an "armed camp for the intimidation of black folk") were all the more depressing because they constituted the ruin of the promises of political equality and economic development that had accompanied Reconstruction. Altogether, Du Bois asserts, the emotional effect is overwhelming: black people remain stuck in "the Valley of the Shadow of Death, where all that makes life worth living—Liberty, Justice and Right—is marked 'For White People Only'" (*Souls*, 163).

I will argue that Du Bois's task in *The Souls of Black Folk* was to help his readers see this objectively depressing situation as a site of potentially victorious struggle. Accordingly, Du Bois analyzes precisely how and why the situation is depressing for African American subjects in order that he can also show how it might not be. Central to this analysis is Du Bois's assessment of African American subjectivity as essentially melancholic, preoccupied with difficult losses, but not necessarily depressing for that. In his investigation of this potentially antidepressive melancholia, double consciousness and the veil emerge as the central terms.

If double consciousness and the veil enable Du Bois and his readers to reflect on African American structures of feeling, Du Bois presents the sorrow songs as the aesthetic practice that originates in and transforms that melancholic structure of feeling. Even as the Songs dwell on loss and disappointment, they do so in a collective form that returns insistently to the promise of justice and of the righteous overthrow of an oppressive order. Thus, I hope to show, for Du Bois the collective affect created in the singing of the Songs holds onto and returns repeatedly to the problem of loss not in order that a therapeutic mourning can be accomplished, but in order to remain attuned to the unfinished work of the past, that is, to the problem of American racism. I will argue that the sorrow songs offer for Du Bois an ideal form of culture, indeed the model for his own practice, one that is not (or is at least not only) compensatory or "affirmative" (in Herbert Marcuse's sense), in contrast to the music of Wagner, which Du Bois presents as affirmative culture par excellence in the "The Story of John."

First, however, I want to examine how Du Bois came to this understanding of his project in *Souls*. For *Souls* was the result of a major reevaluation of his intellectual project, and an examination of it will show us how affect and loss found their way to a central place in Du Bois's understanding of his work.

Sam Hose and the Turn to Propaganda

> Something died within me that day.
>
> —W. E. B. DU BOIS

Du Bois spoke modestly of his hopes for *The Souls of Black Folk,* which he referred to as a collection of his "fugitive pieces"[7] yet the book marked a distinct turning point in his own understanding of his work.[8] Before the book's composition, Du Bois had been firmly committed to the promise of sociological knowledge and its potential for combating racism. "The Negro problem," he recalled, "was in my mind a matter of systematic investigation and intelligent understanding. The world was thinking wrong about race because it did not know. The ultimate evil was stupidity. The cure for it was knowledge based on scientific investigation."[9] This position had been a productive one for him, motivating him to accomplish important sociological work (the most influential of which was *The Philadelphia Negro,* based on research completed in 1896)[10] and to launch his academic career. After the Philadelphia study, Du Bois was offered a job directing an ambitious series of annual studies of black life in the United States at Atlanta University. The statement of purpose for his proposed one-hundred-year project typifies Du Bois's Enlightenment intellectual ideology: "This study is a further carrying out of a plan of social study by means of recurring decennial inquiries into the same general set of human problems. . . . we wish not only to make the Truth clear but to present it in such a shape as will encourage and help social reform."[11]

With his appointment at Atlanta University, Du Bois was, as he put it, happily ensconced in the "ivory tower of race." In April 1899, however, a traumatic event left Du Bois in a state of emotional and intellectual crisis.

At the very time when my studies were most successful, there cut across this plan which I had as a scientist, a red ray which could not be ignored. I remember when it first, as it were, startled me to my feet: a poor Negro in central Georgia, Sam Hose, had killed his landlord's wife. I wrote out a careful and reasoned statement concerning the evident facts and started down to the *Atlanta Constitution* office, carrying in my pocket a letter of introduction to Joel Chandler Harris. I did not get there. On the way news met me: Sam Hose had been lynched, and they said that his knuckles were on exhibition at a grocery store farther down on Mitchell Street, along which I was walking. I turned back to the University. I began to turn aside from my work. I did not meet Joel Chandler Harris nor the editor of the *Constitution*.[12]

In a characteristic attempt to combat (the "stupidity" of) racism with "intelligent understanding," Du Bois wrote a "careful and reasoned statement concerning the evident facts" in order to intervene in the journalistic public sphere, whereas the *Constitution* (along with other local papers) had been reporting where the lynching was to happen, recounting the anticipation of the whites who would be involved—in essence, the newspaper was promoting the event. As Ida B. Wells wrote, "this awful deed was suggested, encouraged and made possible by the daily press of Atlanta, Georgia."[13] When he realized that the event had already taken place, that he was and had been powerless to intercede, and that Sam Hose's knuckles were on display in a grocery store, Du Bois turned back to the university in shock and put aside his work.

The raison d'être of Du Bois's work as he understood it—fighting racism through intelligent understanding—had been fundamentally challenged. The bloody "red ray" cutting across his work "startled" him to his feet, stopped him in his tracks, and caused him to reevaluate his approach to his work *tout court*. "Two considerations thereafter broke in upon my work and eventually disrupted it: first, one could not be a calm, cool, and detached scientist while Negroes were lynched, murdered and starved; and secondly, there was no such definite demand for scientific work of the sort that I was doing, as I had confidently assumed would be easily forthcoming."[14] Du Bois's calm, scientific detachment, what we might call his optimistic Enlightenment mood, suddenly appeared radically inadequate. By "mood" here I mean Heidegger's *Stimmung,* also translated as "attunement."[15] By way of our mood or "mode of attunement" *(Gestimmstein),* as Heidegger explains it, we see a certain set of possibilities for action, interest, and affective attachment in the world; our *Stimmung* determines how things can "matter" to us.[16] As Charles Guignon put it, "nothing would matter to us if we were not already in a mood, if we were not already attuned to the world in a particular way."[17] The "red ray" cut across Du Bois's mode of attunement, and made that mode itself visible to him precisely inasmuch as it left him feeling distinctly *out* of tune with the world. He found himself having been thrown into a world in which "Negroes were lynched, murdered and starved," with no choice but to find a way to come to terms with it, a task for which he realized his "calm, cool," scientific, ivory tower *Stimmung* was painfully inadequate. Changing one's *Stimmung*, however, is not simply a matter of will or decision; one has to figure out how to invoke or awaken a "counter-mood." The nature of the "counter-mood" Du Bois sought to summon is best understood if we examine a little further the nature of the shock that motivated it.

That Du Bois had trouble making sense of Sam Hose's lynching within the ways of thinking and feeling available to him at that moment is underscored by the fact that Du Bois incorrectly recounts the facts surrounding the lynching. Hose in fact killed not his landlord's wife (as Du Bois writes in both *Dusk of Dawn* and his *Autobiography*) but his employer, reportedly in a dispute over wages owed Hose.[18] Indeed, the wife actively participated in the organization and promoting of the lynching, adding to the murder charge the inflammatory accusation of rape.[19] Revisions of memory after the fact such as Du Bois's here have for some time been understood to be likely when the event in question has been impossible to incorporate into a meaningful context in the first instance. The deferred or retroactive memory (the usual translation of Freud's word of choice, *Nachträglichkeit,* later raised by Lacan to the level of a concept) is formed in relation to different conflicting psychic imperatives, with the usual effect of endowing the experience "not only with a new meaning but also with psychic effectiveness."[20] Hose's lynching not only interrupted Du Bois's *Stimmung* but also was what Lacan would call an irruption of the real, a disturbance of the symbolic network with which we process our lives. The revised memory represents an attempt to cover the hole in the symbolic network, to place the event back into a psychically relevant context. We might speculate that replacing the dead white man with a dead white woman in the story allows the memory to rhyme with Du Bois's own experience of racial animus and hostility, which, in his other autobiographical writings, usually feature the rejection or disgust of a white woman.[21] This is the case, for example, in his "Strivings of the Negro People" (which would become the opening chapter of *Souls,* and had been published for the first time shortly before Hose's lynching), which tells the story of his childhood rejection by a white girl at school in Great Barrington, Massachusetts, as the moment he became aware of racial difference and inequality as such (more on this later). At the same time, the revised memory acts as a wish fulfillment, that the wife *should* be dead. Thus the memory allows Du Bois at once to identify with Hose (inasmuch as they share a troubled relation with white women) and to avenge him, thereby (unconsciously) redeeming what he saw in himself as his failure to stop the lynching.

When Du Bois later recollected that he felt something die within him that day, he is likely referring to the death of his optimistic Enlightenment *Stimmung* and the sense of self that went with it. However, there appears to be an identificatory or incorporative mechanism at work here as well. As in the Freudian understanding of melancholia, here too a difficult or confusing loss has led to an internalization of an image of the dead other in order to avoid the difficult work of disattaching from that other. Along such lines, we can say that Du Bois's internal death functions as a compensatorily sympathetic response; like Hose, he also experiences a death, mimetically fragmenting himself in the process. He is left then with his own internal corpse—the corpse of his previous self, his optimistic combat-racism-through-reason self—a corpse, which indexically links to Hose, substituting for him. The incorporation of the death gives Du Bois a local site (over which he might exercise some control) onto which he can direct the complex swirl of emotions that spun out of the Hose lynching. The loss and its attendant affects can be kept inside and saved for a later date, for a time when he might be capable of apprehending and asking what a mourning would or could here take place.

Compounding the disruptive shock caused by the Hose lynching, the very next month Du Bois's only son Burghardt died of diphtheria. As the illness became so serious that it threatened his life, Du Bois and his wife Nina were unable to find a doctor who would see a black patient. David Lewis suggests that after Burghardt's death Nina never forgave Du Bois for having brought her to racist Atlanta, so hostile that, in a spectacular failure of sympathy, passersby yelled "Niggers" as they brought Burghardt's coffin to the train station (*Souls*, 168).[22]

In *The Souls of Black Folk*, Du Bois narrates his son's death in religious, apocalyptic tones, suggesting that it was not an event that startled him to his feet so much as one that left him deeply depressed, hardly able to feel that life was even worth living for a black person in the United States. His depression is here ironically refigured as an "awful gladness."

All that day and all that night there sat an awful gladness in my heart,— nay, blame me not if I see the world thus darkly though the Veil,—and my soul whispers ever to me, saying, "Not dead, not dead, but escaped; not bond, but free." No bitter meanness now shall sicken his baby heart till it die a living death, no taunt shall madden his happy boyhood. Fool I was to think or wish that this little soul should grow choked and deformed within the Veil! . . . Well sped, my boy, before the world had dubbed your ambition insolence, had held your ideals unattainable, and taught you to cringe and bow. Better far this nameless void that stops my life than a sea of sorrow for you. (*Souls*, 168)

Silenus-like, Du Bois here proposes that for a child born within the veil, it is better never to have been born, second best to die young. Death is figured as an escape from a white supremacist world that would thwart his son at every step. Du Bois here echoes the rhetoric of the sorrow songs ("not dead, but escaped; not bond, but free"), in which death and freedom from slavery are often equated, sometimes, as is well known, in order to communicate information about escapes to the North. But here the second meaning (escape from slavery) has been evacuated; Burghardt's is not an allegorical but a real death. Du Bois here seems to allow that he cannot figure out a way to make an African American life worth living, that despair is nearly unavoidable given the current state of affairs, and that we can only wait for the final mourning when "the stars begin to fall."[23] This is a depressive melancholia.

By contrast, and to return to the main point here, while the counter-mood Du Bois awakens after the bloody "red ray" disrupts his ability and desire to work is a decidedly melancholic one, it is also a mood that allows him to reassess and politicize anew his intellectual life.[24] In this instance, the unresolved nature of the loss—keeping the referent of "what a mourning" uncertain—attunes him to the unresolved nature of the political problem at its source, American white supremacy. In addition, one of the things that comes into view in this new *Stimmung* is the problem of attunement itself.

"The cure," Du Bois recalled recognizing, "wasn't simply telling people the truth, it was inducing them to act on the truth."[25] In other words, it was a matter of persuasion, of affecting and motivating people. In order to try to induce people to act, Du Bois decided to become what he calls a "master of propaganda,"[26] which will involve understanding, to borrow from Heidegger, "the possibilities of moods in order to rouse them and guide them aright."[27] As a propagandist, Du Bois entered the domain explored by Aristotle's *Rhetoric*, which is concerned with the affects not so much as psychological problems or issues as what must be studied if we are to understand how it is that we affect each other. Thus, Aristotle asks: why and how do people get angry, feel ashamed, sad, or joyous? In what conditions? In relation to what kinds of objects? In this sense, Heidegger wrote, the *Rhetoric* is "the first systematic hermeneutic of the everydayness of Being with one another."[28]

Du Bois's propagandistic project involves a pursuit of just such a hermeneutic—figuring out how people are affected—and then devising a practice that will make use of that knowledge. *The Souls of Black Folk* is essentially the first text Du Bois produced in this propagandistic mode. Thus, if, as Thomas Holt argues, this book "marks Du Bois's conscious turn toward active political engagement," it also marks a new understanding for Du Bois of what politics *is*.[29]

If rhetoric is the study of "the everydayness of being with one another," then the question in relation to *Souls* is not only how does Du Bois theorize the nature of being-with around and across the color line, but what kind of a being-with does he establish in relation to his audience?

Problem

> The problem of the twentieth century is the problem of the color line.
>
> —W. E. B. DU BOIS, *THE SOULS OF BLACK FOLK*

> To the real question, How does it feel to be a problem? I seldom answer a word.
>
> —W. E. B. DU BOIS, *THE SOULS OF BLACK FOLK*

In the opening lines of the "forethought" to *Souls*, Du Bois writes that "herein lie buried many things which if read with patience may show the strange meaning of being black here in the dawning of the twentieth century." Things the reader may have thought buried and gone, Du Bois will insist, are not dead at all. They remain, and Du Bois beckons as if from the grave, politely inviting the reader to view what he will proceed to disinter. In order to show "the strange meaning of being black," a reorientation of temporal perception will be necessary. For these things that lie buried do not speak to us of the past as something that has passed—what black being *was*—but as something dawning (the "dawning of the twentieth Century") in the here and now of Du Bois's writing. Like a ghost, the being of blackness is at once buried and appearing, in *Souls*, as if for the first time. Clearly, for Du Bois—as it must be for his readers if they are to understand his text—"the work of the past," as Walter Benjamin noted in another context, "is still incomplete."[30]

As if sensing that this gothic opening might not immediately interpellate all his "Gentle Readers," Du Bois maintains that this meaning is not without interest to them, and in his famous phrase dramatically asserts that "the problem of the twentieth century is the problem of the color line." By drawing attention to the "color line" (rather than, say, "race" or "racism" or "white people"), Du Bois locates the problem at the moment of division, that which is *between* the "colors," signaling that the meaning of black being is relational. This is self-consciously addressed in the opening lines of the first chapter proper, "Of Our Spiritual Strivings," which begins with the preposition "between."

> Between me and the other world there is ever an unasked question: unasked by some through feelings of delicacy; by others through the difficulty of rightly framing it. All, nevertheless flutter around it. They approach me in a half-hesitant sort of way, eye me curiously or compassionately, and then, instead of saying directly, How does it feel to be a problem? they say, I know an excellent colored man in my town; or, I fought at Mechanicsville; or Do not these Southern outrages make your blood boil? At these I smile, or am interested, or reduce the boiling to a simmer, as the occasion may require. To the real question, How does it feel to be a problem? I seldom answer a word.

As Nahum Chandler has noted, the sentence could have but does not begin "*There is* an unasked question" or "*in* between me and the other world." These phrases would suggest that there is a being (the "in" of "in between," or the question that *is*) preceding the fact of relation. Instead, this beginning is rhetorically constructed "such that the preposition is introduced as condition of its referent, rather than vice-versa."[31] The relation signified by *between* constitutes and ontologically precedes the "me" and the "other world." Thus, this *between*, like the color line, occupies no space, denoting instead relation as such. The "distance" between "here and there," as Langston Hughes put it, "is nowhere."[32]

The nonplace of this relation is made more difficult to perceive and analyze because it is marked by an absence, the *unasked* question "How does it feel to be a problem?" Power, in this instance, lies with ignorance. That is, the relationship is structured by an unasked question not about the white interlocutor but about the black one: the feeling of the being of white people is not in question. In such a situation, the black person (for the white) remains ontologically and emotionally obscure; the perception of similarity across the color line is handily foreclosed through this preterition.[33] The white interlocutor who can flutter around the question but not ask it has the luxury of having between him or her and, for example, the lynched Sam Hose a lacunae across which identification seems impossible. This would be a paradigmatic illustration of what Du Bois saw as one of the chief supports of white supremacy: the absence of any "point of transference where the thoughts and feelings of one race can come into direct contact and sympathy with the thoughts and feelings of the other" (*Souls*, 145).[34]

By introducing the nonasked question in the context of the color line and the "between" that separates and relates Du Bois and the "other world," Du Bois questions the ground of the question "How does it feel to be a problem?" That is, if the "problem" does not exist in a person but in the relation that constitutes that person and the (un)asker, then the question, inasmuch as it presumes that the problem is locatable in the black person, does not make sense. More exactly, it is already an answer, performatively giving the addressee the status of "problem" through its asking. To "answer" it would involve showing how the question is a problem as well. And although Du Bois will proceed to explain that it is "strange" and "peculiar" to be a problem, he will employ a series of strategies to ensure that the question implicates the reader— on both sides of the color line—as well.[35]

The "other world" that Du Bois references as if it were outside the space his text occupies is also at the same time, of course, composed of the very "Gentle Readers" he addresses. But Du Bois does not write, "Between me and *you*, Gentle Reader, there is ever an unasked question." By substituting "other world" for "you," the "between" created by Du Bois's text distances itself from the "between" that creates the color line. He thereby creates a space for the reader to *not* be the "other world." On the one hand, this is a canny way to pursue a double-voiced strategy, whereby the text addresses an African American audience at the same time it addresses readers who see themselves as "white." On the other, it opens an estranging, problematized readerly position for the white reader.

Readers who recognizes themselves as part of the other world will proceed to be engaged in an alienating situation in which they are at once the "you" and the "they" of the text ("you" *are* the "other world"). As the "they," they are most decidedly a problem, the very source of problematic being (as the askers of "How does it feel to be a problem?"), which becomes ever clearer as the text proceeds. But the possibility is quite open, and in fact Du Bois's first-person narration invites it, for the reader who may otherwise see her or himself on the "white" side of the color line to be affected by Du Bois's sense of shame, outrage, or sadness and to be brought into the emotional orbit of Du Bois's persona in *The Souls of Black Folk* ("Thou too! Hast thou seen sorrow and the dull waters of hopelessness?" [*Souls*, 172]). However, here too the readerly position is rendered problematic, because Du Bois keeps reminding us of the force field created by the color line, from which no person escapes, and by which "the other world" comes back into view. Eventually, readers who dwell outside the veil will remember that they are on the other side of a line having few or no points of transference across it, except the one now created by *Souls* itself. In other words, Du Bois's text performs a strange oscillation between a narrative consideration of the worlds defined by the color line on the one hand and the worlds created through the mode of relationality of Du Bois's text itself on the other. The production of the disjuncture between the two—a kind of "double consciousness"—is the point. This creates a sort of readerly whirligig in which there is no stable position for "white" subjectivity as the readers of the text, no space in which the white readers could experience themselves as existing safely outside the realm of questioned being.

In relation to his readers in the "other world," it would seem, Du Bois hopes to create the scene for something like what Jean-Luc Nancy calls "compassion." However, this reader-relation would not be characterized by the so-called "sympathy" created by a book like *Uncle Tom's Cabin,* which, one might argue, represents slaves as victims to be pitied and helped, nor would it even be the liberal version of sympathy as mutual recognition of equal humanness.[36] "Compassion," in Nancy's sense, "is not altruism, nor is it identification; it is the disturbance of violent relatedness."[37] The point is not to assimilate the other to already existing structures of feeling or modes of identity, nor really even to understand the other through analogy ("this other has had experiences like my own") but to experience a disturbance that problematizes the notion of a separate or separable self. Such a compassion (a disturbance of one's own being by one's relatedness) involves a recognition that one's own being is always already tied up with the being of others, and others not only in the present, but from the past as well. Our mood is never ours alone. And no person's being can be safeguarded against the being of others. Thus, Du Bois's response to "being a problem" is not to somehow reinforce the ontology of blackness but to expand the sense of problematicity so that no ontology escapes it.

"The Shadow": Double Consciousness as Collective Melancholia

> The very soul of the toiling, sweating black man is darkened by the shadow of a vast despair.
>
> —W. E. B. DU BOIS, *THE SOULS OF BLACK FOLK*

> The shadow of a deep disappointment rests upon the Negro people.
>
> —W. E. B. DU BOIS, *THE SOULS OF BLACK FOLK*

> I remember well when the shadow swept across me.
>
> —W. E. B. DU BOIS, *THE SOULS OF BLACK FOLK*

> Thus the shadow of the object fell upon the ego . . . in this way an object-loss was transformed into an ego-loss and the conflict between the critical activity and the loved person into a cleavage between the critical activity of the ego and the ego as altered by identification.
>
> —SIGMUND FREUD, "MOURNING AND MELANCHOLIA"

In his effort to examine and explain the depressing effect of white supremacy on black subjectivity and collectivity, Du Bois addresses a problem similar to the one Freud confronted several years later in "Mourning and Melancholia" (1917). That is, both Du Bois and Freud were struggling to understand why some relations to loss were depressing while others were not, and how one might develop or find a practice for converting one relation to loss into another. Furthermore, they understand the general problem in strikingly similar terms. For Du Bois, as for Freud, a difficult, ambivalent loss (the rejection by a classmate) is preserved through a process of internalization, producing what Du Bois calls "double consciousness." This becomes depressing, in each of their accounts, when the negative affects attached to this internalized object return to cast their shadow on the subject.

Yet where Freud is trying to develop a general theory of melancholia and a general technique for treating it, Du Bois is concerned with a particular group of people at a definite historical moment. For Du Bois, "the shadow of a dark despair" falls not on him alone but on everyone on his side of "the veil." Indeed, the falling of the shadow is itself the moment of racial subjectification. And it does not fall accidentally but as the direct result of the institutions, ideological formations, and practices of white supremacy. Thus, Du Bois (unlike Freud) views (African American) depression and despair not only as a psychological problem but as a social and political one as well, the solution to which must be collective in nature.

All of this is introduced in the few famous paragraphs at the beginning of *Souls,* where Du Bois establishes the two thought-images that serve as linchpins of the discussion—double consciousness and the veil. He does this through an allegorical-autobiographical story of childhood rejection.[38] Here is the passage.

It is in the early days of rollicking boyhood that the revelation bursts upon one, all in a day, as it were. I remember well when the shadow swept across me. I was a little thing, away in the hills of New England, where the dark Housatonic winds between Hoosac and Taghkanic to the sea. In a wee wooden schoolhouse, something put it into the boys' and girls' heads to buy gorgeous visiting cards—ten cents a package—and exchange. The exchange was merry, till one girl, a tall newcomer, refused my card,—refused it peremptorily, with a glance. Then it dawned upon me with a certain suddenness that I was different from the others; or like, mayhap, in heart and life and longing, but shut out from their world by a vast veil. I had thereafter no desire to tear down that veil, to creep through; I held all beyond it in common contempt, and lived above it in a region of blue sky and great wandering shadows. That sky was bluest when I could beat my mates at examination time, or beat them at a foot race, or even beat their stringy heads. Alas with the years all this fine contempt began to fade; for the worlds I longed for, and all their dazzling opportunities, were theirs, not mine. But they should not keep these prizes, I said; some not all, I would wrest from them. Just how I would do it I could never decide: by reading law, by healing the sick, by telling the wonderful tales that swam in my head,—some way. With other black boys the strife was not so fiercely sunny: their youth shrank into tasteless sycophancy, or into silent hatred of the pale world about them and mocking distrust of everything white; or wasted itself in a bitter cry, Why did God make me an outcast and stranger in mine own house? The shades of the prison house closed about us all: walls strait and stubborn to the whitest, but relentlessly narrow, tall and unscalable to the sons of night who must plod darkly on in resignation, or beat unwailing palms against the stone, or steadily, half hopeless, watch the streak of blue above.

After the Egyptian and Indian, the Greek and the Roman, the Teuton and the Mongolian, the Negro is a sort of seventh son, born with a veil, and gifted with second sight in the American world,—a world which yields him no true self-consciousness, but only lets him see himself through the revelation of the other world. It is a peculiar sensation, this double consciousness, this sense of always looking at oneself through the eyes of others, of measuring one's soul by the tape of a world that looks on in amused contempt and pity. One ever feels his two-ness,—an American, a Negro; two souls, two thoughts, two unreconciled strivings; two warring ideals in one dark body, whose dogged strength alone keeps it from being torn asunder.

Du Bois compresses a surprisingly wide-ranging narrative into these two paragraphs. The episode begins in his "wee wooden" schoolhouse, where Du Bois and his classmates were imitating the adult practice, common in Victorian America, of exchanging colorfully illustrated visiting cards.[39] This ritual of childhood consumption and exchange is a paradigmatic moment of ideological interpellation, where one learns to recognize and internalize ("something put it into [our] heads") one's place in the social order, how agency in that order is exercised, what gender and sexuality mean there, and, in this case, the significance of one's appearance. The exchange, Du Bois notes, had been "merry" until a newcomer refused his card "peremptorily, with a glance."[40] Thus, in a relatively public setting, charged not only with the usual social anxieties of childhood but also with the pressures of compulsory heterosexuality, Du Bois is rejected. Adding to the shamefulness of rejection, the tall newcomer's peremptory glance communicates a sense of superiority and contempt, a refusal of any further interaction. The glance (which is to say her facial expression as she looked at him) communicated to Du Bois not only these things but also—as glance—that her emotional response was based on visual information: she only had to look at him to know she would not accept *his* card. Du Bois thus sees himself being looked at but not seen.

Like the "red ray" that later disrupted his cheery scientific outlook, the revelation that "bursts" upon him and shocks him out of his "rollicking boyhood" nestled between the picturesque Hoosac and Tagkhanic,[41] leaves him feeling distinctly unattuned to his environment. At this moment he realizes that he is "different from the others" or, more precisely, that he "may be like in heart and life and longing" but is "shut out from their world by a vast veil." Du Bois goes on to describe the emotional impact this had on him and the others with him in the "shades of the prison house." He notes how he managed to remain "fiercely sunny," first by living above the veil "in a region of blue sky and great wandering shadows." Then, seeing that the "dazzling opportunities" he desired were available only to his white peers on the other side of the veil, he realized that the compensatory pleasures of the blue sky distract him from the task of wresting these prizes away. While he is able to persist in the conviction that through some form of achievement ("by reading law, by healing the sick, by telling the wonderful tales that swam in my head") he will be able to get these prizes, Du Bois sees among the others behind the veil with him a set of varied but almost exclusively negative structures of feeling. Aside from Du Bois's own not exactly sanguine sunniness and the "*half* hopeless" looks at the blue sky above the veil, the affective life of African America is dominated, Du Bois tells us here, by resignation, sycophancy, hatred, distrust, and bitterness. At the same time, however, it is here that we see Du Bois's awareness that this negative affective existence is not his alone but is shared by the persons who are trapped in the "shades of the prison house" with him.

Then, with the beginning of the next paragraph, the tone and topic change dramatically. Suddenly, Du Bois is exclaiming the historic destiny of "the Negro." The descent of the veil, just presented as leading to a series of unpleasant emotional states, is refigured as the *gift* of "second sight." And double consciousness—"that peculiar sensation"—is introduced and developed in a way that underscores the struggle between "two souls, two thoughts, two unreconciled strivings; two warring ideals in one dark body,"a struggle that, although difficult, is nonetheless managed with "dogged strength." The mood of resignation has dissipated, and we can be sure that it is not accidental that this shift in tone is accompanied by the movement from an experiential and autobiographical register to an explicitly collective and historical one.

✦

Much of the scholarship on "double consciousness" has been concerned with establishing the best intellectual context or genealogy for understanding it. In part, this interpretive impulse appears to be generated out of the desire to make up for the relatively spare elaboration of the term in *Souls* and thus give the term a conceptual gravity that would help to describe its influence. So, for example, Dickson Bruce traces earlier uses of the term "double consciousness" in Emerson and nineteenth-century psychology; Shamoon Zamir carefully shows how Du Bois borrows from and revises Hegel; and Adolph Reed examines double consciousness in the context of neo-Lamarckian social science.[42] To varying degrees, the suggestion in this work is that the right context helps us to see what Du Bois *really* meant by "double consciousness."[43] Contextualizing the idea and the use of the word itself is certainly helpful in understanding how Du Bois may have imagined the term's signification at the moment of his writing, and expands our sense of Du Bois's text by widening the range of texts he is seen to be in conversation with.

However, if Du Bois's propagandistic aim is to make white supremacy seem like a combatable and defeatable problem, and to make racism less depressing, and at the same time persuade white people not to be racist, then conceptual rigor is less important than rhetorical tactics and the affective quality of the reading experience *Souls* will offer its various readers. As Du Bois had noted, the key was not "telling people the truth" but getting them to *act* on it. For this reason, seeking to *define* double consciousness may miss what is most powerful about *Souls*. After all, it is often just those ideas or images that are underelaborated, a little bit vague around the edges that generate the widest and most emotionally charged and energetic responses. Thought-images with some pliability are best able to correspond to a changing and variable historical context. With this in mind, the simple fact of the multiple readings of double consciousness would seem to evidence Du Bois's success in resonating with a multitude of readers.[44] Just as Henry James's apparently unintentional lascivious prose encourages his readers to read into him, or as Walter Benjamin's willfully gnomic writing invites a certain imaginative (and innervating) appropriation on the part of readers, so too Du Bois's presentation of the veil and double consciousness provides his readers with figures flexible enough to correlate with a range of particular experiences of racial subjectivity. Rather than philosophical concepts, Du Bois creates something closer to constellations: the image of the veil is surrounded by a rhetoric of light and shadows (as in the epigraphs to this section), and double consciousness appears alongside the feeling of "two-ness" and a range of doublednesses.

This constellation-like quality aids Du Bois in the task of producing the common language necessary for a collective consciousness. Later in *Souls,* in the context of his discussion of a summer spent teaching in a small town in Tennessee, he is explicit about the need for this common language:

> I have called my tiny community a world, and so its isolation made it; and yet there was among us but a half-awakened common consciousness, sprung from common joy and grief, at burial, birth or wedding; from a common hardship in poverty, poor land, and low wages; and above all, from the sight of the veil that hung between us and Opportunity. All of this caused us to think some thoughts together; but these, when ripe for speech, were spoken in various languages. (*Souls,* 57–58)

What brings this world together for Du Bois here is not any kind of essential racial identity but a set of emotional experiences. The problem is that the experiences, thoughts, and feelings common to them all are "spoken in various languages." With the constellations around double consciousness and the veil, Du Bois finds a language in which to articulate and rouse this "half-awakened common consciousness."

The articulation of this common consciousness facilitates the recognition by readers of the collective nature of existence in the "shades of the prison house," allowing for at least the beginning of an escape from the "death and isolation," the sense of being alone in beating one's palms against the "walls of the prison house," which Du Bois describes as one of the chief difficulties of the black situation. The depressive aspects of African American experience are represented as communal and political problems rather than personal ones. In reading Du Bois's narrative of shameful alienation, of feeling imprisoned and internally split, African American readers may feel recognized precisely in their experiences of isolating nonrecognition. The experience of isolation is thereby dissolved, and in this Du Bois's text may be seen to aspire to the performative function of the sorrow songs: "Nobody knows the trouble I've seen"—except all the other people singing "Nobody knows the trouble I've seen."

Thus, if the first goal and effect of the description of this melancholic structure of feeling is a feeling of collectivity that from the start alters that structure, this is not its only value. An additional aim for Du Bois, as it was for Freud, is to make cognitively accessible the experiences of depression and despair in their local, subjective, emotional sense, to allow for a self-analysis of one's own emotional life so that one may begin to exert some agency in relation to it. Here, however, it is critical to make these experiences accessible in a way that relates them not only to other persons but also to the social structures and historical developments in which they originate. For only then can one see with whom one's situation is shared, who one's enemies are, what situations must be avoided, what skills developed and tactics pursued—in short, all the ways one might stave off despair and have some agency in relation to one's own emotional life. In this work, too, the flexibility of double consciousness and the veil permit the articulation of different registers of existence, connecting the subjective and the collective, the emotional and the political, and the present and the past.[45]

It is worth noting, moreover, that the polysemousness of both the veil and double consciousness increases their ability to describe not only an African American structure of feeling but a more generally modern one.

This, for example, is what allows double consciousness to provide a potential point of intellectual contact and/or compassion with Du Bois's white readers, who may see their own experiences of alienation, difficult loss, or depressive interiority as similar to double consciousness.

Here, a comparison with Freud is fruitful, because it helps us to elaborate and appreciate the specificity of the depressive mechanism at work in double consciousness, and to see the places where Du Bois exceeds and expands the personal or subjective out to the historical and collective.[46] (It also, of course, underscores the book's larger suggestion about the more broadly modern experience of melancholia, the idea that in his description of melancholia Freud creates a thought-image capable of characterizing the experience of modernity more generally, becoming thereby useful not as the element of a psychology so much as a point of comparison between different experiences of modernity.)

In its basic contours—to return to the long passage from the beginning of *Souls* cited earlier—Du Bois's story functions as a kind of compressed case history of melancholia. As Du Bois tells it, the white eye of the rejecting other is internalized as a super-ego-like critical agent: "It is a peculiar sensation, this double consciousness, the sense of always looking at oneself through the eyes of others, of measuring one's soul by the tape of a world that looks on in amused contempt and pity." Similarly, in "Mourning and Melancholia," Freud argues that melancholia happens when, after a loss or rejection, the ego identifies itself with the lost object in order to avoid losing it, to keep the emotional tie alive ("by taking flight into the ego love escapes extinction"). Problems arise when, now introjected, the affects that were earlier directed at the lost object are directed at the *I* itself, by what Freud called a new "special agency," created for the purpose of keeping this ambivalent emotional tie alive.[47] The subject is left with "the ego divided, fallen apart in two pieces, one of which rages against the second."[48] The process tends toward depression because the negative affects—the "shadow of the object"—previously directed toward the object now fall back on one's self. ("The self-reproaches are reproaches against a loved object which have been shifted away from it on to the patient's own ego.")[49] We end up, Freud suggests, disparaging ourselves as we would (or as we wish we could) disparage the lost object.

However, in Du Bois's autobiographical allegory, the internal split following on the rejection takes a distinct course. Whereas in Freud the melancholic introjection means that you start judging yourself as if you *are* the forsaken object (seeing oneself *as* the other), in Du Bois's case, the relation is reversed: he starts to judge himself from the *point of view* of the lost object, the person who has refused him ("looking at oneself through the eyes of others"). In other words, in double consciousness, it is the "critical activity," not the ego, that is altered by identification with the object. This means that double consciousness is not depressing in the same way Freud's melancholia is. Rather than directing the affects one had about a lost object back at oneself, one is forever judging oneself from the point of view of someone who "looks on in amused contempt and pity."

To make matters worse, this disdainful point of view is that of those to whom certain "dazzling prizes" are available. Thus the situation is uniquely ambivalent. Inasmuch as Du Bois also wants access to these prizes, he does not only see the world from a white point of view but desires to occupy that very position, at the very same time that he hates white people, inasmuch as they bar access to the privileges they enjoy.[50] Richard Wright writes about this ambivalent, contradictory position, which he describes (borrowing from Nietzsche) as the "frog's perspective," the view of the disempowered from below. "A certain degree of hate combined with love (ambivalence) is always involved in this looking from below upward and the object against which the subject is measuring himself undergoes constant change. He loves the object because he would like to resemble it; he hates the object because his chances of resembling it are slight, remote."[51] Here, the ambivalence Freud suggested is always present in identification is at its most attenuated: the desire to be like someone shifts into the desire to replace and thus destroy that person.[52] For the African American subject this is a drama that plays itself out not just with an external object but as a very part of African American subjectivity.

In further unfolding the logic of this particular melancholic mechanism, it is worth considering the shadow metaphor both Freud and Du Bois used. While the metaphor of the shadow in Freud is meant to reference the negative affects that are transferred from the lost object to the ego, it also suggests that what is introjected is the *relation* between the ego and the object, a relation affected and determined by a third force—the source of light, the sun—that causes a shadow to fall on the ego. The ego is blocked from access to the light—from a sense of visibility, of existence, of desirability, of recognition—by the lost object. This lost object then takes on a new importance because it stands between us and the sun, which would seem here to be a metaphor for the possibility of appearing before others, the fact of visibility as such, or what Jacques Lacan called "the gaze."

Of "the gaze" *(le regard)* Lacan writes: "What determines me, at the most profound level, in the visible, is the gaze that is outside. It is through the gaze that I enter light and it is from the gaze that I receive its effects."[53] In order to imagine ourselves as seen, we picture the point of view from which we are seen, to project the image of the other person seeing us. This, of course, is impossible, not least because the gaze is neither singular nor localizable.[54] We are always more visible, and from more points of view, than we would like to be or can imagine ourselves being. Nonetheless, in order to think of ourselves as existing in the visual world (and indeed, Lacan suggests, to be seeing subjects in the first place) we are forever trying to imagine the point of view from which we are seen.[55]

Inasmuch as the general "they" or the abstracted "person who sees me" constituting the gaze is necessarily imaginary, we may conjecture that nothing is so powerful in forming it as the looks from others that are withheld—the looks one desires but does not receive. The refused look is not only the one we most notice and remember but the one we dwell on precisely because we lack and miss it. Thus, modifying Freud (and Lacan), we might say that our lost love objects do not precipitate to form the ego so much as they combine to form the gaze. Our (bodily) ego, our sense of self, is formed in relation to the picture we imagine was presented to that lost other. Or, to be more precise, it is the difference between the image we imagine we did present and the one we wish *had been* presented, the image that *would have been* seen that is crucial here. We are forever trying to produce the image of ourselves that would allow us to be seen by that lost, absent other and so to somehow regain not just the object itself but the sense of a perfect communion we imagine or fantasize would have been possible there. In Du Bois's case, then, we might say that he feels compelled to produce a self that the girl who refused his card could not refuse, at the very same time that he resents and critiques the very need to produce such a self.

Put in a different language, we could say that the relation Du Bois has internalized is an emotional tie with a particular affective valence, that of shame. Du Bois wrote, for example of the inevitable "self-disparagement and self-questioning" that is the result of "that personal disrespect and mockery, the ridicule and systematic humiliation, the distortion of fact and wanton license of fancy, the cyclical ignoring of the better and boisterous welcoming of the worse, the all pervading desire to inculcate disdain for everything black, from Toussaint to the devil" (*Souls*, 13). He continues: "From the double life every American Negro must live, as a Negro and an American, . . . must arise a painful self-consciousness, an almost morbid sense of personality and a moral hesitancy which is fatal to self-confidence" (*Souls*, 160).[56] What makes "true self-consciousness in this American world" impossible, Du Bois implicitly suggests, is the morbidly acute mode of self-consciousness that characterizes melancholic shame, which, as Silvan Tomkins remarked, "is the affect of indignity, of defeat, of transgression, and of alienation."[57] Indeed, Du Bois at times gives the impression that this persistent sense of shame is the most difficult, most depressing element of black existence.

Tomkins argued that "the classic psychoanalytic theory of depression suffered from the absence of the affect of shame."[58] If, in the Freudian account, depression is caused by the internalization of the lost object and its shadow (the ambivalent libidinal attachment), Freud does not have a theory of affect to help us specify the nature of that internalized shadow.[59] For Tomkins, however, each affect has its own systemic logic that cannot be reduced to anything else (such as its object, or "affect in general"). Tomkins helps us see that if double consciousness is the introjection of an emotional attachment, then we can say that shame is the primary affect internalized.

The shame associated with double consciousness is, in Du Bois's autobiographical-allegorical narrative, a response to the contempt Du Bois has read in the peremptory rejection of the tall newcomer. Contempt, as Tomkins notes, is difficult to respond to, because it is a rejection that precludes the possibility of future communion.[60] Du Bois's first response is a kind of counter-contempt, a corresponding rejection. ("I had thereafter no desire to tear down that veil, to creep through; I held all beyond it in common contempt, and lived above it in a region of blue sky and great wandering shadows.") However initially face-saving this may be, it is (in a white supremacist society) in the long run a dangerously depressive response because it is an acquiescence to the hierarchizing logic of contempt.

Because Du Bois still wishes access to the privileges and rights that are available on the other side of the veil, he puts aside his contempt and, at least as he describes it in *Souls*, opens himself to the experience of shame. In contrast to contempt, shame is a more ambivalent and labile, if also more vulnerable, affective response. As the affect that registers an *interruption* of positive interaction, it exists only where an interesting or enjoyable relation has preceded it or been expected.[61] It mirrors the withdrawal from interaction; its classic signs are a downcast face, eyes averted. This "reduction in facial communication" serves a dual function: "shame is both an interruption and a further impediment to communication, which is itself communicated."[62] That is, the shame response conveys two messages at the same time: while withdrawing from the communication of mutual looking, the downcast face is itself readable as a "semaphore of trouble," not only leaving the door open for communication to resume but soliciting it.[63] Thus, shame at the least keeps the possibility of interaction and recognition open, implicitly presuming that mutual interest or enjoyment can be resumed.[64] This is why, in Tomkins's view, meeting contempt with shame significantly attenuates contempt's hierarchizing function: it refuses to accept the hierarchal relationship that contempt tries to create or enforce.[65]

The veil is symbol and medium of Du Bois's replacement of contempt with shame. For what is the veil but the exemplar of shame's "reduction of facial communication," which at the same time draws attention to itself?[66] In Nathaniel Hawthorne's story "The Minister's Black Veil" (a text likely familiar to Du Bois), the donning of a veil, far from rendering the minister invisible, transforms him into the very center of town attention, provoking great speculation and unease among his parishioners. It gives his words a "subtle power," as the inability to see his face makes the parishioners themselves feel unprotected, naked, open to being observed unawares. In this way it provokes *their* shame, their anxieties and fears. The veil solicits the other's imagination; by making the face visible yet unintelligible, it forces the other to read into the obscured face, creating a rich field for all kinds of transferences. As Lacan put it, "if one wishes to deceive a man, what one presents to him is the painting of a veil, that is to say, something that incites him to ask what is behind it."[67] Thus, in addition to working to theorize the logic of social invisibility, the veil in *Souls* also seeks to replace invisibility: to be seen in a veil is to be precisely *not* invisible.

This does not mean, however, that this shame is any easier to bear. Indeed, in Du Bois's account, the African American subject is perpetually and precipitously shame prone, liable to fall into shame-filled depressiveness with every fresh rejection or exclusion. On the level of daily emotional life, the sense of shame is much more tormenting than reciprocal contempt. It produces a continual sense of failure to be sufficiently interesting, harkening back to the precarious moment in infancy when shame is first registered as a failure to capture the mother's attention, an attention that at that point is not only necessary for survival but constitutes the whole world.

✦

If Du Bois's double consciousness is more specific in its emotional tenor than Freudian melancholia, that emotional specificity is also put more easily into conversation with broader social realities. To see this, it is instructive to go back to the scene of rejection itself. That Du Bois has chosen this particular scene, one in which a girl rejects his visiting card, to allegorize the local mechanisms of racism more generally is, we must assume, strategic.

Part of the of the valence and allegorical significance of the card scene stems from its location in a scene of exchange and the fact that African American persons had not long before been *themselves* objects of exchange in the United States (a fact subtly referenced by Du Bois when he describes himself in this scene as "a little thing").[68] Among other things, these visiting cards introduce the students into the logic and particular advantages (emotional and otherwise) of being an agent (as opposed to an object) of exchange. Of special value here is the seemingly simple ability to have this "gorgeous" card stand in for one's person. In the form of the visiting card, one's specific, embodied, visually apparent person is translated into the neutral but attractive sphere of the "person-in-general." Although we do not know what Du Bois's cards looked like, the implicitly racial quality of this abstraction into a public self is underscored by the appearance of a white hand on many Victorian-era visiting cards.[69] Du Bois's offense was that he acted as if he could access this sphere. Unlike Adrian Piper in her brilliant *detournement* of this scene, he did not have his own, different cards that said "I am black."[70]

As Michael Warner noted, some bodies (such as white, male ones) are "already oriented to the procedure of abstraction."[71] What distinguishes exchanger from the exchanged in American society is the capacity to *become* a thing (and thus resolutely to not *be* a thing), to be able to allow a thing such as a visiting card to represent one's person. This lack of access to an abstracted public self is more consequential than it might first appear. For it was precisely such abstraction that enabled one to leave one's particularities behind as a citizen (protected by the law and able to vote), for example, or consumer (able to eat in restaurants or sit on the bus).[72] The attractions and privileges attaching to this capacity for self-abstraction are dramatized (indeed are *made* attractive) by the presence of persons who *cannot* suppress the body, who have not been able to transcend their specific corporeality in the abstract realm of citizen, and whose hyperembodiment therefore serves as a continual obstacle to power and pleasure.[73] At the moment of the card refusal, Du Bois realizes that there are such nonperson persons and that he is to play the role of one of them.

Not only is the ability to move into the abstracted, public position necessary to access certain rights and privileges in the social order; in addition, with the ability to have a thing stand in for you, you acquire a second, public self (which in turn creates the space for a private self).[74] To become and feel public in this way is to acquire the sort of self-distance one might get from imagining oneself dead, as if one could attend one's own funeral. You get to see yourself as if coherent and whole—and you get to see other people in the act of recognizing you.

In this context, the girl's rejection was a body blow that knocked Du Bois out of the light of personhood, back into a more uncertain, shadowy realm of bodily positivity in which neither citizenship nor self-(mis)recognition are available. Quite different from the agency-expanding objecthood one acquires in allowing a visiting-card to stand in for one, this object-ification restricts and reduces. It is, as Fanon put it, a "crushing objecthood."[75] It is as if this girl, bringing the whole white world with her, has stepped between Du Bois and the sun itself, casting him into shadow and blocking his access to visibility in general. ("I remember well when the shadow swept across me.") Freud's "shadow of the object" has fallen on Du Bois's *I* not only psychically or internally but socially as well.

And although Du Bois acknowledges that the whole world is by no means constituted by white people, and that there is in fact a world made up of black persons on his side of the veil, through which he can also achieve visibility and recognition, he also realizes that certain desires can only be met from the other world, because the sun of social and political visibility (which is necessary to receive the "dazzling" gifts of access to economic and political power, freedom from threat of physical violence, access to health care, and so on) goes through that world before it gets to his.[76] And, as it stands, white people block that sun from reaching him. As Ralph Ellison wrote in *Invisible Man,* his extended elaboration of this Du Boisian idea, "I *was* and yet I was invisible, that was the fundamental contradiction."[77]

Yet, despite these difficulties, invisibility has its own advantages, as does the related capacity to look at oneself from the point of view of white America. Because an oppressed group, as Michel de Certeau remarks, "must play on and with a terrain imposed on it and organized" by someone else, its members "must maneuver 'within the enemy's field of vision' and within enemy territory."[78] The oppressed must be able to see the world from the oppressors' point of view, as this makes it possible to plot movements within the "enemy's field of vision." Thus, the African American subject sees herself or himself "through the eyes of . . . a world that looks on in amused contempt and pity" because that is the point of view of the social formation that must be manipulated, poached on, tricked, or otherwise negotiated in some way if one is to survive. It allows one to be able to predict how white people are going to see you, which is also one meaning of "second sight"—seeing oneself from a second perspective.

Occasionally, as in "The Souls of White Folk," Du Bois brags of his ability to operate in enemy territory. Not only can he see the world and himself from a white point of view but also he can see white folk *unobserved* (another meaning of second sight). He writes of white people: "Of them I am singularly clairvoyant. I see in and through them. I view them from unusual points of vantage. . . . I see these souls undressed and from the back and side. I see the working of their entrails. I know their thoughts and they know that I know."[79]

Otherwise, "second sight" as a metaphor-concept is almost entirely unexplicated in *Souls;* like the musical epigraphs, it is something of a cipher that only slowly becomes unraveled as the book goes on.[80] It is not until we examine the sorrow songs, a form most explicitly concerned with the ghosts of the past and potential futures, that we can fully consider "second sight."

This is appropriate both to the argument and practice of Du Bois's book. As Fred Moten has suggested, central to the African American aesthetic tradition is "the irreducible sound of necessarily visual performance."[81] That is, performances, and performances of subjectivity in particular, which are necessarily visual because they must respond to and resist the visual workings of white oppression, can only come into being because of the sound that subtends them. This is not just the old speech-comes-before-writing line that Derrida so persistently deconstructs. Rather, the point concerns the poetics of invisibility. Put differently: *The Souls of Black Folk* could not exist without the sorrow songs (as I will argue), which are themselves a part of Du Bois's necessarily visual performance, but in a way that cannot enter into the book, except as something translated into visual form. "Second sight," in *this* sense, would thus be the ability to be tuned into the sound of the visual performance, the sound behind, beneath, around, and of the visual performance. This is also to say that if we are to understand the form that, for Du Bois, is actually able to convert the African American relation to loss from a depressing into a compelling one, we have to look to music, about which Du Bois has quite a bit to say.

Du Bois contra Wagner

> Then as the sheen of the starlight stole over him, he
> thought of the gilded ceiling of that vast concert hall,
> and heard stealing toward him the faint sweet music
> of the swan. Hark! was it music, or the hurry and
> shouting of men? Yes, surely! Clear and High the faint
> sweet melody rose and fluttered like a living thing, so
> that the very earth trembled as with the tramp of
> horses and the murmur of angry men.
>
> —W. E. B. DU BOIS, "THE COMING OF JOHN"

Avoiding despair, articulating a collectivity, creating interest in African American lives, receiving respect from whites, imagining a nonracist world—all of these are things that Du Bois presents as the tasks of cultural or aesthetic activity.[82] What I want to examine here, before going on to consider Du Bois's analysis and use of the sorrow songs, is the relationship between the rhetoric of art and culture in *Souls* (as "boon and guerdon" for example, or as "kingdom") and Du Bois's presentation of the practices this rhetoric might describe (Wagner's *Lohengrin* chief among them). While numerous appeals are made to the importance of culture—as a concept and in its concrete forms—throughout *Souls*, what Du Bois means by "culture" is not exactly clear. In fact, he seems to be working with several different, even contradictory ideas concerning culture.

On the one hand, Du Bois appears quite explicitly to champion the specificity of African American cultural production. This occurs nowhere more plainly than in his emphatic and persistent defense of the sorrow songs as "the singular spiritual heritage of the nation and the greatest gift of the Negro people" (*Souls*, 198). The value Du Bois attributes to the songs is related to their production and consumption within the veil, as well as their relationship to the specificity of African American historical experience, musical knowledge, and creative genius.[83]

Yet alongside the valorization of African American cultural production from *within* the veil, we find the celebration of a culture *above* the veil and of African American participation in that culture. Du Bois writes, for example, in "On the Training of Black Men," that "he sits with Shakespeare and he winces not . . . above the Veil, I dwell with Truth" (*Souls*, 88). "Culture" in this sense is a transcendent, timeless space "above the smoke," where "smiling men and welcoming women glide in gilded halls." The value of this culture would appear to lie precisely in its *non-specificity*, its nonraced character. This space is worth defending, Du Bois writes, because the "centers of culture" protect "that higher individualism" that rises above the masses (*Souls*, 78). When Du Bois writes in an apparently central sentence of "Of Our Spiritual Strivings" that the end of "Negro striving" is "to be a co-worker in the kingdom of culture," the assumption is usually made that it is to the "gilded halls" above the veil that he refers. These passages in *Souls* have led at least one critic to argue that *in general* "culture" for Du Bois "has no color."[84]

In sum, in *Souls*, we find one model in which culture is valued insofar as it comes from within the African American community and opposes racism and another in which culture is a timeless space to which one escapes *from* the world of race and racism.[85] Can the sorrow songs be both at the same time? Which kind of culture does Du Bois see himself practicing, and which is he advocating? The dilemma becomes more complex when we realize that this tension is only one of the several that make the terrain into which Du Bois is writing rife with cross-purposes and contradictions. Du Bois must also negotiate the overlapping but not identical conflict internal to the idea of "culture," which, Raymond Williams reminds us, is "one of the two or three most complicated words in the English language."[86] On the one hand, there is the idea of a universal Culture, a singular, transcendent space to which the best products of artistic or intellectual achievement ascend (a kind of Arnoldian "best that has been thought and said"). On the other there is the (Herderian) idea of multiple cultures, in which culture is a "way of life," and cultural achievements are interesting and valuable precisely to the extent that they express and/or exemplify this way of life. In this view, each people (or "folk") has its own "gifts."

What may help us to sort through this convoluted terrain is to again recall that Du Bois subjects all else to the rhetorical project of motivating people to participate in combating white supremacy. Along such lines, while Du Bois of course hopes for that future moment when the veil separating African American persons from what he sometimes depicts as "all that makes life worth living" has been destroyed, it would be foolish to operate in the present as if that world *already* existed. For this reason Du Bois employs a persistently double-voiced strategy, directed at both sides of the color line, hoping to inspire both blacks and whites toward the destruction of that line, but in the meanwhile accepting the historical fact of that line in order to reach his audiences where they currently reside.

It is worth keeping in mind, therefore, Du Bois's later assertion that "all art is propaganda," by which he means that "until the art of the black folk compels recognition they will not be rated as human."[87] Thus, in *Souls,* Du Bois must first of all say to his "Gentle Readers" in effect: do not think that you can justify white supremacy by arguing that African American culture is inferior to white culture, because it is not. Accordingly, his approach to the multiple notions of culture already circulating is to make sure that African American culture cannot be excluded from *any* of them. Whatever concept of culture you hew to, Du Bois will argue that African Americans belong there. Conceptual coherence is not as important here as a kind of political coverage.

This means that I am arguing that the ideal of being a "co-worker in the kingdom of culture" is of the "after the revolution" sort. Being the "end," it does not represent a program or plan for the striving of blacks. To borrow from Benjamin, the existence of a racism-free society cannot be thought at the same time as the struggle against racism is thought.[88] While coworking in the kingdom of culture may be an ideal that serves to motivate both whites (for whom it offers reassurance that blacks desire cooperation, not conflict) and blacks (for whom it signifies a world in which white supremacy has ended) in different ways, it does not represent the present world, in which struggle must be conceived and despair avoided.[89] When Du Bois speaks of the present, he is much more likely to invoke the failures of the past, the shortcomings and contradictory promises of American democracy, and the persistent, ongoing sense of loss and disappointment facing the African American world (more on this shortly).

We get a sense of the rhetorical tactics at work when we examine the one chapter in which Du Bois defends an explicitly colorless culture, "On The Training of Black Men." The chapter (first published in the *Atlantic*) concerns African American education; its overt aim is to persuade whites that it is in their best interests to educate blacks. It sounds, at times, like a fund-raising letter. Hence the emphasis, in the chapter's final paragraph, on (a somewhat vague) black participation in the universal space of truth above the veil, with already recognized "great figures" in the Western tradition. The figures mentioned (Shakespeare, Balzac, Dumas, Aurelius, Aristotle) pointedly include no Americans and feature another member of the African diaspora, Dumas, who in France enjoyed a popularity unimaginable for a black person in the United States. Du Bois thereby underscored the exceptional racism of the United States, and the participation of African Americans in a Western cultural tradition that exceeds the implicitly parochial bounds of the United States.

However, just before he places himself in the company of canonical figures in the Western tradition above the veil, Du Bois speaks of culture in rather different terms. "Herein the longing of black men must have respect: the rich and bitter depth of their experience, the unknown treasures of their inner life, the strange rendings of nature they have seen, may give the world new points of view and make their loving, living and doing precious to all human hearts" (*Souls,* 88). This is not a universal culture, but a particular, Herderian-cum-Hegelian one, in which black people have their own gift, a gift that rises out of the particularity ("the rich and bitter depth") of African American experience. It is valuable—demanding respect—not so much because it rises above the color line but precisely because it articulates the view from one side of that line, giving, as Du Bois writes, "the world new points of view."

Shifting again, the next sentence speaks of the value of culture for its African American *producers:* "[a]nd to themselves in these the days that try their souls, the chance to soar above the smoke is to their finer spirits boon and guerdon for what they lose on earth by being black." Du Bois here makes the case for a culture that is particular (not universal) but nonetheless rises above the veil. Culture has an uplifting quality, not in a social but in an ontological sense. Art, in this understanding, is a kind of utopian compensatory practice. The dazzling welcome that takes place in the gilded halls precisely reverses the scene of contempt Du Bois suffered at the hands of the tall newcomer. There, Du Bois can "summon Aristotle and Aurelius and what soul I will, and they come all graciously with no scorn nor condescension." Such a culture is paradigmatically "affirmative" in the Marcusian sense, in that its value stems from the fact that it is a space opposed to the realm of necessity, and thus distanced from everyday life and that life's interests, emotions, and sufferings. It is thereby "the historical form in which were preserved those human wants which surpassed the material reproduction of existence."[90] By way of this culture, a color-blind, democratic, free space where there is no white supremacy is imaginatively experienced. On the one hand, this serves the invaluable purpose of keeping an oppositional vision alive, but at the same time it serves the quietist function of substituting aesthetic, spiritual freedom for social-political freedom, thereby mediating the contradiction "between the insufferable mutability of a bad existence and the need for happiness in order to make such existence possible."[91] Here, as Marcuse warns, the danger is that "the freedom of the soul [is] used to excuse the poverty, martyrdom and bondage of the body."[92]

Thus, in two paragraphs from *Souls*, we see Du Bois move among at least three ideas about culture, each meeting different rhetorical needs for different audiences. While Du Bois does not anywhere in *Souls* offer some final mediation of these different positions (and I would argue that none is in fact available), he does reflect on their relative social and political function, providing a map no less dialectical in its complexity than Marcuse's (or Adorno's) of the aesthetic-cultural terrain on which the African American person may find herself or himself. We can see this most decisively in the penultimate chapter of *Souls*, Du Bois's most clearly fictional contribution to the collection, titled "The Coming of John."

The chapter (written especially for *Souls*) is an allegorical tale of two "Johns," childhood playmates, one black and one white, both from Altamaha, a small town in Georgia. The color line separates them as they get older. Each embodies the hopes of his respective family and community, and so there is great expectation when they each head off to college. The black John (John Jones) at first finds the new environment difficult, and he is suspended "on account of repeated disorder and inattention to work" (*Souls*, 183). He returns from his suspension with renewed purpose however, and becomes entranced in a "queer thoughtworld," learning to "think and puzzle" for himself, "pausing perplexed where others skipped merrily, and walking steadily through the difficulties where others stopped and surrendered" (184). As he moves toward graduation he looks at the world around him with fresh attention: "[he] wondered how he had seen so little before." In particular, "he slowly began to feel almost for the first time the veil that lay between him and the white world; he noticed now the oppression that had not seemed oppression before, differences that erstwhile seemed natural, restraints and slights that in his boyhood days had gone unnoticed or been greeted with a laugh" (*Souls*, 184). His education discloses the veil to him to the precise extent that it also gives him a new sense of the world's possibilities. He starts to become bitter; depression lurks.

Anticipating his return to Altamaha with anxiety and some dread, John Jones welcomes the opportunity to travel to New York with the school's quartet. Swept up by excitement, he follows "a tall light haired young man and a little talkative lady" to a theater, where he finds himself buying a ticket to see Richard Wagner's *Lohengrin*.[93] There, sitting next to the couple he followed to the theater, he is transported first by the beauty of the place and then by the music.

> [H]e sat in a half-maze minding the scene about him; the delicate beauty of the hall, the faint perfume, the moving myriad of men, the rich clothing and low hum of talking seemed all part of a world so different from his, so strangely more beautiful than anything he had known, that he sat in dreamland, and started when, after a hush, rose the high and clear music of Lohengrin's swan. The infinite beauty of the wail lingered and swept through every muscle of his frame, and put it all atune. He closed his eyes and grasped the elbows of the chair, touching unwittingly the lady's arm. And the lady drew away. A deep longing swelled in his heart to rise with that clear music out of the dirt and dust of that low life that held him prisoned and befouled. If only he could live up in the free air where birds sang and setting suns had no touch of blood! Who had called him to be the slave and butt of all? And if he had called, what right had he to call when a world like this lay open before men? (*Souls*, 186)

There could hardly be a clearer dramatization of the affirmative character of culture. The music transforms him and takes him to a beautiful "dreamland," separate from everyday life, which allows him to see and experience the world other than it is, granting him a bodily and emotional feeling of freedom, a sense for a space where there is no white supremacy. Emphasizing the ability of music to reattune, Du Bois describes John Jones as feeling as if the "infinite beauty" of Lohengrin's wail "swept through every muscle of his frame, and put it all atune." He is so transported in fact, that he does not notice the irritation his Negro presence causes some of the white patrons. Especially disturbed are the woman and man (who turns out, in an over-the-top ironic twist, to be none other than his erstwhile playmate and namesake) sitting in the neighboring seats. His dreamy enthusiasm results in his "unwitting touch" of the lady's arm, which in turn leads to his being kicked out by the theater's management.

The contradiction between the content of the aesthetic experience (liberatory, pleasurable, expansive) and its social location (exclusionary, racist) gives the event a critical edge. For a moment at least, John Jones exists, emotionally speaking, in an alternate, freer world. The disjuncture between the attunement he feels in the space of the musical world of the opera and his feeling on returning to the world outside stimulates his sense of injustice and his desire to participate in a program of social transformation. He resolves to go back home, determined to try to "help settle the Negro problems there" (*Souls*, 188). Here the autonomous work of art works as critique; for the moment, Du Bois appears to be defending the Wagnerian aesthetic.[94]

On his return, however, John Jones is disappointed by the "sordidness and narrowness" of the small town. (In this, his reaction is similar to that of the white John, who also returns and is disgusted by the town because it is filled with "nothing but mud and Negroes.") With his new sense of "striving" and his intent to educate and uplift his community, John Jones is daunted by the scope of his task, and alarmed at the offense his educated, too-proud manner seems to cause at every turn. His alienation reaches a peak at an event organized to mark his homecoming, a "meeting of welcome" at the local Baptist church. There, he gives a slow, reasoned, and "methodical" speech, exhorting the townspeople toward uplift through education and organization, urging them to forget parochial religious differences. A "painful hush" in the crowd follows his speech, "for he spoke an unknown tongue." However, the effect is quite different when, in response to what has been perceived as John's belittling of religion, an old man gets up to speak.

> He seized the Bible with his rough, huge hands; twice he raised it inarticulate, and then fairly burst into the words, with rude and awful eloquence. He quivered, swayed, and bent; then rose aloft in perfect majesty, till the people moaned and wept, wailed and shouted, and a wild shrieking arose from the corners where all the pent-up feeling of the hour gathered itself and rushed into the air. (190)

Unlike John, whose methodical speech left the audience cold, this man knew how to "use and make mood." His performative speech, with its emphasis on movement and emotive sound, engages in an antiphonic, rhythmic relationship with the audience. And in contrast to the aesthetic experience John has at *Lohengrin*, this event involves a collective innervation of emotion. While John's experience of *Lohengrin* was rich with affective import, and while its autonomy generated a critical spur, it was essentially isolating, not only because John was kicked out but inasmuch as each patron is alone, politely isolated in her or his private space. Even at its most affecting moments, the performance did not give him a feeling of belonging to a community. The old man's speech, on the other hand, demonstrates the possibility for the collective release of precisely the "pent-up emotion" that would be necessary for political action, if only it could be directed toward political aims instead of cathartically "gathered and rushed into the air" where it then disperses, undirected.

Du Bois discusses the political potential of such affect in the chapter focusing on African American religion ("On the Faith of the Fathers"). While the churches, Du Bois remarks, are the locus of black collective consciousness and feeling, they play a more or less conservative role, in his view leaving the political potential here untapped. He continues:

> But back of this still broods silently the deep religious feeling of the real Negro heart, the stirring, unguided might of powerful human souls who have lost the guiding star of the past and are seeking in the great night a new religious ideal. Some day the Awakening will come, when the pent-up vigor of ten million souls shall sweep irresistibly toward the Goal, out of the Valley of the Shadow of Death, where all that makes life worth living—Liberty, Justice, and Right—is marked "For White People Only." (*Souls*, 163)

People, get ready. There is a sleeping giant, a collective *Grübler* haunting America, and the power of "pent-up" feeling "broods" just below the surface, awaiting only the spark to set it aflame. What the African American community lacks, Du Bois suggests, is the right "guidance," something that could be provided by a mixture of the "the guiding star of the past" and a "new religious ideal." While Du Bois himself clearly hopes to provide the guidance that the African American world needs to awaken its pent-up feeling, he is aware that he must work from within African American cultural traditions, he must go to the religious context where the collective "vigor" resides.

This begins to give us a picture of the kind of aesthetic experience Du Bois values and seeks, a picture that comes into view even more sharply when we consider the conclusion of the "Coming of John" story. After his school is shut down when the white town leaders learn that *liberté* and *egalité* have become part of the curriculum, John Jones, in a bitter and disappointed mood, encounters the other John harassing his younger sister. In a rage he strikes and kills his sister's attacker. After a brief return home to tell his mother that he is "going—North," he flees to the ocean's edge.

> Then as the sheen of the starlight stole over him, he thought of the gilded ceiling of that vast concert hall, and heard stealing toward him the faint

sweet music of the swan. Hark! was it music, or the hurry and shouting of men? Yes, surely! Clear and High the faint sweet melody rose and fluttered like a living thing, *so that* the very earth trembled as with the tramp of horses and the murmur of angry men. (195, my italics)

The Wagnerian song of the swan fades into the murmur of the lynch mob; indeed it is as if the rising and flutter of the "faint sweet melody" *causes* (although "so that" is an ambiguous phrase), in a dialectical movement, the earth to tremble and the murmur of angry men to occur. As the lynch mob approaches, John hums the "Song of the Bride" to himself.[95] Foreseeing D. W. Griffith's use of Wagner in *Birth of Nation* ("uniquely clairvoyant" as he is regarding the ways of white folks), Du Bois sets the lynching scene to a Wagner soundtrack (although it is, to be sure, a different Wagner song and not the "Song of the Valkyries" used by Griffiths). On the one hand (and more obviously), the story generates a sense of tragic irony here, illustrating the dilemma, described by Du Bois in "Strivings," facing the educated African American who is left alienated from both sides of the color line.[96]

However, Du Bois is also, I think, making a dialectical critique of Wagner and the kind of affirmative culture Wagner represents (in a way that prepares us for what he has to say about the sorrow songs). The rich beauty of the bourgeois concert hall and its music can speak to him of freedom and elevation, can give him a taste of it even, but it offers no way to translate that feeling of freedom back into the world. (That the "gilded" decoration of the concert hall's ceiling recalls the "gilded halls" where "smiling men and welcoming women glide" suggests that Du Bois is also commenting here on that earlier passage.) The feeling of freedom and certainty regarding the injustice of the world is no good to John without a plan of action, without the ability to manipulate whites and mobilize blacks. Inasmuch as the *Lohengrin* experience is possible only because its autonomy renders it powerless, it is, in essence, compatible and complicit with white supremacy.[97] Thus is registered a serious skepticism regarding the idea of culture as a transcendent space that can serve as "boon and guerdon."

Just as Du Bois's cool, rational, scientific approach to the problem of racism was useless in his attempt to stop the Hose lynching, so, too, John's education and his Wagnerian epiphany only go partway toward making him an effective leader in any antiracist project. He has no way to fight off his depression, and he is perplexed by the emotional reactions he produces in Altamaha. He lacks a map to negotiate the affective terrain he has found himself thrown into.

We might say that John has been caught up in what Adorno and Horkheimer called the "dialectic of enlightenment," particularly concerning the nature and function of "culture." Adorno and Horkheimer's commentary on the Sirens episode in the *Odyssey*, which for them allegorizes the situation of art in modernity more generally, is apposite here. As they recount it, the "allurement [of the Sirens] is that of losing oneself in the past."[98] But, they continue, if the Sirens possess the knowledge of the past, they "demand the future as its price, and their promise of a happy homecoming is the deception by which the past entraps a humanity filled with longing."[99] To keep his rowers from falling prey to this dangerous lure, Odysseus plugs their ears with wax. "Odysseus, the feudal baron for whom others labor, reserves the second possibility for himself."[100] He has himself tied to the mast, and "the greater the temptation, the more strongly does he order his bonds tightened." He can hear their message but is powerless to do anything about it. The song becomes for Odysseus "a mere object of contemplation," that is, an art object. The rowers, however, are kept doggedly working, denied access to the song. They reproduce the conditions of their own oppression, aware that the song is dangerous but ignorant of its beauty or message. For each party, the haunting, redemption-promising echoes of the past remain at a safe distance.

John Jones seems to have fallen into the position of Odysseus when he attends the Wagner concert. Like Odysseus tied to the mast, he can hear the Sirens but can do nothing with the knowledge he gains. "The prisoner is attending a concert, listening motionless just like the audience at concerts later on in history, and his enthusiastic call for freedom already sounds like applause as it dies away."[101] When he returns to Altamaha, Georgia, he sees a world made up of uneducated laborers, their ears plugged by force to keep knowledge of history and the outside world safely away. His job, as he sees it, is to "enlighten" them through education. What he fails to see is also what Adorno and Horkheimer fail to see: the rowers are already singing their own song. The black community of Altamaha (especially as it takes shape under the guidance of the old preacher) does not need the song of the Sirens because it is maintaining its own connection to the past; this community already knows how to rescue "the past as something living instead of using it as the material of progress."[102]

Moreover, not only do the sorrow songs (as Du Bois presents them) recall the past in their form (the past both of Africa and of slavery), they are *about* the rescue of "what is gone as the living" on the level of content. And the songs are occupied with the lure of a happy return to the past, not in a nostalgic way (in which one wants to escape into the past) but only inasmuch as that past might be redeemed in a present moment. And while the forces of white supremacy work against them with violence and government support, the world of African America in 1900 is not tied to a mast with bonds that prevent them from acting on the song's message. In fact, the enemy is clear, and every performance of the songs incarnates for the participants the collectivity whose action would be necessary to redeem the past by defeating that enemy.

Shadows of Echoes: The Musical Epigraphs

> The best that we can do, however, with paper and types, or even with voices, will convey but a faint shadow of the original.
>
> —WILLIAM FRANCIS ALLEN, *SLAVE SONGS OF THE UNITED STATES*

Du Bois's citation of the sorrow songs in wordless musical notation as epigraphs to the chapters is perhaps the most puzzling and singular formal element of *The Souls of Black Folk*.[103] Their wordlessness, the choice to cite the songs in musical notation, the fact that they are unidentified, the juxtaposition with Western belletristic epigraphs all pose a considerable challenge to the reader of this book, including the one who reads music. "The interpretable text of the sorrow songs as Du Bois uses them in *The Souls of Black Folk*," Eric Sundquist writes, "turns on the most unstable, quasi-material modes of representation, in which the fluent iteration of the underlying lyric code of African America can only be implied until the text is vocalized within the theater of actual or imagined performance."[104] In other words, Du Bois's text does not, indeed cannot, provide what would be necessary for a reading of the songs. The epigraphs beckon toward an absent performance, recognizable only if or when you can identify the (unidentified) bars of music. In *To Wake the Nations*, Sundquist performs the valuable task of identifying, providing the lyrics for, and explicating the songs, allowing him (and us) to consider the texts of the songs in relation to the chapters they head.[105] What Sundquist leaves less examined, however, are the implications of the readerly demand that Du Bois's use of the cryptic epigraphs creates. Why does Du Bois create this problem for his readers at the perimeter of his text? To what rhetorical end?

Among the interpretive difficulties created by these epigraphs is their apparent negation of much of what is usually considered most valuable and particular to the songs. As nearly every commentator on the songs has noted, the songs are fundamentally untranscribable into musical notation. There simply is no notation system for the slides or blue notes, the complex and varying rhythmic structures, the call-and-response patterns, and the improvisatory quality of the songs.[106] The songs thus transcribed obviously cannot produce anything like the aesthetic experience of listening to them—which is not to say, however, that these epigraphs do not have their own aesthetic and rhetorical effects.

The epigraph is what Gerard Genette calls a "paratext." The function of the paratext is to "surround [the text] and extend it, precisely in order to present it, in the usual sense of the verb, but also in the strongest sense: to make present, to ensure the text's presence in the world, its 'reception' and consumption in the form (nowadays at least) of a book."[107] Along with the title, the cover, prefaces, dedications, and footnotes, the epigraph stands at the edge of the text, a kind of veil between the text and the reader, not belonging to the text proper but not autonomous either. "More than a boundary or a sealed border, the paratext is rather a threshold, or—a word Borges used apropos of a preface—a 'vestibule' that offers the world at large the possibility of either stepping inside or turning back."[108] As such, the paratexts play a large role in setting up the mode of relationality the reader will have with the text: the reader's expectations and presumptions, the context in which the reader will consider and interpret the text, the mood in which the reader will find the text.

As is well known, publications by African Americans (especially before the abolition of slavery) often required an extra layer of paratexts to ensure the book's presence in the world, special vestibules to ease the reader into a racialized territory and to establish that racialization itself. Paratexts such as prefaces, appendixes, attestations, dedications, letters to the author, and letters from the publisher all served to frame the text, hold it up, answer all the questions and doubts a white audience might have about reading a text written by a black person. One of the chief aims of such paratexts, as Robert Stepto has shown, was to guarantee the authenticity of the text.[109] Phillis Wheatley's book of poetry, most famously, was prefaced by an attestation of eighteen white men (including, for example, John Hancock, several other signers of the Declaration of Independence, and the governor and lieutenant governor of Massachusetts) who had examined Wheatley and determined that she had in fact written the poems.[110] In slave narratives, likewise, it was important to have some Important White Person—preferably several—testify that they knew this black person who wrote the book, and "This person is real and this person really did write this book, I swear." In addition, these paratexts—prefaces especially—often tried to tell or teach the reader how to read the text, suggesting, for example, how the slave narrative testified to the inhumanity of slavery, or which passages were especially moving and in what way.[111]

Seen in light of this tradition, Du Bois's epigraphs are a way to establish an authorial presence, as Robert Stepto has argued, and to comment on the need to establish it. *Du Bois* has put the paratext there, not someone else. But *Souls* still needs this extra vestibule. The pairing of the musical epigraphs with lines of verse by famous white authors complicates the gesture, ironizing (or at least drawing attention to) the need for the Important White Person to authorize the text. Most significant, however, is the more simple fact that Du Bois's epigraphs are paratexts that, far from clarifying the relation the reader is to have to the text, obscure or veil the text, posing a challenge or question to the reader as one of its first moves. As musical notation, the epigraphs are not communicative in the way language is; there is no message, no constative sense to bars of music. Inasmuch as the bars of music solicit a directly bodily, mimetic response—playing or humming the music—they reference an absent or potential performance and signal a mode of reading that is discontinuous with the rest of Du Bois's text.[112] Put differently, they point toward that which is outside the text but has been and will be necessary to its existence.[113]

What Du Bois is referencing in the bars of music is not just the sorrow songs themselves but also the phenomenon of their circulation and consumption. The bars of music presume a community of readers who can read music, and in fact, the songs had become popular at this point. Sheet music circulated as popular culture for parlor room piano playing among white and black audiences. Du Bois underscored African American participation in this culture by including in the 1900 Paris Exposition exhibition he curated a photograph of a girl being given a piano lesson in a middle-class African American home.[114]

As Jon Cruz has shown, the interest motivating transcription of the songs first arose in the context of abolitionism.[115] There these "authentic" products of "the Negro" were put to use as testimony to the human feelings of black people, as a way to create sympathy and support for the abolitionist cause. The first two significant transcriptions of the songs (both cited by Du Bois) were published in the collaborative endeavor *Slave Songs of the United States* (1867) and in Thomas Higginson's *Army Life in a Black Regiment* (1869).[116] Most widely circulated, however, were two books associated with the popular singing groups the Hampton Singers (*Hampton and Its Students, with Fifty Cabin and Plantation Songs,* 1874) and the Fisk Jubilee Singers (*The Story of the Jubilee Singers with Their Songs,* 1880), which sold tens of thousands of copies.[117] (Sundquist writes that Du Bois appears to have appropriated the bars of music from these two books.)[118] In the opening paragraphs of the chapter entitled "The Sorrow Songs," Du Bois celebrates the transatlantic popularity of the Fisk Jubilee singers and their ability to raise the money for the founding of Fisk University.

So Du Bois was appropriating the bars of music not from some secret black culture behind the veil but from a widely consumed early black mass culture, in the process of being standardized. In other words, Du Bois is appropriating the bars of music from the appropriators. In part he is referencing the fact of the music's circulation and the contested cultural terrain it occupies. In so doing, he is also wresting the songs away from the other discourses appropriating them. These would include not only the straight-out racist derogations or dismissals of the form and white anthropological uses of the songs but also emerging black middle-class tastes, which disdained the songs as springing from a past better forgotten.[119] Just because white people have appropriated and transformed the music by writing it down does not mean that Du Bois cannot appropriate it again for his own (political) purposes.

In appropriating the music thus, Du Bois is also demonstrating the persistent mobility of the songs. Their transcription, even though it may be a mistranslation of an essentially untranscribable form, and although it may be appropriated into other discourses and projects, is in any event inevitable.[120] Laments for the loss of the original form in the musical transcriptions are akin to a leftist melancholia that indulges in nostalgia for a past moment of political possibility without attention to what might be possible in the present. In Walter Benjamin's famous remark, "articulating the past historically does not mean recognizing it the way it really was. It means appropriating a memory as it flashes up at a moment of danger."[121] The musical epigraphs are not meant to somehow represent the spirituals as they "really were" but are a visual emblem of the reseizure of the songs at this moment of danger. They visually convey the fragmentary nature of the survival of African traditions, the necessarily splintered fashion in which the messages from the slave past can be received. There is no coherent, total narrative to be had; only fragments to shore against one's ruin.

Du Bois's epigraphs are a kind of invitation to a performance—to be arranged by *us*—at the same time that they mark the absence of any such performance from the present scene of reading. As such Du Bois welcomes sound into his text as that which cannot be represented in the text, by the text, but precisely as such must be represented there because it is the condition of possibility for the text to come into being.[122] The songs are the origin of the African American tradition in which Du Bois sees his own text participating. In one respect, Du Bois is forced to put the songs into a visual form, into notation, because that is the form in which "culture" circulates (and in which the songs were already circulating) and in which the songs can be recognized *as* "culture."

The text's attachment to the songs might, for this reason, be called melancholic, in the sense that the songs are lost from the text, they are what cannot be there; all the text can do is incorporate an image of them in the form of the epigraphs. Yet this incorporated image is also a kind of identification with the songs. The songs become the text's ego-ideal, the model in relation to which Du Bois's own text is to be judged. In a way, the absence of the songs is the most important thing about them.

Echo

> Doesn't a breath of air that pervaded earlier days
> caress us as well? In the voices we hear, isn't there an
> echo of now silent ones? . . . If so, then there is a secret
> agreement between past generations and the present
> one. Then our coming was expected on earth. Then,
> like every generation that preceded us, we have been
> endowed with a *weak* messianic power, a power on
> which the past has a claim.
>
> —WALTER BENJAMIN, "ON THE CONCEPT OF HISTORY"

> And so, before each thought that I have written in this
> book I have set a phrase, a haunting echo of these
> weird old songs in which the soul of the black slave
> spoke to men. Ever since I was a child these songs have
> stirred me strangely. They came out of the South
> unknown to me, one by one, and yet at once I knew
> them as of me and of mine.
>
> —W. E. B. DU BOIS, *THE SOULS OF BLACK FOLK*

"They came out of the South unknown to me, one by one, and yet at once I knew them as of me and of mine."[123] Many readers take this statement to be an attempt on Du Bois's part to assert his own black authenticity, his down-with-the-people-ness.[124] To be sure, in part he *is* saying that he must share something with the community and tradition whence these songs have come, if he so immediately recognized himself in them; therefore, the logic continues, he has the authority to speak of life within the veil, an important element of his case for supplanting Booker T. Washington as leader of African America.[125]

But Du Bois is also making a strong claim for the songs themselves. Inasmuch as they have the power to provoke a moment of self-recognition in him, they disclose the historicity and the plurality of his subjectivity: other people feel like he does, not only the people singing now but people who have sung in the past, and the other audiences who have recognized their emotions in the songs. The songs' existence is thus, for Du Bois, powerful evidence of an already existing African American collective consciousness.

In a direct manner, the songs evince the survival of an African musical tradition, common not only to African America but across the African diaspora. That is, the songs are *known* by Du Bois first of all because he recognizes the musical tradition in which the songs are located. As Lawrence Levine notes (following Alan Lomax), "musical style appears to be one of the most conservative of culture traits and even when an entirely new set of tunes, rhythms, or harmonic patterns is introduced a musical style will remain intact and yield to change only very gradually."[126] It has been well established that characteristic elements of the style of African American music, such as its "antiphony, its group nature, its pervasive functionality, its improvisational character, its strong relationship in performance to dance and bodily movement," as well as its "complex rhythmic structure, percussive qualities, polymeter, [and] syncopation," survive from its West African origins.[127]

It makes sense then that Du Bois could hear in the sorrow songs echoes of an African song passed down in his family.[128] The song ("do bana coba, gene me, gene me") originated with his grandfather's grandmother, who, he tells us, had been "seized by an evil Dutch trader two centuries ago." Isolated, enslaved, and cold, she "looked longingly at the hills and sun" and sang the song to her child. Then "the child sang it to his children and they to their children's children, and so two hundred years it has traveled down to us and we sing it to our children, knowing as little as our fathers what its words may mean, but knowing well the meaning of the music" (*Souls,* 200). Note the shift here from the third person singular ("the child sang") to the third person plural "they" and then finally to "us" and "we." In this way, Du Bois narrates the diachronic movement from the isolation of exile to collective identification and activity, with music as the mechanism of this transformation.

The fact that the knowledge collectively held onto and passed down is fragmented or partial only increases its power. As Sundquist notes, the unknownness of the words signifies "the utmost sign of the loss of ancestral language (or in a more accurate sense, of its fragmentary survival in the words and phrases that have entered American English), remaining a secret language that cannot be correctly translated even by those who remember and repeat it."[129] The juxtaposition of the now senseless words with the meaningful music underscores that the musical style is itself the *sole* carrier of historical memory, and that the words that accompany the music of the sorrow songs are foreign, appropriated by necessity. Like ruins, the music allegorically signifies the world that once surrounded it and is now gone. This loss remains necessarily obscure and unknown; it is a loss that precedes and exceeds the African American subject. In its abstraction, however, this sense of loss makes the songs an ideal site for the transfer of the affects attached to any presently troubling loss, allowing for the connection between these present losses and a long history of loss. The sorrow songs are a fruitful site for emotionally charged allegorical brooding, for imaginative fixation, and this, as much as anything, gives them their expansive power.[130] And just as the songs signal missing histories, absent worlds, so too Du Bois's epigraphs allegorically signify the absence of the music and singers themselves, encouraging an imaginative reflection on or, in humming the melody or striking it on the piano, an identification with those singers. Thus Du Bois solicits the melancholic mode of reading that he describes here: one that focuses on absences and lacks precisely in order to engage the reader in a reflection not only on history but on the historicity of the reader herself or himself.

The melancholic force of the music is amplified and the evidentiary value of the songs increased by the fact that Du Bois recognizes not only fragments of musical knowledge there but also the *Stimmung*. The mood he finds there is a mix of disappointment and hope, shaped by the preoccupation with "death and suffering and unvoiced longing toward a truer world" (*Souls*, 199–200). The songs "stir him strangely," indeed haunt him, because the "articulate message of the slave to the world" resonates with Du Bois's *present;* he recognizes himself in the structures of feeling of slaves. The songs thus disclose what Jacques Derrida called the "non-contemporeneity with itself of the living present."[131] Du Bois's subjectivity is itself haunted by the voices of the past, his emotions are not entirely his, or not his alone.

The structures of feelings of the slaves endure in the post-Reconstruction period because the social, economic, and political realities of slavery persist as well. As Du Bois details in chapters 7 and 8 ("Of the Black Belt" and "On the Quest of the Golden Fleece"), many (even most) former slaves in the South live in the de facto slavery of peonage. While the situation is worst for these African Americans, the persistence of Jim Crow and the failure of Reconstruction to provide access to education, property, the right to vote, and equal protection under the law leaves no African American unaffected by state-sanctioned and -enforced white supremacy.

Du Bois finds the neoslavery of the South deeply depressing. He remarks on his arrival in the "strange land of shadows" that "the whole land seems forlorn and forsaken." There, "a resistless feeling of depression falls slowly upon us" (*Souls*, 95). He continues:

> It is a depressing place,—bare, unshaded, with no charm of past association, only a memory of forced human toil,—now, then, and before the law. They are not happy, these black men whom we meet throughout this region. There is little of the joyous abandon and playfulness we are wont to associate with the plantation Negro. At best, the natural good–nature is edged with complaint or has changed into sullenness and gloom. And now and then it blazes forth in veiled but hot anger. (95)

Here especially, the "swarthy specter" of the past haunts the present, as "forced human toil" characterizes the now as much as the then. The songs, which are, Du Bois argues, "the music of an unhappy people, of the children of disappointment," describe the South Du Bois sees no less than the world of the slaves. Indeed, the fact that the slaves (of whom

Du Bois writes "few men ever worshipped Freedom with half such unquestioning faith as did the American Negro for two centuries [10]) had imagined "in one divine event the end of all doubt and disappointment" (10) makes the despair arising from the failure of Reconstruction all the deeper. The question is how can the fierce anger under the resistless depression be directed toward collective action.

Somewhat counterintuitively, and contrary to prevailing opinion black and white, Du Bois insisted that it is precisely by dwelling on the past of "forced toil," on the failures of Reconstruction, that we might direct the affective force of the "veiled but hot anger" toward the goal of racial justice. This is a direct attack on the belief in progress, the desire to see the past as past, which was more often than not an excuse for complacency. This was true of the federal government, which pretended that progress would somehow happen by itself, but was also a dangerous component in the thinking of an emerging black middle class, anxious to forget slavery.[132] The sorrow songs offer a powerful corrective to this desire to leave the past in the past, Du Bois maintains, modeling a historical and aesthetic practice that African America ignores at its peril.

It is instructive at this point to see how Du Bois's understanding of the aesthetic experience offered by the songs and the political function that experience might serve differs importantly from Frederick Douglass's, perhaps the most influential commentary on the songs up to that point. Du Bois made a different case, in part because the political demands of the African American situation had changed. As we know, Douglass was involved in the abolitionist cause, and thus with making arguments concerning the humanity of the slaves and the human suffering caused by the realities of slavery in the present moment. Du Bois, however, finds himself addressing a situation in which slavery, in principle, has been "abolished." He therefore must draw attention to the ways abolition has failed; he needs to reorient the historical gaze of the reader who might not see this fact yet at the same time to ward off the aforementioned despair overwhelming those who see it all too well.

That said, Du Bois and Douglass agree on several key things. Like Douglass, Du Bois insists that the songs oppose and lament slavery;[133] and that whites who claim to the contrary are foolishly and ignorantly mistaken.[134] Each also noted, in different ways, the ambivalent emotional quality of the songs, about which Douglass wrote, "while on their way, they would make the dense old woods, for miles around, reverberate with their wild songs, revealing at once the greatest joy and the deepest sadness."[135] But Douglass also emphasizes several aspects of the music that Du Bois more or less ignores. For example, Douglass is more interested in the function the music served for the slaves who sang it, pointing out the collective, improvisatory, indexical quality of the music. ("They would compose and sign as they went along, consulting neither time nor tune. The thought that came up, came out—if not in the word, in the sound;—and as frequently in one as in the other.")[136] And Douglass was concerned with the formal qualities of the music, emphasizing the tensions internal to the songs' performance: "They would sometimes sign the most pathetic sentiment in the most rapturous tone, and the most rapturous sentiment in the most pathetic tone."

Regarding the emotional *effects* of the songs on listeners and singers—and this is the point I want to stress here—Du Bois departs from Douglass. Douglass wrote: "slaves sing most when they are most unhappy. The songs of the slave represent the sorrows of his heart; and he is relieved by them, only as an aching heart is relieved by its tears."[137] In other words, he suggests that the songs allowed pent-up emotion to be innervated, that they are, in effect, cathartically therapeutic.[138] The critique that might be leveled at such an argument, were it transferred to Du Bois's context, would be the one Marcuse makes regarding affirmative culture: the songs serve a basically compensatory and thus quietist function.

For Du Bois, although the songs articulate sadness, loss, disappointment, and "unvoiced longing," they do not themselves *relieve* sadness. Du Bois writes that "through all the sorrow of the sorrow songs, there breathes a hope—a faith in the ultimate justice of things. The minor cadences of despair change often to triumph and calm confidence" (*Souls*, 206). Rather than allow for an expressive release of sadness, they create a counter-mood in which a different relationship can be established with the historical situation that has caused suffering, in which what mourning can or will take place can be rearticulated. This creation of a counter-mood might work in several ways.

First, the songs rearticulate that loss within an historical context. Recollecting the slave past can be politically useful, as Frank Kirkland writes, because it might allow "African Americans to highlight fragments torn from the past and define them as motives for rending 'the Veil'; it enables them to conceive themselves as breaking the repetition of unfulfilled expectations regarding what counts as good and just in their future-oriented present."[139] By bringing the *now* and the *then* together, such a melancholic practice disrupts our sense of progression through what Benjamin called "empty, homogeneous time," rendering time discontinuous, interruptible, in a word *messianic* (more on this shortly). On the one hand, the sorrow songs distance listeners from the present, inasmuch as they allow one to see the world from the point of view of the past, and, at the same time, inasmuch as the present world similar to that past—as if it *were* the past.[140] This may embolden one to act in order to *in fact* make it into the past by changing it. On the other hand, the songs also reconnect singers and audiences to a longer historical view with new clarity, insofar as concrete elements of a past world, affectively defamiliarized, now jump out at us.

The sorrow songs (or at least Du Bois's use of them) would also appear to support Benjamin's argument that our forms of emotional investment in the present are generated out of remembrance. Our "image of happiness," he writes, "is indissolubly bound up with the image of redemption."[141] In other words, we are motivated most by the possibility of returning to and redeeming past losses and repairing past wrongs. Our "happiness is founded on the very despair and desolation which were ours."[142] For Benjamin, history too shares in this messianic logic, on a larger scale. Our collective happiness too is only imaginable in relation to a formerly despair-filled but presently redeemable situation. Likewise, spleen and the spirit of sacrifice are "nourished by the image of enslaved ancestors rather than that of liberated grandchildren." Exemplifying this phenomenon more recently, participants in the civil rights movement cited to powerful effect the music and words of the spirituals, as in the stirring conclusion to M. L. King Jr.'s most famous speech: "in the words of the old Negro spiritual, 'Free at last! free at last! thank God Almighty, we are free at last!'"[143]

The historical practice described here is best performed by a subject with a talent for being attuned to the fragmented images that surface from the past (such as the achievements of "single black men" who have "flashed here and there like falling stars," dying before "the world has rightly gauged their brightness" [*Souls*, 9]), but who can at the same time be attentive toward present emotionally urgent concerns. In other words, here we have another meaning of "second sight": the ability to keep two temporal registers in view at the same time. The sorrow songs, inasmuch as they combine a ghostly return of the past with an emotional awareness of the present, promise such a second sight.

Second sight in this sense makes it possible to "brush history against the grain," to see histories otherwise obscured. Unlike that inventory of spoils displayed by the victors before the vanquished that we call "culture" (e.g., Shakespeare, Balzac, and Wagner), the sorrow songs reanimate the voices of the oppressed. The sorrow songs are the paradigm of the antidepressive melancholic aesthetic, inasmuch as they link together a present oppression with those who have come before, demonstrating the history that is 'condensed' within one's own emotional life, allowing one to feel as if one's own personal life were "a muscle strong enough to contract the whole of historical time."[144] When struggle is conceived in this way, the battle against the racists who yelled "Niggers" as Du Bois and his wife were bringing their son's body home to be buried, for instance, is at the same time a possible victorious encounter with the whole history of white supremacy itself.

In addition, the songs testify to the possibility, more generally, of constructing usable pasts from the remains of other suppressed histories. "Culture" itself is opened up. The songs are the opposite of a universal, transcendent culture, composed not by an isolated genius but collaboratively by persons brought together (across the world and hundreds of years) by the similarities of their emotions in relation to a situation of oppression. This then is one moment among several where Du Bois's use of the sorrow songs suggests how the songs, and the model of historical and musical activity they instantiate, might be useful to others not as pseudoethnographic evidence of African American humanity and depth of feeling but as a form for articulating the losses and hauntedness that characterize the experience of modernity more broadly. The striking influence and popularity of African American music surely is connected to this capacity, to greater effect (when we consider the history of twentieth-century popular music) than even Du Bois had foreseen.

The particularity of the sorrow songs stems not only from their ability to articulate a past with a present but also from their flexibility, which enables them ("the siftings of centuries") to contain an *accumulation* of pasts. They are able to do this inasmuch as they instantiate a form that can be "adapted, changed, and intensified" under new circumstances, for different purposes. Du Bois writes of the music: "sprung from the African forests, where its counterpart can still be heard, it was adapted, changed, and intensified by the tragic soul-life of the slave, until, under the stress of law and whip, it became the one true expression of a people's sorrow, despair, and hope" (*Souls*, 151). Not only, then, has the music been changed by the experience of slaves, but it will be changed again. Like the "weary traveler" of Du Bois's concluding song, or like the story in Benjamin's essay "The Storyteller," the music itself has been and will continue to be mobile.[145] Many commentators have noted the improvisatory nature of the songs, the way each song, in each performance, serves the emotional purposes of the moment and is embedded in the life of the singers. In her discussion of the singing of the spirituals during the civil rights movement, Mahalia Jackson, for example, notes that "when the students began to go to jail during the sit-ins they began to make up new words to the spirituals and hymns and old gospel melodies that the Negroes had been singing in their churches for generations. Some got printed, some got put on records and some just got passed around."[146] This built-in adaptability means that the music incorporates along the way the experiences and emotions of its many singers.[147] Du Bois suggests that it is in fact *through* the emotions ("sorrow, despair, and hope") of the singers that the historical context of the slave ("the stress of law and whip") makes it into the song.

The songs thereby become a kind of mnemonic tool, a portable collective madeleine, where communal involuntary memories can be lodged and recalled. Here, as in few other places, "certain contents of the individual past combine in the memory with material from the collective past."[148] In each singing of a Sorrow Song, past sufferers are resurrected, and through them history itself. The songs are moving machines for the abstracting of affective life in its historicity.

Furthermore, because the singers know the songs will be repeated and because they know they will leave their traces in the songs, the songs afford them the ability to see themselves from the point of view of collective remembrance.[149] The self-estranging, memento mori effect is amplified because part of this process involves asking oneself how one's affects can be put in a repeatable, narrative, collective, musically structured form. And no plot feature appears more frequently in the narratives of the sorrow songs than the contemplation of one's own death. ("Of death the Negro showed little fear, but talked of it familiarly and even fondly as simply a crossing of the waters, perhaps—who knows?— back to his ancient forests again.") The songs thus insistently narrate the experience they promote. In doing this, the songs (and by extension, *Souls* itself) provide a nugget of affective experience for the audience, and then tell the audience how and why that experience is valuable, interesting, historically and politically relevant. This is the moment of what I have been calling affective mapping: the practice evokes and then also narrates, locates, or maps the very affects it solicits and produces.

Although many of the songs Du Bois discusses involve the contemplation of death (such as "I Hope My Mother Will Be There," "Swing

Low, Sweet Chariot," and "I'll Hear the Trumpet Sound"), "Lay This Body Down" may be taken as exemplary, especially since Du Bois himself prioritizes it, using its lyrics as the epigraph to the sorrow songs chapter (the only such instance), and highlighting it as one of the songs that "have always attracted [him]."

> I walk through the churchyard
> To Lay this body down;
> I know moon-rise, I know star-rise;
> I walk in the moonlight, I walk in the starlight;
> I'll lie in the grave and stretch out my arms,
> I'll go to judgment in the evening of the day,
> And my soul and thy soul shall meet that day,
> When I lay this body down.

Here we have a literal consideration of one's corporeal death. Death is depicted as a moment of rest and spatial freedom, a place where one can stretch out one's arms. At the same time, death is also a moment of meeting someone ("my soul and thy soul"), a someone who is the *you* of the song but is otherwise abstract. Thus, this *you*, can be whomever the singer wishes it to be, indeed the song requires the singer to read this *you* (Jesus? a lost love? an absent lover? a missed parent?) into the song. But in the moment of singing, "thy soul" is of course also the audience or other singers themselves. The song thus narrates the experience it promotes in another way: it tells of being brought together with an other or others as the singing does in fact bring one together with others. And just as the singing of the songs is collective, so is the death the songs narrate. If Rousseau could say that he "never began to live until [he] looked upon [himself] as a dead man," then perhaps we can also say that group life cannot come into existence until we can see our own collective death.

The songs indeed seem to make such a Rousseau-ian suggestion, for the one topic that may exceed in frequency the consideration of death in the songs is the image of a collective, righteous resurrection. Seeing one's collective self as living follows closely on the heels of seeing one's collective self dead. Mourning, the songs suggest, in both the experience they solicit and the narratives they tell, is always also a resurrection, an awakening. Nowhere of course, is this relation clearer than in the remarkable song "My Lord, What a Mourning," which was transcribed also as "What a Morning." That "mourning" and "morning" would be interchangeable is a rather spectacular illustration of the advantages of an oral musical tradition, capable of such feats as this yoking of the homonymic words together, making an explosive indeterminacy ever available. Du Bois's choice to use the spelling "mourning" while borrowing the bars of music from the *Hampton* text in which the spelling "morning" appears indicates that he was fully aware of the textual variability, and also suggests that he wished to emphasize the significance of "mourning" to the "waking of the nations."

However it is spelled, the song narrates a massive uprising of the "nations underground" at the moment of final judgment. This messianic moment is always a "mourning," even the ideal or fantasy of melancholic mourning, in that the dead and gone are resurrected. As such it is a literalization of the melancholic process of incorporation, which is itself a kind of resurrection, a way to render the lost object alive after its death. The bursting of the tombs that is repeatedly narrated in the sorrow songs is thus a mirror image of the feelings of loss, disappointment, and abandonment also treated in the songs. In this sense the depiction of the final judgment is not utopian, in the sense that there is no specific social order imagined but simply an *end* to the suffering and injustice of the past and present worlds.[150] For this reason, what is to happen at the moment of the waking nations, when "the stars begin to fall," is left necessarily vague and open. The "what a" of "what a mourning" is a way of acknowledging the uncertainty regarding what that "mourning" will be and how that "morning" will look, at the same time registering its inevitably exclamatory quality.[151]

The messianic, Derrida notes, is the thinking of the event to come, an event about which by definition we cannot be certain. It involves "awaiting without horizon of the wait" for an "alterity that cannot be anticipated."[152] And, paradoxically, the future moment of rupture will only come by virtue of an attentiveness to the past. The repetition within and of the sorrow songs signals that theirs is a mourning with an indeterminate future, one to which one insistently returns with the hope of interrupting the present. In the conclusion to this final chapter of *Souls*, Du Bois underscores one last time that the way to welcome such a future is by continuing to echo the past.

In the final paragraph, Du Bois writes optimistically of a future when the veil has been rended and the prisoned go free. Such a freedom, he writes, would be like the freedom of "the sunshine," or the freedom of the "fresh young voices welling up to me from the caverns of brick and mortar below." Like the unknowing souls of Plato's cave allegory, these singers, whom he calls "my children, my little children," may themselves be located out of the sun, down in the caverns, still behind the veil. And even if they cannot see the sun, their voices nonetheless address it: his children, Du Bois happily declares, "are singing to the sunshine." The shadow cast by the lost object is no longer relevant, not so much because the singers have transcended it as because they have moved to another register of being. If they cannot move into the sun as visual beings, then they will do so as voices. By bringing sound into the sun, the visible is problematized: that which is out of the sun but which nonetheless subtends the world of the visible comes into the light not as a stepping out of the shadows, or a pulling aside of the veil, but through the movement of sound, that which the veil cannot block. Indeed, the veil only increases the power of the voice as the invisible becomes visibly invisible.[153] The place in the sunlight becomes haunted.

In part, Du Bois's metaphor references the Fisk Jubilee Singers' concrete successes in moving out of the shadow of invisibility and despair by way of their voices, raising money for the university, playing to appreciative audiences throughout Europe, and contributing to the sorrow songs' entrance into the world of American popular culture—and

And the traveller girds himself, and sets his face toward the Morning, and goes his way.

into a visual world—by way of sheet music. But he is clearly also indicating something about black fugitivity, by which I mean African American practices for evading and avoiding white supremacy—sidestepping and outwitting it, which is, as Fred Moten argues, the primary mode of black freedom. Black fugitivity and freedom exists in the realm of the aural, the musical, the singing voice, but exists there not only in itself, as it were, that is, as the living presence of sound, but also exists as it is translated into the visual, as having moved into the visual. And it is precisely there that its excess, its uncapturability, its unfixability is most clearly communicated, proliferated, and reproduced.

Du Bois's readers, who do not *hear* the voices, but can only *see* them as they are narrated on the page, must project, transfer, or imagine what these sounds are like, an inevitably mimetic practice, one that might take shape in a humming or singing along. As if in complete sympathy with this readerly movement, Du Bois cites nearly a full page with lyrics and musical notation at the very end of his book, giving readers everything they need to sing along.

The singers—who may at this point also be Du Bois's readers—exhort us to cheer the weary traveler. And then Du Bois responds as if to affirm that the cheer has been successful, that the weary traveler, having girded himself, is now ready to keep moving. He "sets his face toward the Morning"—or is it the Mourning?—"and goes his way."

CHAPTER FIVE

Andrei Platonov's Revolutionary Melancholia

Friendship and *Toska* in *Chevengur*

"I was wondering 'what am I depressed about?' It was because I was missing socialism."

—ANDREI PLATONOV, *CHEVENGUR*

Socialism as antidepressant: this is indeed how socialism is presented in Andrei Platonov's *Chevengur,* the 1927 novel about peasant life in the Russian steppe in the years leading up to and following the October revolution. While the notion of socialism as salve for depression may in the present-day context of Prozac and capitalist triumphalism seem counterintuitive at best, for the reader of *Chevengur,* the realization by the self-named peasant "Dostoevsky" about halfway through the novel that he has been depressed by lack of socialism does not come as a surprise. It is no surprise first of all because we have already seen that loss, death, intense privation, and the danger of depression and despair are the basic facts of existence for the people of Platonov's novel. Indeed, the readers of *Chevengur* may be slightly taken aback by the deaths they encounter in even the first few pages of the novel: a hermit accidentally poisons himself with a lizard he has eaten in desperate hunger; several children have starved and others been given a "medicine" to ease them into death before they starve; and a fisherman has committed suicide by jumping into the lake so that he can "live with death a little bit" in order to see what it is like. The orphan left behind by this fisherman, Sasha Dvanov, becomes a central character of the novel, and it is suggested that orphanhood is paradigmatic of the human (or at least the Russian) condition more generally. In this world, maintaining interest in life presents itself as a task, not as something that in any way comes naturally. In short, the ubiquity of death and suffering and the persistent threat of depression are the basic facts every person must cope with in some way or another and to which, therefore, *any* ideology or social formation would have to respond.

But it was not just any ideology or social formation that managed these problems, it was Soviet socialism, and Platonov's novel shows us, in affectionate detail, various uses the idea and discourse of socialism were put to in the years following the October revolution. These fashionings are by and large idiosyncratic and homemade, but the thing that they all share in addition to the melancholic preoccupation with loss is a powerful interest in the communal, collective friendship that depends on and transforms this shared melancholy. Take, for example, the impressively mournful Stepan Kopenkin, who has devoted his search for communism to the memory of Rosa Luxembourg and whose dearest hope is that in communism Rosa might be resurrected. Here, in a passage I will return to, he reflects on his friendship with Sasha Dvanov: "[I]n the open fields . . . he had been riding beside Sasha Dvanov and when he started to feel melancholy [*toskoval*], Dvanov also felt melancholy [*toskoval*], and their melancholy [*toska*] went toward each other, and having met, stopped in the middle" (249/274).[1] When pluralized by the relational dynamic established by friendship, melancholia is transformed into a mode of intimate and imitative emotional connection and at the same time functions as an alibi for that intimate relation. In *Chevengur,* melancholia reminds and returns one again and again to the need for friendship. In this emphasis on friendship *(druzhba),* a friendship that would appear to be an intensification of a more general comradeship *(tovarishchestvo),*[2] Platonov not only offers an original addition to the long history of the dialectic between melancholia and utopia;[3] he also supplies a contribution to the more local project of giving a tangible shape to socialist society. Indeed, Platonov suggests that socialism is friendship. Or, as one of the peasants in Chevengur remarks, "we eat and make friends; there's your Soviet" (166/185). Even though Chevengur was censored at the time, and despite the fact that Platonov was later hailed in the West as a critic of Soviet socialism, Platonov seriously desired to participate in the construction of socialism and, I will argue, presents in Chevengur a concrete and compelling case for the emotional attractions of the socialist project.[4]

✦

Before going any further, however, several prefatory notes are needed. First, it is important to distinguish Platonov's understanding of melancholia or depression from ours; his involves a paradigmatic Russian "untranslatable," the word *toska*. (Platonov uses the word frequently enough that one of his recent translators, Robert Chandler, has suggested that we introduce the word into English, as we have with *ennui*.)[5] The *Oxford Russian-English Dictionary* translates *toska* as "melancholy, torment, longing, depression," but as Vladimir Nabokov has noted, "no single word in English renders all the shades of *toska*." Like "melancholy," *toska* has a rich connotative field. Nabokov gives a sense of its range: "at its deepest and most painful, it is a sensation of great spiritual anguish, often without any specific cause. At less morbid levels it is a dull ache of the soul, a longing with nothing to long for, a sick pining, a vague restlessness, mental throes, yearning. In particular cases it may be the desire for somebody or something specific, nostalgia, lovesickness. At the lowest level, it grades into ennui, boredom."[6] *Toska* can suggest a feeling of various intensities as well as different levels of specificity.

While its range and usage is in some ways similar to the English "melancholy," *toska* can take an object in a way that neither depression or melancholia (at least in current usage) can. While one can be depressed or melancholy *about* something, this does not suggest the same active feeling in relation to an object as is indicated by having toska *for* something (home, a friend, socialism). Hence, for example, *toska* is the word used for homesickness—*toska po rodine*. Relatedly, toska has a verb form. As a verb, the word underscores the potentially and paradoxically active nature of lacking something; one can *toskovat* for things.[7] (For an English equivalent we would have to borrow the now antiquated "melancholize" from Robert Burton.)[8] This is what the peasant quoted in the epigraph is doing: rather than "being depressed," which suggests a mood one is in and that one has been put there, here our peasant *toskuyet,* feeling the absence of he's not sure what, until, that is, he realizes that what he lacks is socialism.

A second note concerns the Russian philosopher Nikolay Fyodorov. Fyodorov's influence on Platonov is well known and much discussed in the scholarship on Platonov.[9] However, outside of the Russian reading world the surprisingly influential Fyodorov is virtually unknown, as only small fragments of his work have appeared in English translation.[10] Fyodorov's lifelong work, of which I will only give a bare outline here, was the explication of what he called "the common task" *(obshchevo dela).* For Fyodorov, the central problem of human existence was death, closely followed by birth, both of which exemplified our sorry state of subjection to the (hostile) forces of nature. The loss of our parents (fathers in particular), indeed all of our ancestors, was for Fyo-dorov a trauma from which we never recover, damaging our capacity for human attachment more generally. We are all, in some basic way, orphans. His rather fantastical utopian response to the problem of orphanhood was to envision the sublimation of sexual energies into technological-scientific ones so that we could develop the means to ac-tually physically resurrect the dead, and at the same time explore the cosmos in order to find the space to put them all. In addition to allow-ing us to overcome death and render birth unnecessary, this "common task" would in the meanwhile solve the problem of our alienation from one another because it would bring us together to work on this mourn-ful project.[11] Inasmuch as his project was hostile to birth and reproduc-tion, it also sought to make women (linked to nature in Fyodorov's vision) unnecessary.[12] Accordingly, Fyodorov is hostile to the nuclear family and heterosexual couple, which, in his view, isolates us from a broader collectivity, and draws us away from the real problem—our in-ability to mourn the death of our parents—while producing more chil-dren who will be left in this state of orphanhood.[13]

The emphasis on loss and the past, the fantasy of resurrection, the state of orphanhood, the idea that our shared losses can bring us to-gether, as well as a skepticism concerning the isolating effects of the nuclear family and the heterosexual couple all find their way into Platonov's work.[14] However, whereas Fyodorov's project sought to abolish death, I will argue that Platonov (in *Chevengur* at least) drama-tizes the dangers of such an apocalyptic desire, instead emphasizing the ways practices motivated by and stemming from a melancholic dwelling on loss without the hope for a final mourning can themselves be a source of people's reconnection to each other, to the past, and to a com-mon, collective project of social transformation.

Finally, it may be helpful also to provide a quick sum of the key per-sonages and events in the novel, which non-Russian readers are unlikely to know.[15] This is somewhat difficult, given that, as Thomas Seifrid notes, "the emplotment of events is often maddeningly diffuse";[16] many episodes in the novel have nothing to do with the development of the story as such, characters appear and disappear without any narrative indication of which ones are central, and temporal shifts occur without so much as a warning.[17] That said, the novel opens by introducing us to a kind of wandering tinkerer, Zakhar Pavlovich, who makes things in order to prevent himself from dwelling on the suffering and death that surrounds him. His mode of existence is in some ways juxtaposed to

that of the fisherman who drowns himself in the lake, leaving the orphan Sasha Dvanov. Sasha moves in with a large family, from which he
is eventually driven by one of the children, Prokofy, or Proshka, who
sees Sasha as a drain on the family's already meager resources. Learning
that Sasha is homeless, Zakhar Pavlovich adopts him; the preternatu-
rally sensitive boy grows up with Zakhar, and they see the arrival of the
revolution together. Sasha is then sent off to the front by the Party, and
shortly thereafter he meets up with Stepan Kopenkin, an out-of-work
Bolshevik soldier, whose horse is named Proletarian Strength and who
fights, as I mentioned, for the memory and resurrection of Rosa Luxembourg; he in fact carries inside his cap a picture of Rosa to remind him
of this. Sasha and Kopenkin develop an intimate friendship, indeed the
reader may be inclined to say that they are in love, except that one of
the particularities of Platonov's style is that there is a kind of affective
deadpan-ness to the narrative that leaves it entirely to the reader to
make suppositions about the interior emotional lives of his characters
(more on this later). Dvanov and Kopenkin enjoy a series of Don
Quixote–like misadventures while searching for socialism in the countryside before Sasha decides to go back home in order to study some
more and reconsider his situation. Kopenkin joins up with a group of
peasants, almost exclusively male, to create communism in the town
called Chevengur. They abolish work and aim to live off the bounty of
the sun, they move the houses around every Saturday in order to keep
the space of socialism dynamic, and they kill the local bourgeoisie, that
is, the property-owning peasants (understanding that this is one of the
basic requirements for socialism to come into being). They also send
Proshka, who has become a sort of party ideologist for the town, to
search for the most nonbourgeois people he can find, to populate the
now mostly empty town. Proshka returns with "the miscellaneous"
(prochie). Meanwhile, Kopenkin pines *(toskuyet)* for Sasha while
doubting the veracity of the socialism the peasants think that they have
created. He sends for Sasha, whose arrival not only cheers Kopenkin
but seems to fortify the mood of the village more generally. For a time,
this has the happy effect of redoubling the Chevengurians' commitment
to cultivating friendship, and they busy themselves creating tokens of
affection: not only growing food and cooking for each other but also
building statues and writing poems. A visiting party official from
Moscow describes them as "happy, but useless." The miscellaneous,
however, demand that some women be brought to the town, which
Proshka does, at which point the miscellaneous cease living the com-

radely life and settle into a kind of domesticity. The novel ends when a group of Cossacks, perhaps dispatched by the government to bring the offbeat town into line, attacks it and slaughters most of its inhabitants. Dvanov, having survived the attack, returns to the village where he was born and drowns himself in the same lake where his father killed himself. The novel ends with Zakhar Pavlovich missing Dvanov, and, not knowing that he is dead, asking Proshka to look for him.

Platonov's characters tend to take on an allegorical quality, in the sense that they instantiate certain paradigmatic positions in relation to the social forces they must contend with. However, they are not allegorical in a way that is immediately translatable back into everyday life; they are not, for example, the recognizable and central social types of the great realist novels celebrated by Lukacs nor the ideal types of socialist realism.[18] Rather, Platonov's characters are closer to Baudelaire's melancholy heroes of modernity (the widow, the dandy, the lesbian, the flaneur, the prostitute) who are allegorical in a dialectical way, for what they are not and for the ways they are marked by what they have lost. The types of characters populating Platonov's world—orphans, mechanics, hermits, soldiers, and wanderers—are all shaped by loss of one kind or another, and through these characters Platonov maps out different ways of relating to loss, and the aesthetic-political implications of these different melancholic practices.

The Wooden Frying Pan versus the Wisdom of the Fish

The first of *Chevengur*'s melancholic allegorical figures is Zakhar Pavlovich, the wandering craftsman-inventor, whom we meet in the opening lines of the book.

There are worn-out edges to old provincial towns. People come straight out of nature to live there. A man appears, with a piercing face that has been exhausted to the point of sadness [*grust'*], a man who can fix up or equip anything but who has lived through his own life unequipped. There was not one man-made thing [*izdeliye*], from a frying pan to an alarm clock, that had not in its life passed through the hands of this man. Nor had be refused to resole shoes, to cast shot for wolf hunting, or to turn out counterfeit medals to be sold at old-time village fairs. But he had never made anything for himself—neither a family nor a dwelling. In summer he simply lived in nature, carrying his tools in a sack and using the sack as a pillow, more for the protection of the tools than for softness. To protect himself from the early morning sun he put burdocks in his eyes in the evenings. Winters he lived on the remnants of his summer earnings and paid the church watchman for a room by ringing the night hours. He was not particularly interested in anything—not people or nature, only in every kind of man-made thing [*izdeliye*]. And so he treated people and fields with an indifferent tenderness, not infringing on their interests. During the winter evenings he would sometimes make unneeded things [*nenuzhnie veshchi*]: towers out of wire, ships from pieces of roofing iron, glued paper airships, and so on—exclusively for his own pleasure. Often he even delayed someone's chance order; for example, he would have been given a barrel to re-hoop, but he would be busy with the construction of a wooden clock, thinking it should work without winding up—from the earth's rotation. (3/5)[19]

Zakhar comes "straight out of nature," but his abiding fascination is with its transformation. He concerns himself with *izdeliye,* which is often translated as "object" or "product" but which more literally means "that which has been made out of something," a work, creation, or manufactured object.[20] At first glance, the uninstrumentalized and strictly speaking "needless" nature of Zakhar's carefully crafted *izdeliye* recalls Kant's classic definition of art as "purposive and purposeless." But Zakhar's tinkering tries to use this space of needlessness to invent things that could in fact make it back into the world of use; this is not an autonomous art. For example, in addition to the wooden clock that would work by the power of the earth's rotation, Zakhar is also fascinated with the idea of a wooden frying pan.

When Zakhar Pavlovich made an oak frying pan the hermit was astonished since all the same they wouldn't be able to fry anything in it. But Zakhar Pavlovich poured water into the wooden frying pan and succeeded in bringing the water to a boil over a slow fire without burning the pan. The hermit was frozen in amazement. (4/7)

We see here the desire to change the relationship that we have to our everyday lives to make them more "needless" in their essence and, just as important, more open to the possibility of surprise and invention. Who would expect a wooden pan? Such a thing may be "unneeded," but it is not exactly without use. The fact that one can boil water in it is important because it produces the crucial effect of amazement, jolting us out of our own means-ends rationality and reminding us at once that the things we make may surprise us, and that our tinkering, needless activities might nonetheless turn out to produce surprisingly usable things.[21]

In working on a piano, Zakhar is not motivated by an interest in the music as such. Rather, he wants to know "how the *izdeliye* was constructed," this *izdeliye* "that could move any heart, that could make a person kind" (8/11). The music made by the piano, like the water boiled by the wooden pan, compels Zakhar because of what it reveals about the power of human making, and the extent to which made objects can outlive humans and operate in and according to a logic that exceeds the human but nonetheless affects people in surprising ways. Zakhar's interest is thus one that not only seeks nonalienated labor but also hopes for a labor with unexpectedness in its results, waiting, as Derrida puts it, "for what one does not expect any longer or yet" and welcoming the possibility of the apparently impossible.[22]

It becomes evident that the unnecessariness Zakhar finds pleasing in his *izdeliya* is attractive precisely to the extent to which it negates the extreme need that characterizes everyday life. "In order to forget his hunger," Platonov writes, "Zakhar Pavlovich worked all the time and trained himself to make from wood everything he had previously made from metal" (4/7). Not only hunger, moreover, but also Zakhar's persistent sense of grief must be somehow be addressed by his aesthetic practice: "Grief and orphanhood [*sirotstvo*] touched him powerfully— some unknown conscience which had been appeared in his chest made him want to walk about the earth without rest, to meet grief in all the villages and to sob over other people's graves. But he was stopped by the various *izdeliya* that came his way—the elder gave him a wall clock to repair and the priest a piano to tune" (8/11). There is a clear sense of transference or substitution here—work on the *izdeliya* replaces the practice of sobbing over other people's graves. It would appear to be a question of innervation: the affects need somewhere to go. And innervation, as Benjamin reminds us, accompanies imagination. Thus, unimaginative, noninventive work, such as cutting stakes, Zakhar learns, is insufficient to keep his *toska* at bay.[23]

Zakhar does not know or understand whence his grief, and Platonov does not explain it as such. Yet enough evidence is presented for us to conjecture about the sources—after all, we have just been introduced to Zakhar Pavlovich, and we have seen him witness the death of his companion the hermit, and then remember the suicide by drowning of his fisherman acquaintance, and his attempt to comfort the mourning orphan, Sasha. There is no shortage of death over which Zakhar may need to grieve.

Nonetheless, the fact that the reader must figure this out, must read into the text in order to speculate about the sources of Zakhar's grief, is a crucial aspect of the reading experience Platonov solicits. In general, there is a kind of affective and epistemological flatness to Platonov's writing: emotions, actions, bodies, events are all described from an impersonal distance. As Valery Podoroga puts it, "what is represented is deprived of traditional novelistic props: it is depersonalized, depsychologized, and not definable by any inner teleology." This means that "Platonov's prose . . . suffers from a rupture between the literality of the depiction of the event and its meaning."[24] The reader is left to supply the meaning and to determine, or indeed to feel, its affective intensity. Like the blank affect Freud advocated for the ideal therapist, Platonov's prose requires that one transfer affects from one's *own* past onto the scenes and events he describes, even if (or especially because) the events described may bear little apparent similarity to one's own life.

Platonov actively plays with this distance between event and meaning, continually putting the reader into undecidable situations. Thus, when Zakhar says to the dying hermit "Don't be afraid . . . I'd die right now myself, but, you know, when you are busy with different *izdeliya* . . ." (5/8), one is tempted at first to laugh. After all, Zakhar's response is so unanticipated, absurd even, a moment of comic relief: offering to die with the hermit, as if dying was a potentially interesting task like going on a trip that one might choose to do at any moment, an activity that in principle Zakhar fully supported. But then one reflects on Zakhar's earnest attempt to sympathize with the man to the point of considering dying too, and one realizes that perhaps Zakhar's offer to die is not ridiculous at all and is instead an accurate expression of his tenuous hold on the desire to live. Perhaps it *is* only his *izdeliya* that give him a reason to live. As readers we find ourselves oscillating between two positions. Podoroga describes this as the alternation between comic and tragic readerly distances, but quickly adds that in fact "we are dealing with one and the same distance, which, while making us independent of what is being read, even its judges, suddenly returns us almost instantaneously to ourselves, through some unknown parabola, though now to a 'different ourselves,' transforming us from autonomous subjects into objects of provocation, revulsion, and melancholy."[25] This moment of self-alienation, we will see, is not only the aesthetic effect Platonov seems to solicit from his readers (one akin, it may also be noted, to the one described by Adorno and discussed earlier in relation to the "aesthetic shudder") but also a moment he allegorizes in an almost pedagogical way in several places throughout the novel (including in the surprising figure of the "eunuch of the soul," on which more later) but first of all in the figure of Zakhar himself.

From the fascination with wooden frying pans and wire towers Zakhar develops an intense attraction to the burgeoning machine culture, and he gets a job at an nearby train yard. Like his handmade things, the train is interesting to Zakhar not as instrument but as something that people have made that then acquires its own independent life. Here, for example, Zakhar sits before the door of the steam engine's firebox:

> This replaced for him the enormous pleasure of friendship and conversation with people. Watching the living flame, Zakhar Pavlovich himself lived—within him his head thought, his heart felt and his entire body quietly enjoyed. Zakhar Pavlovich respected coal, angle iron, every sleeping raw material and semifinished product, but he really loved and felt only the *izdeliya,* that into which something had been made by means of a person's labor and which then continues to live its own independent life. . . . Zakhar Pavlovich was not solitary—machines were like people for him, constantly arousing within him feelings, thoughts and desires. (27/32)

The trains and *izdeliya* can be Zakhar's people, inasmuch as they have their own, semiautonomous, immanent logic that is not reducible to the human but is nonetheless similar to it. Whereas, for example, the "complete little living world" of ants that Zakhar notices when he sits down to smoke is completely separate from him, the world of things-we-have-made is one we can understand and, more important, is one into which our emotions may travel. Thus, for the trains Zakhar had "light tears of sympathy." He "greatly enjoyed one constant thought," Platonov writes, the thought of "how man's latent vital power would suddenly appear in the agitated machines, which were greater in size and significance than the skilled workers" (29/35). It is not that Zakhar Pavlovich *identifies* with the machines so much as that he is able to transfer his affects—his own latent vital power—into the alternative, imaginable world instantiated by them.

However, one day, the ultimately inadequate compensatory nature of Zakhar's love of machines is disclosed to him through a chance encounter with a young boy traipsing through town begging for crusts of bread and money. He recognizes the boy, Proshka (of the family that adopted Sasha the orphan) and he feels a burst of sorrow and sympathy. Looking at Proshka, Zakhar began for some reason to doubt the value of machines and *izdeliya* as being higher than a man. . . . Proshka fell at the bend of the tracks. He was alone, small, and without defense. Zakhar Pavlovich wanted to bring him back to himself forever, but it was a long way to catch up.

In the morning Zakhar Pavlovich did not want to go to work like he usually did. In the evening he grew melancholy [*zatoskoval*] and lay down to sleep immediately. The bolts, valves, and old manometers that he always kept on the table could not dispel his ennui [*skuka*]—he glanced at them and did not feel himself to be in their company. Something was drilling inside him, as if his heart was gnashing in unfamiliar reverse. Zakhar Pavlovich could in no way forget Proshka's small thin body wandering along the tracks into the distance, a distance crammed with an enormous nature that seemed to have collapsed. (34/40–41)

Zakhar's affection and sympathy for Proshka interrupts his machine love, throwing a wrench in the transferential logic that sustained it. In seeing Proshka's small, thin body, Zakhar remembers that bodies are "defenseless" when alone, that they became thin when not fed, and that people die and leave others behind who mourn and miss them. Whereas previously Zakhar thought that time was not real, that it was just the "even taut strength of the spring" (30/36) in the clock, now he sees "that time was the movement of grief and the same as a tangible object, like any substance, although it was unfit for being worked on" (32–33/39). Time as humans experience it is not made by the movement of the clock. Rather, mortality and loss and the ensuing grief creates an awareness of time. This is one natural thing that cannot be transformed into something produced by human labor. Grief is in this sense irreducible, unavoidable, and shared by everyone. But if it cannot be "worked on," it must nonetheless be responded to, and indeed it is the sharing of what we might call this general affect of grief, and the need to absorb or represent it collectively, that brings the characters of *Chevengur* together.

Machines may exist outside this world of loss and bodily time, and indeed this is part of their attraction, but Zakhar is no longer able to compensate for his grief with his *izdeliya*; he no longer feels like he belongs among the bolts and tools, because the image of Proshka that sticks in his head reminds him of the gap between his world and the world of machines. He cannot forget that the train tracks that run alongside Proshka are absolutely no help to him against the force of collapsing nature that surrounds him. Platonov uses a technical phrase— *na obratnom khodu* ("in reverse")—to explain what has happened to Zakhar's internal emotional machine: the affects that had been transferred from the world of people to the machines are now sent back as if they are "drilling through him," reaching on return a different Zakhar. His love for the machines has disappeared, his sense of being transformed:

The fisherman had drowned in Lake Mutevo, the hermit had died in the woods, the empty village had overgrown with a thicket of grass, and yet the church watchman's clock ran, and the trains ran on schedule, and now Zakhar Pavlovich felt depressed and ashamed about the accuracy of the trains and clocks. . . .

The warm fog of love for machines in which Zakhar Pavlovich had lived peacefully and hopefully was now blown away by a clean wind, and before Zakhar Pavlovich opened the defenseless, solitary life of the people who live naked, with no self-deceiving belief in the aid of machines. (35/41)

The process that sees its end here began when Zakhar had become attached to machines as if they were friends. His affects from the world had found their way into the warm fog of this aesthetic space. And when he feels a similar mode of connection to Proshka—by surprise, without meaning to—the same affects find their way back into a corporeal human world. He is reminded of the grief and naked life from which he has been escaping into the world of machines and sees that grief and that life defamiliarized, as if for the first time. Thus, Zakhar can see the nature of his emotional attachment to the machines, and the extent to which this has involved a negation of the everyday, material, finite human world in which he lives. His unsettling encounter with Proshka also leads him to recognize that the ordered, eternal, transcendent moment of the machine cannot be translated back into the world of the body. Although he can feel affection for the machines and fantasize about the greater-than-human world they comprise, the relation is not symmetrical: the machines cannot sympathize with him nor with Proshka. The train will not save Proshka; only another person can help him. And he needs help. So the machines make Zakhar feel ashamed— in their orderliness and precision they ignore the *toska* of life in the world. He therefore abandons them: "for just a monetary payment, it turned out to be difficult even to hit the head of the nail correctly" (34– 35/42). Shortly thereafter he tracks down and begins to take care of Sasha Dvanov.

I have dwelled on this moment because I think Zakhar's experience with the machines is an ideal form of aesthetic experience for Platonov, and, as I mentioned, is analogous to the readerly experience he seeks to solicit. It opens up and encourages a new space of relationality or connectedness, one that becomes occupied by friendship, a sublation, we might say, of the "unneeded" activity Zakhar comes to appreciate in the space of the machines. Thus, although he abandons the machines,

Zakhar's experience with them has allowed him to find a way to inner-vate and externalize his affects. Just as, in psychoanalysis, we cannot have the moment of recognition regarding the emotions we have been unconsciously transferring from our past onto the analyst without first transferring them, so too Zakhar could not have been jolted by the move-ment of his heart in unfamiliar reverse if his heart had not already been moving ahead. The transformatively self-estranging moment when the "warm fog of love" blows away would be impossible without the initial step into the fog.

The value of Zakhar's antidepressive aesthetic strategy here is under-scored by its juxtaposition with the one pursued by the fisherman, who dreamed of seeing life from the point of view of a fish, and who imag-ined death as "another province," one more interesting than the one he presently occupied.

> Zakhar Pavlovich knew one man, a fisherman from Lake Mutevo, who had questioned many people about death and who was melancholy [*tosko-val*] from his curiosity; this fisherman loved fish not as food, but as special beings that probably knew the secret of death. He would show the eyes of a dead fish to Zakhar Pavlovich and say, "Look—true wisdom! A fish stands between life and death, and that's why he's mute and stares without expression. I mean even a calf thinks, but a not a fish—it knows everything already." Contemplating the lake through the years, the fisherman always thought about one and the same thing—about the interest of death. Za-khar Pavlovich tried to talk him out of it: "There's nothing special there, just something cramped." A year after that, the fisherman couldn't bear it anymore and threw himself into the lake from his boat, having tied his feet with a rope so that he wouldn't start to swim accidentally. In secret he didn't believe in death at all, the important thing was that he wanted to look at what was there—perhaps it was much more interesting than living in a village or on the shores of a lake; he saw death as another province, lo-cated under the sky, as if at the bottom of cool water, and it attracted him. Some of the *muzhiks* the fisherman talked with about his intention to live with death for a while and return tried to talk him out of it, but others agreed with him: "True enough, Mitry Ivanich, nothing ventured, nothing gained. Try it, then you'll tell us." Dmitry Ivanich tried: they dragged him from the lake after three days and buried him by the fence in the village graveyard. (6/9)

Like Zakhar, the fisherman is trying to find within his workaday life an aesthetic utopian space to negate that life. Also like Zakhar, the fisher-man finds the site for his fantasies of escape in the product of his labor, the fish themselves. And, just as Zakhar values most the *izdeliye* for which he does not get paid, the fisherman finds value in the fish by de-instrumentalizing them, by not thinking of them as something to eat but as "special beings" with great wisdom.

Yet the fisherman's fantasy has an escapist and apocalyptic aspect lacking in Zakhar's. Zakhar's melancholy aesthetic is also a praxis, an engagement with the world that also transforms that world. Although Zakhar experiences the world of machines as a compensatory departure from the world of grief, his *izdeliya* are dialectically linked to the world they come from and negate.[26] The fisherman, on the other hand, is not engaged in a practice but in a dream. Moreover, he does not feel in the *company* of the fish (as Zakhar did, and then did not, with his bolts and manometers) but rather sees the fish as the inhabitants of some other, unknown, abstractly better and more interesting place, where some kind of knowledge beyond life exists. No affects can actually be transferred from everyday life into such a space, because there is no there there, no material, immanent other logic to imaginatively inhabit. Such a place can only be leapt into by an act of faith. Thus, the fisherman is not ready-and-waiting for the unexpected in an experimental open-ended way (as Zakhar is) so much as he hopes to end his present mode of existence through a dramatic act of will.

The fisherman is also clearer that what he seeks is the point of view of death. This desire has a precedent in Russian literature in Dostoevsky's Kirilov, one of the alienated young revolutionaries of *The Demons (B'esy)*. Kirilov's hopes are even more grandiose than the fisherman's: he believes not only that he can overcome death through suicide, but that the moment of willful self-negation involved in killing himself will elevate him to a god-like Archimedean position and inaugurate a new moment in human history.[27] But, of course, as Blanchot puts it, "whoever dwells with negation cannot *use* it . . . one who espouses negation cannot allow it to be incarnated in a final decision which would be exempt from that negation."[28] Thus, where Zakhar's *izdeliya* lead him toward a renewed sense of connection to the world, to other people and the adoption of Sasha, the fisherman's dream of transcendence through self-negation ends simply in suicide, and the abandonment of Sasha.

The implicit comparison between the fisherman and Zakhar that begins the book is important as the initial situation for Sasha, but also because it establishes two paradigms that serve as points of reference for the modes of interest in communism throughout the rest of the book. Thus, for example, to the fisherman's individual utopian impulse,

Platonov parallels one mode of interest in Soviet communism as a collective, Fyodorovian fantasy of finally leaving death and the past behind and thus escaping from the world of *toska*.

> [C]ommunism tormented [*muchil*] Chepurny the way the secret of posthumous life had tormented Dvanov's father, and Chepurny could not bear the secret of time, so he cut short [*prekratil*] the length of history with the urgent construction of communism in Chevengur, just as the fisherman could not bear his own life and turned [*prevratil*] it into death, in order to try out in advance the beauty of that world. (259/285)

Chepurny, the Chevengurian who organized (as he put it) a "second coming" for the local bourgeoisie, is attracted and tormented by communism in the same way Dvanov's father was attracted by the utopia of death. Like Dvanov's father, he is impatient to end time and to escape into the beauty of an unknown world.

Dvanov, on the other hand, "did not love himself too deeply to achieve communism for his own personal life, but he went forward with everyone else because everyone was going and it was terrifying to remain behind alone" (259/285). Because Sasha can only do or feel anything in solidarity and sympathy with others, his interest in communism is quite different.

> His father was dear to Dvanov not because of his curiosity and he liked Chepurny not because of his passion for immediate communism—in and of himself his father had been essential to Dvanov as a first lost friend [*pervyi utrachennyi drug*], and Chepurny—as a homeless comrade who, without communism, would have nobody to hold onto him. Dvanov loved his father, Kopenkin, Chepurny, and many others because all of them, like his father, would perish of impatience with life while he would stay alone among strangers. (259/285)

For Dvanov, communism is not attractive as a way to redeem life or end history but as a way to access forms of affinity. Where Chepurny and his father wanted to get over their loss, leave *toska* behind, and celebrate something totally new, Dvanov holds onto loss. His father and the Chevengurians are dear to Sasha precisely because they are friends he has lost or he knows he will lose (more on this shortly). As Derrida reminds us, "all phenomena of friendship . . . belong to spectrality."[29] Here, *toska,* far from being something from which to escape, is the shared condition that enables friendship, and by extension, communism itself. In Sasha Dvanov, then, we have another allegorical figure, whose melancholic practice offers a protosocialist response to the "movement of grief."

"I Am Like It"

> The child plays at being not only a shopkeeper or
> teacher but also a windmill or a train. . . . What
> advantage does this schooling in mimetic conduct
> bring to a human being?
>
> —WALTER BENJAMIN, "THE DOCTRINE OF SIMILARITY"

Although Zakhar Pavlovich and the fisherman dramatize two divergent modes of sustaining interest in the world, two different kinds of melancholic aesthetic practices, they share a basically solipsistic orientation (at least until Zakhar's crisis with Proshka). Theirs are individual practices. The orphan Sasha Dvanov, by contrast, develops a melancholic practice that moves him toward collectivity, bringing him into community not only with persons but also with everyday objects, machines, and animals. In this, Platonov presents the orphan Dvanov as in many ways the paradigmatic subject-ready-for-socialism, emotionally prepared to establish a noninstrumental, nonreified relation to the world around him. What distinguishes him is his unusual capacity for perceiving and producing likenesses, what Walter Benjamin called the mimetic faculty.[30] Indeed, it is hard to imagine a better exemplar of this faculty (which, in Benjamin's view, was withering under the assaults of capitalist modernity) than Sasha Dvanov. Distinguishing Sasha from Zakhar and his father, Platonov writes:

> His attraction was not curiosity, which ends together with the discovery of the secrets of the machine. Sasha was interested in machines as he was in other acting and living things. He wanted more to feel them, to experience their life [*perezhit' ikh zhizn'*], than to get to know [*uznat'*] them. For this reason, returning from work, Sasha imagined himself to be a locomotive making all the noises an engine does as it runs. Falling asleep he would think that the chickens of the village had long ago gone to sleep, and this consciousness of community with the chickens or the locomotive gave him satisfaction. Sasha could not enter into anything separately: at first he sought out some similarity [*podobie*] to his action and only then did he act, not from his own necessity, but from sympathy toward something or someone. (38/44)

Where Zakhar is motivated in part by the desire to see how *izdeliya* are made in order to appreciate their madeness, Sasha's interest in the world is based on a desire to be-with others in order to "feel them," to experience, or literally "live through" *(perezhit')* their lives, which Platonov distinguishes from recognizing or getting to know *(uznat')* others. Insofar as knowledge requires a subject who knows and an object who is known, it creates a relationship of negation, whereas Sasha desires maximal proximity. He accomplishes this by perceiving or creating a similarity between his behavior and the "active or living thing" he is interested in. Platonov suggests that Sasha does not seek to be like things *because* he is interested in them; rather, he cannot take any action or "enter into anything" without *first* seeing how his own act is in a relationship of similarity to something else. For Sasha, the perception of similarity and being-similar is primary.

Similarity or likeness here, it is worth emphasizing, is not sameness but a third term aside the identity difference binary. As Jean-Luc Nancy puts it, "the like is not the same." Sasha does not think that he is the *same* as the train or the chickens; there is neither an identification at work nor an appropriation. Nancy: "A like-being resembles me in that I myself resemble him: we resemble together, if you will. That is to say there is no original or origin of identity."[31] Thus, it may be most accurate to say that Sasha has no sense of self or being that precedes his sense of being-in-common with others.

In his desire to feel or experience other lives, Sasha is not limited to things that bear some kind of immediately sensible similarity.

> "I am like him," Sasha often said to himself. Looking at the ancient fence he thought in a sincere voice, "It stands for itself!" and also stood someplace without any need. In the fall when the shutters creaked dismally and Sasha was bored with sitting home in the evenings, he listened to the shutters and felt: they are also bored!—and then stopped feeling bored.
>
> When Sasha got fed up with going to work, he calmed himself with the wind, which blew day and night.
>
> "I am like it," he thought when he saw the wind. "I only work in the day and it has to work in the night too. The wind has things even worse." (38/44–45)

Sasha does not find likenesses so much as he creates them, often doing something *in order* to feel like something else, turning his body, his self, into an instrument of imitation. In this way, feeling bored or tired, Sasha finds comfort in the shutters or wind—who are like him, but who have things even worse. It is not only by way of actions of behaviors (making the sounds of a train, standing alone) that Sasha finds ways to be similar but also through affective states. In this, he returns to what

Daniel Stern has proposed is the initial moment of infant relationality and perhaps a basic mechanism of relationality in general.

As I mentioned in chapter 1, in his study *The Interpersonal World of the Infant,* Stern examines the ways parents share affective states with infants, arguing that "the sharing of affective states is the most pervasive and clinically germane feature of intersubjective relatedness."[32] The capacity for infant relationality, and (I would add) perhaps for having affects at all, depends on the parent's ability to engage in what Stern calls "affective attunement." Interestingly, he finds that parents accomplish this attunement by performing "some behavior that is not a strict imitation but nonetheless corresponds in some way to the infant's overt behavior."[33] So, for example, in one instance, "the intensity level and duration of the girl's voice is matched by the mother's body movements." In another case, "features of a boy's arm movements are matched by features of the mother's voice."[34] That is, the mother engages in an activity that is not identical to the infant's but similar to it, a similarity that is marked by way of a translation between modes or senses, from sound to movement, or vice versa, often by way of "amodal" characteristics such as intensity, shape, or rhythm. In this way, Stern writes, "what is matched is not the other person's behavior per se, but rather some aspect of the behavior that reflects the person's feeling state." He continues, "the capacities for identifying cross modal equivalences [what Stern calls similarity across senses, from one sense to another] that make for a perceptually unified world are the same capacities that permit the mother and the infant to engage in affect attunement to achieve affective intersubjectivity."[35] That is to say that precisely the capacity for perceiving what Walter Benjamin called "non-sensuous similarities" is essential for affective attunement.

When Sasha hears the shutters creaking and feels that they are also bored, looks at the fence and thinks it is "standing for itself," or sees the wind blowing and senses that it works even longer hours than he does, he is also imitating crossmodally, finding correspondences across differences. As if he had stepped into the world of Baudelaire's "Correspondances," everything looks at Sasha with familiar eyes; nothing is excluded in advance from like-being. In fact, Sasha's striking capacity for seeing and creating similarities seems to enable him to attune himself to different modes of feeling and being almost at will.

Stern's research also suggests that affective states or experiences are in some sense originarily or fundamentally communal. One of the most surprising aspects of the interactions he observed was that while the infant took no apparent notice of attunement behaviors on the part of the mother, when the mother abruptly stopped these behaviors or acted in a way that was noncorresponding through mismatches of intensity or rhythm, the infants interrupted their activities, often displaying confusion or uncertainty. Without the sharing of an affect, the infant stops engagement in a behavior because the infant is not sure how to continue—as if affects *require* a plural existence in order to come into being.

Sasha seems to need to return repeatedly to this moment of affective attunement, sharing affects with other beings in order to have an emotional life at all. This turns out to be additionally important because his ability to see the ways he is like things offers him a way to combat his feelings of loneliness, exhaustion, and ennui. Just as, later in the book (cited earlier), Kopenkin will feel his *toska* relieved when it meets up with Sasha's, here too the feeling that the shutters are also bored relieves Sasha's boredom or depression.[36] In such an instance, one's own boredom is externalized into a shared space, as one's own subjectivity is dissolved into a *we*. The attraction and effect of this pluralizing of affect would appear in this instance not to be that it allows an historical mode of thinking about one's affects (as, for example, in Du Bois) but rather that it dissolves the isolating, affect-inhibiting effect of depression itself. His mimetic talents provide Sasha with a way to exert agency over his affective life by giving him a way to reconnect with the world, to reinterest himself first of all in this person or thing with which he is sharing an experience, even (or especially) if it that experience is the failure to be interested or to connect.

As Platonov presents it, Sasha's mimetic talents appear to have been stimulated by the experience of loss; they originate in his orphanhood. We can see this in Sasha's response to being "chased out to beg" from "the house in which he had lived, had loved Prokhor Abramovich, Mavra Fetisovna and Proshka." When this happens he realizes that this house "turned out not to be his house [and] . . . in his half-childish saddened soul, undiluted by the comforting water of consciousness, was clenched a full, crushing insult, which he felt up into his throat" (19/23). Rejected by his foster family, abandoned twice over, Sasha experiences his own singular being: "for the first time he thought now about himself and touched his chest: here I am—and everywhere it was alien and unlike him" (18/23).

Unable to bear his singularity, Sasha wanders to his father's grave. There, in an attempt to commune with his (dead) father, Sasha appears to return to and stage a strange reversal of an early scene of parent-infant relatedness. He says, "Papa, they chased me out to beg. Now I'll die to you—its boring there for you alone, and I'm bored." Sasha offers to "die to" his father *(umru k teb'e)*, as if dying were a verb of motion, an act that one could undertake to bring one closer to someone else. And in fact, by thinking of his own death as a journey to someplace else (where his father is) he imitates his father's own earlier desire to visit with death, and in doing so is "with" him in that sense as well. Then, in an apparent paradox, feeling *bored* becomes for Dvanov a way of being *interested,* because he can feel his father being bored as well. That the *we* thereby invoked in this allegorical episode includes a corpse only underscores the extent to which being-like is motivated from the first by loss and enabled by an awareness of death.

In *Memoires for Paul de Man* Derrida writes: "the terrible solitude which is mine or ours at the death of the other is what constitutes that relationship to self which we call 'me,' 'us,' 'between us,' 'subjectivity,' 'intersubjectivity,' 'memory.' The *possibility* of death 'happens,' so to speak, 'before' these other different instances, and makes them possible."[37] There is neither a *self* nor an *us* before our awareness of the death, the finitude, the potential absence of the other. We imitate our first lost friend in order to preserve something of her or him "in" our "self," *as* our initial self. The "self" is at once the instrument and creation of this like-being. Out of this moment springs the dynamic in which "liking" someone else is dependent on our ability to "be like" them, to have created a likeness of them inside us, as *us.* We all mime what we lack, repeating over and again a melancholic process creating the very possibility of relationality. It is in this sense that "his father had been vital to Dvanov as a first lost friend." We all need a first friend to lose in order to have friends at all. "There is no friendship without this knowledge of finitude."[38]

Shortly after Sasha's encounter with his father's corpse, his mimetic talents begin to expand, as we saw, to fences, sleds, shutters, and trains. And if the world of objects seems like a field of potential similarities, with other persons Sasha's need to feel something in common, to sense and experience a feeling of similarity, is nearly compulsory. Sasha could, Platonov writes, "feel a distant stranger's life to the point of hot flashes, but imagined himself only with difficulty" (43/51). No other character embodies more thoroughly what Podoroga called the feeling, shared by everyone in Chevengur, that it is "a burden to be integrated, to exist within a sphere that is particular to them."[39] Where his father wanted to "live a little with death," Sasha "always felt a painful discomfort when he could not imagine a man closely and even just briefly live his life a bit" (142/158). It is not hard to see how this gives him a special skill for friendship, as well as a tendency to be emotionally compelled by collective, historical movements. And the discourse of socialism, with its emphasis on comradeship, collectivity, and togetherness appeals quite precisely to his talents.

Through Sasha, Platonov articulates a powerful vision of subjectivity in a noncapitalist modernity, giving us a sense of what a socialist *Stimmung* might look like. Where Benjamin argues that modernity in its capitalist form has thus far been unkind to the mimetic faculty and the capacity for relationality that comes with it, Platonov presents in Sasha Dvanov an allegory for a socialist modernity in which the traumas of Russian modernity—orphanhood, loss, and grief—*stimulate* the mimetic faculty.

The nature of Sasha's mode of melancholic relationality is dramatized by contrast with the miscellaneous *(prochie)*, the "shards of people" Proshka brings to be the new proletariat of Chevengur, after the bourgeois departed. Their new arrivals' lack of a capacity for friendship is indicated immediately on their appearance in Chevengur, where they are seen huddling close together "not out of love and family feeling, but rather from their insufficiency of clothing" (225/248). They neither know nor expect friendship.

This is because they never had a first friend to lose and thus never learned how to lose. Without this initial loss they do not know, or do not have the capacity, to turn to friendship as an antidepressive melancholic praxis. As Platonov describes it, in a Fyodorovian alternative to Freud's Oedipal scenario, while the mother gives birth, it is the relationship with the father, the "first comrade and friend," that is crucial in developing the capacity for future relationality. "Not one of the miscellaneous had seen his father," Platonov writes, and "they all remembered their mothers as a vague *toska* of the body for that lost peace, a *toska* which in the adult years was transformed into a devastating sadness" (230/254). This leaves the miscellaneous too damaged for friendship; they are unable to "live each other's lives." Indeed, Platonov writes that they lack the "higher signs" of "mind and sensitive sincere despondency [*zaunyvnost'*]" (229/253) altogether.

Struggling to create themselves with only the "last traces of a mother's warmth inside them" left the miscellaneous tired when they reached Chevengur. Thus, they appear to be "powerless and nonproletarian elements" (231/255). Nonetheless, the miscellaneous "had made of themselves exercises in endurance, and within the inner substance of the bodies of the miscellaneous had formed minds full of curiosity and doubt, quick feelings capable of exchanging permanent bliss for a brother comrade who also had no brother and no property, but who could make one forget the one and the other. The miscellaneous still carried hopes within themselves, hopes that were sure, successful and sad [grustnuyu] as loss itself" (231/255). The miscellaneous still *feel* loss, no one does not; and so they are in need of some technique or practice for dealing with grief. But lacking that vital first lost friend, the miscellaneous are without the ability to be-with others, to create an "in us" or "between us" by way of imitation. Their "quick feelings" and hopes lead them to be more susceptible to apocalyptic, sudden solutions—as if loss itself could be overcome or death abolished—even if that required "leading the entire world to its final grave" (231/255). But, as Platonov writes, "there is not enough time to catch that which is lost," and if they do not find themselves actively needed by someone else and thus distracted from their grief, the miscellaneous are left in a state of perpetual and devastating sadness, forever looking for that which cannot be found, without compensatory practice or pleasure.

Before concluding with an examination of this friendship of which the miscellaneous seem incapable, I want to return to the question of the aesthetic experience Platonov's text solicits from his reader. For it is this experience that prepares us for—even teaches us—the mode of melancholic relationality Platonov portrays.

The Eunuch of the Soul

Platonov introduces the surprising figure of the "eunuch of the soul" in the context of a description of Sasha Dvanov's interiority at a moment of psychic crisis. Sasha has been shot by an "anarchist detachment" and then saved from these anarchists by Stepan Kopenkin, whom he thereby meets for the first time. Kopenkin brings Sasha back to a nearby village and the home of Sasha's erstwhile girlfriend of sorts, Sonia (about whom Sasha has been thinking in an affectionate, obliquely libidinal way). There Sasha, Kopenkin, and the other men lie down to sleep, in a room separate from Sonia.

> The five men lay down in a row on the straw and soon Dvanov's face grew pale from sleep. He snuggled his head into Kopenkin's stomach and grew quiet again, while Kopenkin, who slept with his sword and in his complete uniform, put his arm around Dvanov for protection. (79/90)

Inasmuch as Platonov (in characteristic fashion) sets no emotional context for this encounter, it is unclear what kind of affective significance one should attach to Kopenkin's uniformed protective embrace, or to Dvanov's seemingly more than comradely snuggling with this man who he has just met. What kind of a friendship is this? As if in sympathy with the reader's potential uncertainty and perhaps curiosity, in the midst of this tender scene, Dvanov wakes up:

> "But where then is socialism?" Dvanov remembered and peered into the murk of the room, searching for his thing. It seemed to him that he had already found it, but then had spent it in sleep among these strangers. In fear of future punishment, Dvanov went outside without hat and in socks, saw the dangerous unanswering night, and dashed off through the village into its distance. (79/90)

In the middle of this moment of intimate contact with Kopenkin and other men, Sasha wakes up with sudden, dreamlike anxiety about the location of socialism. Remembering the desire for socialism and wondering where it is, the uncertainty about the location of socialism is displaced onto a search for his "thing" (veshch'), which then seems to stand in for this socialism he lacks. (Like Lacan's object petit a, this "thing" would seem to be a representation of Sasha's desire, the instantiation of a structural, unconscious desire—and in this instance a desire for socialism as such, a desire that, as Jameson remarks, does not yet have its Freud or Lacan.)[40] This desire, it then becomes clear, is linked in Sasha's unconscious to his relations with "strange men." Platonov writes that it seemed to Sasha that he has "lost" or "spent" (utratil) the thing he found while sleeping with these strangers. His fear would appear to be that he found the thing—socialism, or an emotional substitute for it—among these men, with whom he now has relations that may seem perilously close to improperly sexual.

So in this state of unconsciousness and anxiety, Sasha rushes off in a sleepwalking haze, and gets on a train. At this point, Platonov offers the following commentary.

> Two days later Alexander remembered why he lived and where he had been sent. But within man lives a little spectator: he participates in neither actions not suffering—he is always cool and the same. His service is to see and be a witness, but he is without the right of voice in a person's life and it is not known why he solitarily exists. This corner of the person's consciousness is lit both day and night, like the doorman's room in a large building. All day and night the wakeful doorman sits in the lobby of the person, he knows all the residents of the building, but not a single resident

asks the doorman's advice about his affairs. The residents come and go, and the observer-doorman accompanies them with his eyes. Due to his powerless knowledge, he sometimes seems sad, but he is always polite, set apart, and has an apartment in another building. In the event of fire the doorman telephones the fireman and observes the events that follow from the outside.

While Dvanov rode and walked in unconsciousness, the spectator saw everything in him, although had did not once warn or help. He lived parallel to Dvanov, but he was not Dvanov.

It was as if he existed as the person's dead brother: everything human seemed to be at hand, but something small and crucial was lacking. The person never remembers him, but always entrusts himself to him, as the resident leaving his wife at home is never jealous of the doorman.

This is the eunuch of the human soul. It was to this that he was witness. (80/90–91)

In terms of narrative development, Platonov introduces this figure in order that he can narrate what Dvanov experiences during the ensuing two-day period where he is "asleep on his feet," in a stupor or state of unconsciousness (*bespamyatstvo*, a word Fyodorov used to describe our relationship to our dead ancestors).[41] So, at first, one might think that the "this" of "it was to this that he was witness" seems to refer only to what happens during these two days before Sasha "remembered why he lived and where he had been sent." But then one realizes that there has been no substantial shift in style; nor is it as if the moment when we *stop* seeing from the point of view of this watchman is clearly indicated with a marker or stylistic break. We have been seeing from the point of view of this oddly described "little spectator" all along. As Podoroga has suggested, Platonov is offering us here an allegory for his own "prose-gaze."

Like the watchman at the border of Freud's unconscious, this internal doorman never sleeps. He witnesses everything that happens to the person, but without the ability to influence or participate. At most, Platonov explains, he can call for help. But then, in a typically unexpected elaboration, Platonov adds that this watchman is "like a man's dead brother." With this, Platonov underscores the sense of a closely related but uninvolved observer, like the angel in Wim Wenders' *Wings of Desire* who looks upon the world but lacks the possibility of living in it, who cannot experience the pain and pleasures of corporeal life. Yet one is also reminded here of the desire of Sasha's father to see the world from the point of view of death. Platonov appears to be indicating that the aesthetic experience he is offering responds to the same desire to visit with death and return (which, of course, is not at all a new sort of claim to make about the attraction of writing).[42] This deathly view, as Platonov presents it, is not outside the subject or opposed to life or living subjectivity. Rather, it is as if we have always already lost a "brother," a first friend, whom we have internalized, and who watches over us. The specular structure that enables Dvanov to say to himself "here I am" is already inhabited by the trace of the other. That is to say, the point of view of death that Sasha's father thinks he sees in the eyes of the fish is interior and essential to subjectivity itself, and Platonov is proposing to see the world from there, and to remind us that we might as well.

But this is far from all he is accomplishing with his strange prose-gaze. In giving us a distanced, almost lifeless view of the world, he allows for a radical step not only out of the daily world of means-ends rationality but, even more simply, out of the thinking and feeling world in which we ask: what does this mean? what should be done? how do I feel about this? Platonov's gaze enables him to represent a range of affects that are very much "in solution" (to use Raymond Williams's phrase)[43]—affects that are in no way reducible to or understandable in terms of already existing or fixed institutions or frameworks, indeed that do not even make sense to the people experiencing them. As Podoroga has pointed out, "It is precisely the radical injunction to describe and to witness what is capable of no comprehension that defines the Platonovian gaze."[44] Thus we do not really know what is going on in the novel; the narrator does not tell us—it is left to us, as I noted, to comprehend that Kopenkin is in love with Dvanov, or that Dvanov's father was suicidally depressed, or that Dvanov has his first orgasm while clinging to the leg of a horse after he is shot in the leg by the anarchists . . . and so on. This lack of narrative knowledge is especially evident and relevant in relation to sexual desires and practices.

With the figure of the eunuch of the soul, Platonov indicates that this nonjudging, noninterpretive gaze is particularly indifferent to matters of sexual desire: no male desire here. Alluding perhaps to the eunuchs who were supposed to have guarded harems, or the Russian *skoptsi*, who castrated themselves in a literal-minded identification with the chastity of Jesus, the "eunuch of the soul" is nondesiring, asexual—indeed castrated.[45] Thus, no matter what behaviors, feelings, bodily acts, and emotional ties are represented in the field of vision of this watchman, none will be subjected to that will to knowledge that determines the "sexuality" of them. From the eunuch of the soul's point of view, it is not only the distinction between different kinds or modes of sexuality that is displaced but the distinction between the sexual and the nonsexual itself. All actions, pleasure, behaviors, relationships are on an equally neutral terrain, which becomes more and more significant as the relationships between the men in Chevengur become more apparently sexual—that is to say, bodily, intimate, and emotionally intense. Take for example, the following reunion scene between Sasha and Kopenkin.

> Kopenkin came up to Dvanov from the back; he looked at Dvanov with the greed of his friendship for him, then forgot to get off his horse. Proletarian Strength was the first to whinny at Dvanov, and then Kopenkin also got down. Dvanov stood with a sullen face—he was ashamed of his excessive feeling for Kopenkin and was afraid to express it and make a mistake.
>
> Kopenkin also had a conscience about secret relations between comrades, but he was encouraged by his happy, neighing steed.
>
> "Sasha," Kopenkin said, "you've come now? . . . let me kiss you a bit, in order to quickly stop suffering." (259–260/286)

This is one of many scenes of male affection and attraction throughout the novel.[46] Men kiss, they sleep together, they look at each other's naked bodies. At least one critic takes this as evidence of the novel's promotion of homosexuality, writing that "*Chevengur* is a *gnostic utopia resting on homosexual psychology.*"[47]

While the value of male friendship is clearly a central theme in *Chevengur,* and although the relationship between Sasha and Kopenkin looks more physically and emotionally intimate than heterosexuality would allow, it is worth remembering that in the early Soviet period there was a general "normative uncertainty" regarding sexuality, as Igor Kon put it.[48] Or as one doctor wrote during that period, "the majority of us are not clear what normal sexual attraction is."[49] There is no clear and demonstrable public and institutional interest in the distinction between homosexual and heterosexual identity (as there was, for example, for the world in which Henry James operated).[50] This is not to say that sexual relations between men were any more or less tolerated than previously, but that the epistemological pressure placed on bodies and practices associated with the emergence of a homo-hetero distinction was not present in the same way as it was in western Europe and North America. There *was,* however, debate concerning the nature of properly proletarian sexuality, and about how to produce or liberate collective desires. To some extent, inasmuch as it presupposed that sexuality was a social and not a psychological matter, this debate displaced the model that allowed for the creation of the "homosexual" as a "species" (as Foucault put it) in western Europe. In the early Soviet context, attention to the discovery or liberation of "one's own" desires was seen as a sign of a decadent, bourgeois sensibility.[51] Nevertheless, as Eric Naiman has argued in *Sex in Public,* it appears that the dominant Soviet discourse about sexuality, as it emerged through the 1920s, tended to emphasize a restrained, ascetic orientation; "sexuality" as such, inasmuch as it was articulated or discursified, was hard to disassociate from a bourgeois worldview. How this affected actual practices is less than clear.

The point, however, is that Platonov does not provide his readers with the knowledge that would allow them to say "Aha, here we have homosexuality," or "Oh that's just normal behavior among soldiers during wartime," or even "Platonov is depicting a gay utopia." This has two complementary effects. First, as I have been arguing, relieving epistemological pressure on the acts of persons is a way to displace questions of sexuality precisely in order that previously questionable acts, behaviors, and modes of affiliation can be permitted, explored, and elaborated. Platonov is freed up to depict relations between men as if sexual identity did not exist, to explore what socialist modes of affinity might look like without having to defend them against the accusations of abnormal, homosexual, perverse, or decadent sexualities. The vision of friendship Platonov is therefore allowed to present here is notable because it neither excludes nor includes what was then or would now be recognizable as "homosexuality." Thus, the emotional ties in *Chevengur* never become identities but remain situations—affects that originate not from some inner (sex or gender) core identity but from a shared space.

As readers, we can observe what bodies do, the affects that appear, and the internal workings of the mind—but it is in any event up to us as readers to supply the epistemological or ethical framework for any judgments or conclusions. This is the second effect of Platonov's narrative gaze. As readers we are thrown back on ourselves in a way it is difficult not to notice; our specific readerly reactions are difficult to attribute to the text itself. The text insists on its own indifference to its meaning.

Precisely inasmuch as it refuses to "know" anything about the world or its characters or to provide any kind of moral context for evaluating their lives and actions, Platonov's text solicits an affective, innervating response from us, what Platonov calls a "searching *toska*." "The warden held that there are no boring or meaningless books when the reader vigilantly seeks the meaning of life in them. Boring books come from boring readers, for in books it is the reader's searching *toska*, not the writer's talent, at work" (101/114). In this remark by a peripheral character, Platonov offers another of his pedagogical-allegorical moments. The move is at once self-effacing and confrontational in relation to the reader. On the one hand, he suggests that if you don't like this book (i.e., *Chevengur*), it is your fault for failing to seek the meaning of life in it attentively. But he is also saying that in any case, this book here that you happen to be reading is not special or exceptional in any way, nor is it making any claims to be the product of a talented writer. *Any* book will do if you pay attention to it in the right way. However, even if he is not making any claims for what he thinks his book can accomplish, he is making it clear what kind of reading experience he values and hopes to solicit: one in which the reader's *toska* can go to work in the text, as Zakhar's went to work in his *izdeliye*.

Ultimately, however, Platonov suggests, our searching *toska* can go to work there only in order that it may eventually shift into reverse and work its way back out (which it most certainly will do by the end of the novel if not sooner). He thus will leave us alone with a sense of our limitedness and mortality, ready for—perhaps even in desperate need of—new modes of relationality. And he shows us what these new modes might look like.

"Mutual Futile Attractions"

> Grasses passed by the carriage in the other direction, as though they were returning to Chevengur, while the half-asleep man drove forward, not looking at the stars that shined above him from the thick heights, from the eternal but already achieved future, from that quiet system in which the stars moved as comrades, not so far apart that they might forget one another and not so close together that they would flow into one and lose their differences and mutual futile attractions.
>
> —ANDREI PLATONOV, *CHEVENGUR*

As I mentioned, as Platonov describes it in *Chevengur*, there is in the early Soviet period what amounts to a general state of orphanhood. No character in *Chevengur* is not trying to develop a practice to respond to *toska* and remain interested in the world. This common emotional situation or general affect at once requires and serves as the basis for the forms of human community that come into being in *Chevengur* under the rubric of socialism. As it turns out, "making friends" becomes the main activity of Platonovian socialism, and what is necessary in order to "make friends" is the capacity for affective attunement. Thus, "the proletarian's thought works in feeling, not under the bald spot" (141/156). And this "thought working in feeling" is something for which, as we saw with Dvanov, the orphan may be particularly suited. This is one reason, as Sasha asserts, orphans are "the raw material of socialism."[52]

The star-comrade metaphor in the epigraph suggests that similarity is natural, something that one finds everywhere. In Platonov's world, similarities proliferate. "Nothing occurs without being similar to something" (101/114), remarks the same warden who made the observation about "searching *toska.*" Therefore, the making of friends is something for which the resources exist all around us. Weeds and grasses, for example, are also cited as exemplars of community and comradeship along with stars, and thus as comforts at moments of doubt or depression. "Chepurny touched a burdock—it too wanted communism: the entire weed patch was a friendship of living plants . . . just like the proletariat, this grass endures the life of heat and the death of deep snow" (198/219). As a "friendship of living plants," the weeds are inspiring, awakeners and confirmers of Chepurny's own desire for friendship and communism. Benjamin, who singled out the stars as one of the earliest sites of mimetic impulses, suggests that we "must assume in principle that processes in the sky were imitable, both collectively and individually, by people who lived in earlier times; indeed, that this imitability contained instructions for mastering an already present similarity."[53] For Platonov, as for Benjamin, the perception of similarity is linked directly to the compulsion to "become similar and behave mimetically."[54] As Sasha was comforted by his similarity to the shutters or chickens, here too Chepurny, feeling that "after all, it's scary to be alone on the eve of communism," manages to feel community at least with the weeds: "If not for the weeds, if not for the brotherly, patient grasses, similar to unhappy people, the steppe would have been unacceptable" (197/219).

Like the comrade-stars in the epigraph, the citizens of Chevengur are "not so far apart that they might forget one another and not so close together that they would flow into one and lose their differences and mutual futile attractions." Neither incommensurate nor identical, the stars make up a "plurality which persists as such."[55] Like Benjamin's collection, the socialism that forms in Chevengur is akin to a "magic circle" in which persons and objects have been relieved of their usefulness and instead placed into a constellation of similarities.[56] The incompatibility between friendship and use (a mainstay of theories of friendship since Aristotle) is a regular theme throughout *Chevengur*.[57] In the context of a burgeoning Soviet socialism, this incompatibility serves as a key element of the argument against capitalism and for the attractions of socialism. Unsuprisingly, the particular form of use that takes form in property is singled out as a special barrier to friendship: "When property lies between people, then people calmly expend their powers on worrying about the property, but when there is absolutely nothing between people, then they begin not to part from one another and to preserve one another from the cold as they sleep" (225/249).

Accordingly, uselessness or "futility" is turned into a positive goal in Chevengur. Chepurny notes that "the bourgeoisie wanted labor to have uses, but that didn't work out" (310/341). Upon his arrival in Chevengur, Serbinov observes the unusual proliferation of useless items.

> That morning Serbinov noticed on a table a frying pan made of fir wood and up on a roof an iron flag attached to a pole, a flag that could not submit to the wind . . . There were wooden wheels twelve feet across, tiny iron buttons, clay statues that resembled portraits of beloved comrades, including Dvanov, a perpetual motion machine made of a broken alarm clock, a self-heating oven stuffed with all the pillows and blankets in Chevengur, but in which only one person at a time, the coldest, could warm himself. There were other things, the functions of which Serbinov could not even imagine. (308–309/340)

Zakhar's *izdeliya* have returned, but now they are part and parcel of the production of friends. "The soul of man—that's a basic profession," a Chevengurian asserts. "And its product is friendship and comradeship! How is that not an occupation for you, tell me now" (175/195). Friendship itself has come to replace Zakhar's wooden frying pan, a noninstrumental act of creation, an "invention," as Foucault has it, of "a relationship that is still formless."[58] As Chepurny declares, "See, we don't work for usefulness [*pol'zy*] but for each other" (310/341). The Chevengurians are "happy, but useless" (310/342). Or as Serbinov remarks, perhaps it would be more accurate to say they are happy *because* useless.

Nowhere is the active production of friendship more evident than in the relationship between Kopenkin and Dvanov. "[Kopenkin] plowed not for his own food, but for the future happiness of another man, for Alexander Dvanov" (302/332). Here, Kopenkin mediates his love for Dvanov through the figure of Rosa. "Kopenkin had unstitched the portrait of Rosa Luxembourg from his cap and was now sitting, copying from his picture, because he wanted to give Dvanov a picture of Rosa Luxembourg, so that maybe he falls in love with her too." He wanted, Platonov continues, "to imperceptibly attract Dvanov to the beauty of Rosa Luxembourg and so to make some happiness for him since it was embarrassing immediately to embrace and fall in love with Dvanov" (280–281/308–309). Recalling Zakhar's earlier tinkering, Kopenkin transfers his melancholy desire to attract Dvanov onto the portrait of Rosa Luxembourg. Kopenkin's effort seems designed to sustain the shared space of mournfulness for Rosa Luxembourg, as if it is not beautiful Rosa herself that is so important but the fact that there is a *toska* to share and an occasion for sharing it.

Put differently, we might say that the portrait of Rosa is a place where Dvanov's *toska* and Kopenkin's *toska* can meet up. Before Sasha had arrived in Chevengur (to return to a passage cited earlier), Kopenkin wistfully remembered their time spent travelling in the "open fields" where "no organization was possible." There, "he had been riding beside Sasha Dvanov and when he started to feel melancholy [*toskoval*], Dvanov also felt melancholy [*toskoval*], and their melancholy [*toska*] went toward each other, and having met, stopped in the middle" (249/274). Before Dvanov's arrival, Kopenkin did not have a comrade to meet his *toska* halfway, and so instead it "continued out into the steppe, into the emptiness of the dark air, coming to an end in the lonely world." Having a comrade with his own *toska* pluralizes Kopenkin's *toska*, since the two *toskas* having met up now become a collective *toska*, *their* *toska*. Inasmuch as this affect no longer belongs to one alone but to both together, they are each also alienated from it. Resting there in this space between, the *toska* is as if concretized—there it is, halfway between us—and thus defamiliarized as well, making it available for contemplation, reflection, and as a source of motivation. The *toska* that fades away by itself in the dark, lonely world never comes to light as such; it fades away with its origins and nature unclear, never coming to rest or to a shared space.

It would appear that having Dvanov next to him not only means that Kopenkin has someone to "meet his *toska*" and stop it but that the *toska* itself is what generates the need to have someone coming toward you. And Dvanov is more than happy to return the favor.

In order to get Kopenkin to settle down in Chevengur with him, every day Alexander wrote for him from his own imagination the story of Rosa Luxembourg's life, and for Kirei, who now walked behind Dvanov with the *toska* of his friendliness and watched over him at night so he would not suddenly disappear from Chevengur, for Kirei Dvanov dragged up from the bottom of he river a small stump of black wood, because Kirei wanted to carve a wooden weapon from it. (302/332)

Sasha's time in Chevengur is devoted primarily to practices that create a place or space where *toska* can meet up. We might say that the mutual attraction between Kopenkin and Sasha is "futile," in the sense that they will never come together, instead perpetually sending out affects to meet halfway. But this space between is, for Platonov, the sine qua non of friendship. It is the place where the emotional "work" of friendship takes place, the site for its collaborative, goalless invention. Here, friendship, as a practice that distances us from one's own *toska* at the same time that it brings it into existence, invites the ferment of self-estrangement to enter one's life.

The novel, as I mentioned, ends with the slaughter of almost everyone in the village by a band of marauding Cossacks of uncertain origin and purpose. After the killing is over, Sasha, having survived, gets on Proletarian Strength and returns to his hometown, where he drowns himself in Lake Mutevo, joining his father. In the very last lines of the book we see Zakhar Pavlovich arriving in Chevengur, having decided to come look for Sasha because he misses him so much. He sees Proshka in the ruins of Chevengur, and asking him if he knows where Sasha is, offers to give him a ruble, as he did earlier, to find Sasha. Proshka offers to get him for free.

One may be tempted to read the end of the novel as a depressing allegory about the inevitable failure of utopias, or of the soon-to-come forced collectivization, purges, and other violences associated with the name of Stalin. I do not think this is what is happening here, however. On the contrary, I believe the ending is designed to at once stimulate our readerly *toska* and then blow it away like the fog of Zakhar's machine love.

Our own readerly sense of loss at the death of Sasha is amplified through our identification with Zakhar Pavlovich, who does not know Sasha is dead. Like the viewers of Hitchcock's "bomb under the table" who want to warn the characters in the film about the bomb, we too wish to tell Zakhar that Sasha is dead, that Proshka will not find him. As we imagine Zakhar's future grief, our own sadness and longing comes into existence. And then the book ends, leaving us nowhere to go with our in-the-process of transferring emotions. With Hitchcock's bomb under the table, the audience is stimulated into twenty minutes of involved anticipation—when will it go off? will they find out in time?—whereas the emotionally charged speculation Platonov initiates is abruptly truncated. We never learn whether Zakhar finds out that Sasha is dead, when or if Zakhar gives up searching, or how he feels about all this.

In other words, as the book ends, it evokes sympathetic, imitative emotions, stimulating our desire for human contact, and then leaves us nowhere to go with that desire. We are left hanging, as it were. We thus leave the novel with a *toska* for the very friendship the book has modeled and solicited, before it withdraws the offer in a final moment of loss. We are thereby disabused of any compensatory pleasures we might have gained from *Chevengur*. Just as Zakhar no longer felt in the company of his bolts and manometers after the fog of his love for machines had blown away, so too Platonov propels us away from the world of books, reminding us that in the final analysis books, like Zakhar's trains, will not help us. Instead, it is to other people and to the practice of making friends that we must turn.

Notes

Introduction

1. On the history of ideas about melancholia see the following: Jennifer Radden, "Introduction: From Melancholic States to Clinical Depression," in *The Nature of Melancholy from Aristotle to Kristeva*, ed. Radden (New York: Oxford University Press, 2000), a helpful collection of writings on melancholia; Stanley Jackson, *Melancholia and Depression: From Hippocratic Times to Modern Times* (New Haven: Yale University Press, 1986), traces the history of melancholia and depression from a more clinical point of view; Raymond Klibansky, Erwin Panofsky, and Fritz Saxl, *Saturn and Melancholy: Studies in the History of Natural Philosophy, Religion and Art* (New York: Basic Books, 1964), is organized around a reading of Dürer's *Melencolia I*; Andrew Solomon, *The Noonday Demon* (New York: Scribner, 2001), 285–334, also traces the history of views about melancholia.

2. I do not mean to suggest, however, that this is always the case or that the sense of the availability of this more positive melancholia has been equal in different historical moments or different contexts. Acedia, a medieval version of melancholia, for example, was seen as a sin. Even here, in the medieval context, we find in William Langland's *Piers Plowman*, for instance, an extended consideration of the relationship between acedia and intellectual reflection, and the suggestion that acedia may in fact promote a thoroughgoing evaluation and thus deepening of one's faith. More recently, in relation to the discovery of selective serotonin reuptake inhibitor (SSRI) antidepressants, Andrew Solomon and Peter Kramer have each argued that there is nothing redeeming about depression, that depression should absolutely be avoided when possible, a position with which I would basically agree, even as I insist on the interest and value of the opposition to depression (an opposition, of course, that would not exist without depression itself)— the attempts to avoid depression through aesthetic or other practices—by

those who know what it is to be depressed. Unlike Solomon and Kramer, I am not making a normative case about how things should be, but a descriptive one about how things have been.

3. Aristotelian Problem XXX. Probably not written by Aristotle, although authorship is unclear.

4. Robert Burton, *Anatomy of Melancholia: What it is, with all the kinds, causes, symptomes, prognostickes and severall cures of it* (New York: Vintage Books, 1977), 22. Burton's assertion that his knowledge is gotten by melancholizing and not by books is not a little ironic, since the assertion is made by way of a citation from a book, which is being read in a book, which, moreover, is thickly, almost manically, allusive to other books. On Burton, see Lawrence Babb, *The Elizabethan Malady: A Study of Melancholia in English Literature from 1580 to 1642* (East Lansing: Michigan State College Press, 1951); Ruth A. Fox, *The Tangled Chain: The Structure of Disorder in the Anatomy of Melancholy* (Berkeley: University of California Press, 1976); Bridget Gellert Lyons, *Voices of Melancholy: Studies of Literary Treatments of Melancholy in Renaissance England* (New York: Routledge and Kegan Paul, 1971), esp. 113–148; Juliet Schiesari, *The Gendering of Melancholia: Feminism, Psychoanalysis, and the Symbolics of Loss in Renaissance Literature* (Ithaca, N.Y.: Cornell University Press, 1992), 243–257.

5. Completed in 1928–1929, *Chevengur* was scheduled to be published and was reportedly at the printer when it was at the last minute censored. It was not published in full until 1988, in the Soviet journal *Khudozhestvennaya Literatura*. On the censoring of *Chevengur,* and Platonov's correspondence with Maxim Gorky about it, see Mikhail Geller, *Andrei Platonov V Poiskakh Schast'ya* (Moscow: MIK, 1999), 180–187.

6. In *The Standard Edition of the Complete Psychological Works of Sigmund Freud,* vol. 14, trans. and ed. James Strachey (London: Hogarth Press, 1957), 243–258 (hereafter MM). Strachey tells us that while the essay was not published until 1917, it was written in 1915.

7. In approaching the problem this way, my book differs from one that proposes a theory of melancholia that is then put to use in readings. One excellent book written in this mode is Esther Sanchez-Pardo, *Cultures of the Death Drive: Melanie Klein and Modernist Melancholia* (Durham, NC: Duke University Press, 2003), which develops a Kleinian paradigm. Julia Kristeva, *Black Sun: Depression and Melancholia,* trans. Leon Roudiez (New York: Columbia University Press, 1989), is probably the most influential book of this type.

To be clear: inasmuch as this book does not seek to offer a general theory of melancholia, it differs from Kristeva's and Sanchez-Pardo's work in its basic approach. Unlike Kristeva, I am interested in the emergence of a new theory of melancholia around the beginning of the twentieth century not as a more "correct" or "better" theory, but as one of many attempts to understand and explain the new affective terrain of modernity, one in which loss has become newly problematic. In this, my approach bears some similarity to the one taken by Svetlana Boym in her brilliant work *The Future of Nostalgia* (New York: Basic Books, 2001), which treats nostalgia as a kind of historical symptom or historical phenomenon itself. Kristeva, as a psychoanalyst, is more interested in an all-purpose theory with real clinical value. Questions of historical formation and collective politics, in my view, are obscured in such an approach.

As a point of reference, it may be nonetheless useful to position myself in relation to Kristeva's theory, which develops (via Lacan) the Freudian paradigm I discuss here. Kristeva writes: "I shall try to bring out, from the core of the melancholy/depressive composite, blurred as its borders may be, what pertains to a common experience of object loss and of a modification of signifying bonds" (10). For Kristeva, melancholia has a basic psychic structure that has not varied over time, even if it has taken different forms. She focuses on the key moment in child development when the infant realizes that it and the mother are not the same thing and that she can leave and does leave and will leave. This loss is as unmournable as it is foundational; it occurs before we acquire language. Indeed, for Kristeva, language arrives in order to compensate for this loss. Linguistic representation becomes necessary only when we become aware of absence and loss. Kristeva argues that this first loss must be "negated," or put aside, in order to move into language. She writes: "'I have lost an essential object that happens to be, in the final analysis, my mother' is what the speaking being seems to be saying. 'But no, I have found her again in signs, or rather since I consent to lose her I have not lost her (that is the negation), I can recover her in language'"(43).

Problems arise when we do not negate that loss but deny or disavow it. In such situations, we do not put the loss aside and instead become prone to depression, permanently rejection-sensitive. "Depressed persons . . . disavow the negation: they cancel it out, suspend it, and nostalgically fall back on the real object (the Thing) of their loss, which is just what they do not manage to lose, to which they remain painfully riveted. The denial of negation would thus be the exercise of an impossible mourning, the setting up of a fundamental sadness and an artificial unbelievable language, cut out of the painful background that is not accessible to any signifier and that intonation alone, intermittently, succeeds in inflecting" (44).

In this situation, that original loss, Loss itself, still lingers on with its full force. Every time we lose something or suffer some disappointment in adult life, it hits us with the full force of this first loss. We are left mute sufferers of our moods, incapable of transferring our affect into the symbolic realm. At best, in such a case, affects can express themselves in the semiotic realm of sighs, sounds, movements, and rhythm. Aesthetic or literary activities, then, are a way to keep at bay full-fledged symbolic collapse. They are not so much curative in a final sense; through them we do not mourn this first Loss. But they are therapeutic, providing readers with a symbolic system to borrow, as it were. With this borrowed symbolic language providing a way to put affect into language, Kristeva argues, depressive episodes can be temporarily staved off. "Aesthetic and particularly literary creation, and also religious discourse in its imaginary, fictional essence, set forth a device whose prosodic economy, interaction of characters, and implicit symbolism constitute a very faithful battle with symbolic collapse. Such a literary representation is not an elaboration in the sense of 'becoming aware' of the inter and intra psychic causes of moral suffering; that is where it diverges from the psychoanalytic course, which aims at dissolving this symptom. Nevertheless, the literary and religious representation possess a real and imaginary effectiveness that comes closer to catharsis than to elaboration; it is a therapeutic device used in all societies throughout the ages" (24).

I should perhaps emphasize here that I do not think that Kristeva is *incorrect*. She has proposed an impressive and viable paradigm, one that can explain not only some modes of depression for some people but also one important way aesthetic activity has served a not quite curative but nonetheless helpful function for some depressed persons. And, in fact, some of the texts here, certain aspects of Du Bois and Platonov, for example, could be interestingly read in relation to this Kristevan paradigm. My difference with her, as I mentioned, lies on the level of project. Rather than a universal theory focused toward the development of individual cures, or an emphasis on the more universal aspects of melancholia, I am much more concerned with the way modernist melancholias are responses to a historical situation, responses that encode resistances to that situation and solicit a collective participation in such resistance.

8. *The Psychic Life of Power: Theories in Subjection* (Stanford: Stanford University Press, 1997). Judith Butler's examination of the tension between Freud's two different positions on melancholia and its implications for our understanding of gender identification in the "Melancholia of Gender" section of *Gender Trouble: Feminism and the Subversion of Identity* (New York: Routledge, 1990) was important for my earliest thinking about this project; see also her *Bodies That Matter: On the Discursive Limits of "Sex"* (New York: Routledge, 1993), and on mourning more specifically see *Antigone's Claim: Kinship between Life and Death* (New York: Columbia University Press, 2000).

9. Walter Benjamin, "N [On the Theory of Knowledge, Theory of Progress]," in *The Arcades Project*, trans. Howard Eiland and Kevin Mclaughlin (Cambridge: Harvard University Press, 1999), 481.

10. This remark is from a section entitled "Something for the Industrious," in *The Gay Science*, trans. Walter Kaufmann (New York: Vintage Books, 1974), 81–82.

11. Heidegger defines and discusses *Stimmung* in *Being and Time*, trans. John Macquarrie and Edward Robinson (San Francisco: Harper and Row, 1962), esp. 172–179, from the German edition, *Sein und Zeit* (Tubingen: Niemeyer,

1979) (hereafter BT), 134–140. References hereafter will be to this translation rather than the more recent one by Joan Stambaugh (Albany: State University of New York Press, 1996). The Stambaugh version has its advantages, and I frequently consulted it, but her translation of *Befindlichkeit* as "attunement," while much better than Macquarrie and Robinson's "state-of-mind," is confusing because "attunement" is also often a translation of *Stimmung*. For a helpful review of the Stambaugh translation see Theodore Kisiel, "The New Translation of *Sein und Zeit*: A Grammatological Lexicographer's Commentary," in Kisiel, *Heidegger's Way of Thought* (New York: Continuum, 2002), 64–83.

A somewhat more approachable and differently developed examination of *Stimmung* can be found in Heidegger's lectures of 1929–1930, collected as *The Fundamental Concepts of Metaphysics: World, Finitude, Solitude* (Bloomington, Indiana: Indiana State University Press, 1995) trans. William McNeill and Nicholas Walker (hereafter FCM), esp. 59–69. McNeill and Walker translate *Stimmung* as "attunement," which has the benefit of communicating the sense of the noun *Stimme*, which can refer to the voice, and the verb *stimmen*, one meaning of which is "to tune." Whichever word I use here (and I will use both), I have tried to keep in mind both the everyday-ness of the word *mood* and the metaphorics of tune and tuning in *attunement*.

12. Guignon, "Moods in Heidegger's Being and Time," in *What Is an Emotion?* ed. Cheshire Calhoun and Robert C. Solomon (New York: Oxford University Press, 1984), 239.

13. See Leo Bersani, *The Culture of Redemption* (Berkeley: University of California Press, 1989), for an analysis and critique of this redemptive tendency within modernism.

14. As one example among many, see Donald Kuspit, *The Cult of the Avant-Garde Artist* (New York: Cambridge University Press, 1993), where he argues for the fundamentally "therapeutic" nature of modernist art.

15. On melancholy in Baudelaire, see Ross Chambers, *The Writing of Melancholy: Modes of Opposition in Early French Modernism*, trans. Mary Seidman Trouille (Chicago: University of Chicago Press, 1993); on melancholy in nineteenth-century French literature more broadly see Naomi Schor, *One Hundred Years of Melancholy* (Oxford: Clarendon Press, 1996).

16. The full sentence reads: "The decisively new ferment that enters the *taedium vitae* and turns it into spleen is self-estrangement." From "Central Park" (hereafter CP), in *Walter Benjamin, Selected Writings*, vol. 4 (Cambridge: Harvard University Press, 2003) (hereafter SW4), 163. Here "self-estrangement" is a translation of *Selbstentfremdung*, *Entfremdung* being the "alienation" of Marx and not the Brechtian *Verfremdung* of the "V-effect" or "alienation effect."

17. See, for example, Joseph Brodsky, "Catastrophes in Air," in *Less Than One: Selected Essays* (New York: Farrar, Straus, and Giroux, 1986), and

Tatyana Tolstaya, "Andrei Platonov's Unusual World," in *Pushkin's Children: Writings on Russia and Russians* (New York: Houghton Mifflin, 2003), 218–226.

18. Recent excellent books of this type would include, for example, Paul Gilroy, *The Black Atlantic* (Cambridge: Harvard University Press, 2000), and Brent Edwards, *The Practice of Diaspora* (Cambridge: Harvard University Press, 2003). Concerning the relation between the Russian and the African American traditions in particular, of which there is much of interest to be said, see Kate Baldwin, *Beyond the Color Line and the Iron Curtain: Reading Encounters between Black and Red, 1922–1963* (Durham, NC: Duke University Press, 2002), and Dale Peterson, *Up from Bondage: The Literatures of Russian and African American Soul* (Durham, NC: Duke University Press, 2000).

Glossary

1. In the humanities, a nonexhaustive list of recent books focusing extensively and explicitly on theories of affect or emotion might include: Sianne Ngai, *Ugly Feelings* (Cambridge: Harvard University Press, 2005); Sara Ahmed, *The Cultural Politics of Emotion* (New York: Routledge, 2004); Charles Altieri, *The Particulars of Rapture: The Aesthetics of the Affects* (Ithaca, NY: Cornell University Press, 2003); Philip Fisher, *The Vehement Passions* (Princeton: Princeton University Press, 2002); Brian Massumi, *Parables of the Virtual* (Durham, NC: Duke University Press, 2002), esp. "The Autonomy of Affect" 23–45; William Reddy, *The Navigation of Feeling: A Framework for the History of the Emotions* (Cambridge, UK: Cambridge University Press, 2001); Rei Terada, *Feeling in Theory* (Cambridge: Harvard University Press, 2001). In philosophy, the most formidable recent contribution is Martha Nussbaum, *Upheavals of Thought: The Intelligence of Emotions* (Cambridge, UK: Cambridge University Press, 2001). Also see Aaron Ben Ze'ev, *The Subtlety of Emotions* (Cambridge: MIT Press, 2000); Paul Griffiths, *What Emotions Are: The Problem of Psychological Categories* (Chicago: University of Chicago Press, 1997); Michael Stocker with Elizabeth Hegeman, *Valuing Emotions* (Cambridge, UK: Cambridge University Press, 1996). From a more continental/intellectual history perspective see Paul Redding, *The Logic of Affect* (Ithaca, NY: Cornell University Press, 1999). While *Shame and Its Sisters: A Silvan Tomkins Reader* ed. Eve Kosofsky Sedgwick and Adam Frank (Durham, NC: Duke University Press, 1995) (hereafter designated SIS), was a compilation of earlier work by Silvan Tomkins, it contributed, along with Sedgwick and Frank's "Shame in the Cybernetic Fold: Reading Silvan Tomkins" included therein and Sedgwick's essays collected in *Touching Feeling: Affect, Pedagogy, Performativity* (Durham, NC: Duke University Press, 2003), to the resurgence of interest in affect, not least my own. Paul Ekman, *Emotions Revealed* (New York: Holt, 2003), introduces a general audience to his influential research on fa-

cial behavior and emotion; Daniel Goleman's bestseller *Emotional Intelligence* (New York: Bantam, 1995), despite its ideological bent toward normality, offers a surprisingly wide-ranging and helpful survey of and introduction to work on affect and emotion in psychology and neuroscience; Rosalind Picard's lucid *Affective Computing* (Cambridge: MIT Press, 1997) examines the fascinating attempt to theorize and create computers with affects. There is also a great deal of recent neuroscientific research; on this, see Joseph LeDoux, *The Emotional Brain: The Mysterious Underpinnings of Emotional Life* (New York: Simon and Schuster, 1996), and Antonio Damasio, *Descartes' Error* (New York: Harper, 1995), *The Feeling of What Happens: Body and Emotion in the Making of Consciousness* (New York: Harcourt, Brace, 1999), and *Looking for Spinoza: Joy, Sorrow, and the Feeling Brain* (New York: Harcourt, 2003). I should also mention here two helpful recent anthologies: Robert Solomon, ed., *What Is an Emotion? Classic and Contemporary Readings* (New York: Oxford University Press, 2003), assembles important writings on emotion from the history of philosophy and psychology along with influential recent work; eds., Paul Ekman and Richard J. Davidson, *The Nature of Emotion: Fundamental Questions* (New York: Oxford University Press, 1994), excerpts important work (mostly) in psychology from different representative positions and organizes these writings around key debates on such questions as whether there are basic emotions and whether we can control our emotions.

Other books engaged with affect thematically, historically or theoretically that have influenced my thinking about these matters include Ann Cvetkovich, *An Archive of Feelings: Trauma, Sexuality and Lesbian Public Cultures* (Durham, NC: Duke University Press, 2003); Ranjana Khanna, *Dark Continents: Psychoanalysis and Colonialism* (Durham: Duke University Press, 2003); Douglas Crimp, *Melancholia and Moralism: Essays on AIDS and Queer Politics* (Cambridge: MIT Press, 2002); Anne Anlin Cheng, *The Melancholia of Race: Psychoanalysis, Assmilation, and Hidden Grief* (Oxford: Oxford University Press, 2001); Svetlana Boym, *The Future of Nostalgia* (New York: Basic Books, 2001); José Esteban Muñoz, *Disidentifications: Queers of Color and the Performance of Politics* (Minneapolis: University of Minnesota Press, 1999).

2. Happily, books such as Redding, *The Logic of Affect*, LeDoux, *The Emotional Brain*, and Altieri, *The Particulars of Rapture* supply accessible overviews of the range of work on affect from usefully different intellectual perspectives. In his *Logic of Affect*, Redding traces the emergence of "cognitivist" approaches to affect in relation to Jamesian views and then the reaction to cognitivist views. See his introduction and chap. 1, "Affect in Twentieth Century Thought." Altieri engages and argues with much of the recent work in philosophy, examining how debates there relate to the relation between affect and aesthetics. I found Le Doux's presentation of recent neuroscientific work on the emotions in *The Emotional Brain* most readable and persuasive of the several such accounts. But also see useful sum-

mary accounts of recent work in the aforementioned works by Reddy, Ngai, Terada, and Ahmed.

3. This difference is underscored by the etymology of the words, *emotion* originating in the Latin *emovere,* or to move out. *Affect,* on the other hand, is linked to acting or acting on; affect refers to the effect of actions on one, how one has been affected.

4. Aristotle, *Rhetoric,* 1378a20, in *The Basic Works of Aristotle,* trans. W. Rhys Roberts, ed. Richard McKeon (New York: Modern Library, 2001), 1380.

5. For an overview of Tomkins's theory of affect see his "What Are Affects," in SIS, 33–74, and "The Quest for Primary Motives: Biography and Auto-biography of an Idea," in Tomkins, *Exploring Affect: The Selected Writings of Silvan S. Tomkins* ed. E. Virginia Demos (Cambridge, UK: Cambridge University Press, 1995), 27–63.

6. Tomkins, "Quest for Primary Motives," 32. Tomkins notes, for instance, how pilots during World War II experienced no panic as the result of the deprivation of oxygen from flying too high, indeed appeared to experience pleasure, which was of course a problem because it prevented them from taking action to save themselves.

7. William James, "What Is an Emotion?" (1884), 66–76, in Solomon, *What Is an Emotion,* 67.

8. Stanley Schachter and Jerome E. Singer, from "Cognitive, Social and Physiological Determinants of Emotional State" (1962), in Solomon, *What Is an Emotion,* 111–118.

9. Martha Nussbaum takes a strong version of the cognitivist position, arguing that emotions are rational judgments that are valuable precisely for this reason. She sums up her view this way: "This view holds that emotions are appraisals or value judgments, which ascribe to things and persons outside the person's own control great importance for that person's own flourishing. It thus contains three salient ideas: the idea of a cognitive appraisal or evaluation; the idea of one's own flourishing or one's important goals and projects; and the idea of the salience of external objects as elements in one's own scheme of goals" (*Upheavals of Thought,* 4).

It should be said, however, that to a great extent, where one falls in the cognitivist debate depends on where one draws the line around cognition, and one's investment in the rhetorical leverage one gets by calling something cognitive or not. Tomkins, for example, does contend that affects process information and in effect make judgments; for Nussbaum this would make them "cognitive." Tomkins would insist, contra Nussbaum, on the specific feeling quality of affect, on the particular phenomenology of the world experienced by way of affects, and on the specific way affects process information as being essentially different from "reason." The affects serve a function, for Tomkins, that thinking in itself cannot; thinking cannot make us *care* about things. Thus, if for no other reason, because of the central importance of this function for human life, it is worth emphasizing the specific nature of affect in order to value and appreciate this function. Also see Altieri for a sustained critique of Nussbaum's argument.

10. Tomkins, "Quest for Primary Motives," 35. See Tomkins's critique of cognitive theory also in *Affect, Imagery, Consciousness*, vol. 3 (New York: Springer, 1991), 44–62.

11. Other influential defenses of the irreducibility or autonomy of affect include those made by Robert Zajonc, "Feeling and Thinking: Preferences Need No Inferences," *American Psychologist* 35 (1980): 151–175, and the synoptic "On the Primacy of Affect," in *Approaches to Emotion*, ed. Paul Ekman and Klaus Scherer (Hillsdale, NJ: Erlbaum, 1984), 259–270, and Jaak Panksepp, in *Affective Neuroscience: The Foundations of Human and Animal Emotions* (New York: Oxford University Press, 1998), and "The Basics of Basic Emotion," excerpted in Ekman and Davidson, *The Nature of Emotion*, 20–24.

12. Le Doux, *Emotional Brain*, 69.

13. Le Doux sums up his argument for the separateness of emotion and cognition in ibid., 69–70. Damasio talks about one of these brain-damaged patients in *Descartes's Error*, 43. See also Le Doux, "The Emotional Brain Revisited," in his later *The Synaptic Self* (New York: Penguin Books, 2002).

14. There are several different ideas about what the basic affects are, although fear, anger, distress, and joy appear on most lists. Tomkins, for example, at first theorizes that there are eight basic affects (shame, disgust, interest, joy, fear, anger, surprise, and distress) and then later revises the number to nine as he distinguishes "dismell" from disgust. Deciding for once and all which affects are basic and which are not seems less important to me than the heuristic value of considering the implications of basic affects and treating some affects if they were evolutionarily developed basic human systems like the senses or our capacity to comprehend spatial relationships.

15. Darwin, *Expression of the Emotions in Man and Animals* (New York: Philosophical Library, 1955) (orig. pub. 1872); Ekman, *Emotions Revealed*, and, among others, Paul Ekman, E. R. Sorenson, and W. V. Friesen, "Pan-Cultural Elements in Facial Display of Emotions," *Science* 164 (1969): 86–88; Carrol Izard, *The Face of Emotion* (New York: Appleton-Century-Crofts, 1971).

16. Ekman's first study, in which he showed images of facial expressions to people in Chile, Argentina, Brazil, Japan, and the United States, found that the majority in each cultural setting agreed about which emotion was being expressed by which facial behavior. He refined and repeated his studies in many different contexts, including preliterate cultures in Papua New Guinea. Ekman tells this story in "Emotions across Cultures," the first chapter of *Emotions Revealed*. Unsurprisingly, Ekman's argument has been contested from a number of different positions; Reddy surveys some of these from the area of cognitive psychology in *The Navigation of Feeling*, 12–13; see also Nussbaum's critique, *Upheavals of Thought*, 158–160.

17. Reddy does a good job of summarizing and synthesizing recent anthropological work on emotion in *The Navigation of Feeling*. For one influential anthropological account of emotion see Catherine Lutz, *Unnatural Emotions* (Chicago: University of Chicago Press, 1988).

18. For more on systems theory see William Rasch and Cary Wolfe, "Introduction: Systems Theory and the Politics of Postmodernity," in *Observing Complexity: Systems Theory and Postmodernity* (Minneapolis: University of Minnesota Press, 2000). Also see Steven Joshua Heims, *Constructing a Social Science for Postwar America: The Cybernetics Group, 1946–1953* (Cambridge: MIT Press, 1993), and Sedgwick and Frank, "Shame in the Cybernetic Fold."

19. The phrase is from Niklas Luhmann, "Modernity in Contemporary Society," in *Observations on Modernity* (Stanford: Stanford University Press, 1998), 1.

20. Ronald de Sousa, for example, writes: "For a variable but always limited time, an emotion limits the range of information that the organism will take into account, the inferences actually drawn from a potential infinity, and the set of live options among which it will choose." *The Rationality of Emotions* (Cambridge: MIT University Press, 1987), 195.

21. Gilles Deleuze and Felix Guattari, *Anti-Oedipus: Capitalism and Schizophrenia*, trans. Robert Hurley, Mark Seem and Helen R. Lane (Minneapolis: University of Minnesota Press, 1983), 6.

22. Along similar lines, Brain Massumi writes that "an emotion is a subjective content, the sociolinguistic fixing of the quality of an experience which is from that point onward defined as personal"; "The Autonomy of Affect," in *Deleuze Reader*, ed. Paul Patton (Oxford: Blackwell, 1996), 221. While I am not at all certain that emotions cannot be collective, I see the usefulness of having a term to talk about those experiences of affect that *are* more fixed and located squarely in the personal. But, for my purposes, Massumi's concepts of emotion and affect are too specific; they leave too much out. This is especially true regarding his understanding of affect, which he, very much like Schachter and Singer, sees as a kind of irreducible, nonassimilable intensity ("intensity is the inassimilable"). Whereas affect is nonsubjective because it exceeds subjectivity, as a moment of disorienting intensity, emotion would be the term to describe our internal, iterable, recognizable experience of an affect: "emotion is qualified intensity, the conventional, consensual point of insertion of intensity into semantically and semiotically formed progressions, into narrativizable action-reaction circuits, into function and meaning. It is intensity owned and realized" (221). It is the apparent valorization of affect as the "inassimilable," and the all too handy opposition between (pure? transcendent?) affect-as-intensity and ("conventional," "owned") emotion that seems least helpful to me here.

23. "If an imputed characteristic of an object is capable of evoking a particular affect, the evocation of that affect is also capable of producing a subjective restructuring of the object so that it possesses the imputed characteristic

which is capable of evoking that effect. . . . The object may evoke the affect, or the affect find the object." "What Are Affects," in SIS, 54–55.

24. Benjamin famously discusses the distinction between *Erfahrung* and *Erlebnis* (which he parallels to the distinction between voluntary and involuntary memory) in the opening sections of "On Some Motifs in Baudelaire," in *Walter Benjamin: Selected Writings*, vol. 4 (Cambridge: Harvard University Press, 2003) (hereafter SW4).

25. Benjamin, "One Way Street," in *Walter Benjamin: Selected Writings*, vol. 1 (Cambridge: Harvard University Press, 1996) (hereafter SW1), 449.

26. "In this picture," Benjamin wrote, "all factuality is already 'theory' and therefore it refrains from any deductive abstraction, and prognostication, and, within certain bounds, even any judgment." He hoped "to take materialism so seriously that the historical phenomena themselves were brought to speech." From a 1927 letter to Martin Buber, in *The Correspondence of Walter Benjamin*, ed. Gershom Scholem and Theodor Adorno, trans. Manfred Jacobsen and Evelyn Jacobsen (Chicago: University of Chicago Press, 1994), 313. Benjamin is writing here apropos his trip to Moscow, which he hoped would result in this concept-less writing.

27. Jean Paul Sartre, *The Emotions: Outline of a Theory*, trans. Bernard Frechtman (New York: Philosophical Library, 1948).

28. Ibid., 58–59.

29. Another relevant example is Sartre's explanation for "passive sadness," i.e., depression. See ibid., 65.

30. Emotions are, he writes, "a spontaneous and lived degradation of consciousness in the face of the world." Ibid., 77. It should be noted that Sartre's theory does have the dialectical advantage of making emotions into a kind of photographic negative of the world; insofar as they are magical transformations in response to obstacles, our emotions then offer us a picture of what is missing, and thereby, indirectly, point the way toward transformation.

31. Although I am appropriating Heidegger's understanding of *Stimmung* here, I do not, however, want to give the impression that mood has not been explored in other contexts. Indeed, within psychology, depression is frequently understood as a "mood disorder," and there is some general agreement that moods, in distinction from affects, are nonintentional and longer in duration. The historical, collective emphasis we find in Heidegger, however, is relatively unique. For a more specifically psychoanalytic perspective on depression as a mood, see Edith Jacobsen, *Depression* (New York: International Universities Press, 1971). Also see the second section of Ekman and Davidson, *The Nature of Emotion*, "Question 2: How Are Emotions Distinguished from Moods, Temperament, and Other Related Affective Constructs?" 49–96.

32. Heidegger: "The dominance of the public way in which things have been interpreted has already been decisive even for the possibilities of having a mood—that is for the basic way in which Dasein lets the world 'matter' to

it. The 'they' prescribes one's state of mind, and determines what and how one 'sees.'" *Being and Time*, trans. John Macquarrie and Edward Robinson (San Francisco: Harper and Row, 1962) (hereafter BT), 213.

33. Charles Guignon, "Moods in Heidegger's Being and Time," in *What Is an Emotion? Classic Readings in Philosophical Psychology*, ed. Cheshire Calhoun and Robert C. Solomon (New York: Oxford University Press, 1984), 233. I also found helpful the commentaries on Heidegger and *Stimmung* in Michel Haar, "The Primacy of Stimmung over Dasein's Bodiliness," in *Heidegger and the Grounds of the History of Being*, trans. Reginald Lilly (Bloomington: Indiana University Press, 1993), 34–46; Hubert L. Dreyfus, *Being-in-the-World: A Commentary on Heidegger's Being and Time, Division I* (Cambridge: MIT University Press, 1991), esp. 168–183; Bruce W. Ballard, *The Role of Mood in Heidegger's Ontology* (Lanham, MD: University Press of America, 1991). There are also discussions of *Stimmung* in Stephen Mulhall, "Can There Be an Epistemology of Moods," in *Verstehen and Humane Understanding* (Cambridge, UK: Cambridge University Press, 1996), 191–210; William D. Blattner, *Heidegger's Temporal Idealism* (Cambridge, UK: Cambridge University Press, 1999), esp. 31–53; Miguel de Beistegui, *Thinking with Heidegger: Displacements* (Bloomington: Indiana University Press, 2003), esp. chap. entitled "Boredom," 61–80. See also Thomas Pfau, *Romantic Moods: Paranoia, Trauma and Melancholy, 1790–1840* (Baltimore: Johns Hopkins University Press, 2005), and Sianne Ngai, *Ugly Feelings*, esp. chap. 5, "Anxiety," 209–247.

34. It seems as if every commentator and translator has a different translation of *Befindlichkeit*: "state-of-mind," which the Macquarrie and Robinson translation uses, everyone agrees is wrong, inasmuch as it is precisely not "mind" Heidegger is concerned with; Joan Stambaugh's translation of *Being and Time* settles on "attunement," which is confusing since it is also a common translation of *Stimmung*, as in William McNeill and Nicholas Walker *The Fundamental Concepts of Metaphysics*; Herbert Dreyfus translates it as "affectedness;" Charles Guignon as "situatedness"; several others use "disposition."

35. Haar, "Primacy of Stimmung," 37.

36. "A mood assails us. It comes neither from 'outside' nor from 'inside', but arises out of Being-in-the-world, as a way of such Being." BT, 176.

37. I reference here the opening poem of *Les Fleurs du Mal*, "Au Lecteur" ("To the Reader").

38. This was depicted in the excellent film *This Is What Democracy Looks Like* (2000).

39. On the League of Black Revolutionary Workers, see the very interesting film *Finally Got the News*, and Dan Georgakis and Marvin Surkin, *Detroit, I Do Mind Dying: A Study in Urban Revolution* (Cambridge: South End Press, 1998).

40. His most detailed discussion of "structure of feeling" is in *Marxism and Literature* (New York: Oxford University Press, 1977); he offers occasional

elaborations of the concept in different places throughout his writing; see in particular *Drama from Ibsen to Brecht* (London: Hogarth Press, 1987).

41. *Marxism and Literature*, 132.
42. Jameson, *The Political Unconscious* (Ithaca, NY: Cornell University Press, 1981), 102.

1. Modernism and Melancholia

1. On modernity and time see Matei Calinescu, "The Idea of Modernity," in *Five Faces of Modernity: Modernism, Avant-Garde, Decadence, Kitsch, Postmodernism* (Durham, NC: Duke University Press, 1987), which provides a useful history of the word "modernity"; Peter Osborne, *The Politics of Time: Modernity and Avant-Garde* (London: Verso, 1995); Reinhart Koselleck, *Futures Past: On the Semantics of Historical Time*, trans. Keith Tribe (Cambridge: MIT Press, 1985); and David Harvey, *The Condition of Postmodernity* (Oxford: Blackwell, 1989), esp. pt. 3, "The Experience of Space and Time," 201–323.
2. In *A Singular Modernity* (London: Verso, 2002), Fredric Jameson proposes: "Modernity is not a concept, philosophical or otherwise, but a narrative category" (40).
3. In *Five Faces of Modernity*, Calinescu writes that the "maxim about the dwarf standing on the shoulders of a giant and thus being able to see farther than the giant himself can be traced back to Bernard of Chartres, who died in 1126" (15).
4. Dava Sobel, *Longitude* (New York: Walker, 1995).
5. See F. W. Taylor, *The Principles of Scientific Management* (New York: Norton, 1967). Also see David Harvey on the Taylorist and Fordist projects and on space-time compression, in *The Condition of Postmodernity* (Cambridge, UK: Blackwell, 1989).
6. Cited by Walter Benjamin in "The Storyteller: Observations on the Works of Nikolai Leskov," in *Walter Benjamin: Selected Writings*, vol. 3 (Cambridge: Harvard University Press, 2002) (hereafter SW3), 150.
7. On the more recent Bolivian peasant response to the arrival of capital, see Michael Taussig, *The Devil and Commodity Fetishism in South America* (Chapel Hill: University of North Carolina Press, 1980).
8. On the phrase "all that is solid . . ." from *The Communist Manifesto* as a figure for the experience of modernity more broadly (not only in relation to religion) see Marshall Berman, *All That Is Solid Melts into Air: The Experience of Modernity* (New York: Penguin, 1982), and Perry Anderson's provocative response to it, "Modernity and Revolution," in *A Zone of Engagement* (London: Verso, 1992). Berman discusses the destructive elements of modernization, but emphasizes the liberatory aspect of the destruction of tradition and the possibility of constant change. Anderson objects to Berman's essentially liberal reading of Marx, reminding readers

that when Marx and Engels wrote of all that is solid melting into air, they were describing a specific destructive aspect of capitalism, and in fact, one of the elements of capital that would eventually lead to its undoing. On modernity and modernism in relation to religion, see Harvie Ferguson, *Melancholy and the Critique of Modernity: Soren Kierkegaard's Religious Psychology* (New York: Routledge. 1995), which argues that Kierkegaard's "religious psychology of modern life" is devoted to the task of overcoming a modern, despair-inducing melancholy.

9. See Wolfgang Schivelbusch, *The Railway Journey* (Berkeley: University of California Press, 1987), on this phenomenon.

10. See Georg Simmel, "The Metropolis and Mental Life" (1903), in *Georg Simmel on Individuality and Social Form* (Chicago: University of Chicago Press, 1971), 324–339, and Walter Benjamin's discussion of Simmel in "On Some Motifs in Baudelaire" (hereafter MB), in *Walter Benjamin: Selected Writings*, vol. 4 (Cambridge: Harvard University Press, 2003) (hereafter SW4), 313–355.

11. Here I am thinking of Foucault's studies of new discourses and institutions of normalization, in particular *Madness and Civilization, Discipline and Punish*, and the *History of Sexuality*, vol. 1.

12. "The Fact of Blackness" (1952), in *Black Skin, White Masks*, translated Charles Lam Markmann, 109–140 (New York: Grove Press, 1967).

13. On this theme see Alexander and Margarete Mitscherlich's now classic study *The Inability to Mourn: Principles of Collective Behavior*, trans. Beverly R. Placzek (New York: Grove Press, 1975).

14. Freud wrote several texts dealing with the war and death more directly during the period in which he wrote "Mourning and Melancholia," in particular "Thoughts for the Times on War and Death," and "On Transience," both in *The Standard Edition of the Complete Psychological Works of Sigmund Freud*, vol. 14, trans. and ed. James Strachey (London: Hogarth Press, 1957). It was not only the sheer quantity of deaths that was shocking but also the unexpected and complete refutation of the Enlightenment and ideas of progress offered by the human capacity for mass violence.

15. Habermas's defense of the project of modernity as well as his refined development of what that project is can be found in pointed polemic form in "Modernity: An Unfinished Project" (1980), in *The Anti-Aesthetic*, ed. Hal Foster (Port Townsend, WA: Bay Press, 1983), 3–15. See *The Philosophical Discourse of Modernity* for his extended consideration of the philosophy of modernity. Richard B. Pippin, *Modernism as a Philosophical Problem* (Cambridge: Blackwell, 1991), is also helpful in sorting through philosophical responses to modernity.

16. Peter Hamilton, "The Enlightenment and the Birth of Social Science," offers a good overview of the ideologies and social formations comprising the Enlightenment. In Stuart Hall, Kenneth Thompson, Don Hubert, and David Held, eds., *Modernity; An Introduction of Modern Societies* (London: Blackwell, 1996), 19–54.

17. The "learned helplessness" model of depression was developed by Martin Seligman; see *Helplessness: On Depression, Development and Death* (New York: Freeman, 1975). It was based initially on observations of the depressive effects of contrived helplessness in laboratory animals. Basically, Seligman found that the repeated experience of powerlessness produced the symptoms of depression. The theory is clinically and conceptually suggestive, but kind of thin theoretically, in that he basically defines depression *as* learned helplessness, without really engaging with the full range of experiences that have been understood as depression, nor with other theories of depression.

18. Tomkins writes: "In contrast to the paranoid, the depressed one has not been driven out of the Garden of Eden by the flaming sword of the guardian angel, by terror. He has rather been lectured and reproved by a more loving but more ambitious God, who has tried to show him the error of his ways and who has expressed not only his scorn but his deep disappointment in his favorite son. This god wishes to make man in his own image, to form his will, not to break it, to inspire love and respect and identification with himself rather than to forbid complete identification," in *Shame and Its Sisters: A Silvan Tomkins Reader*, ed. Eve Kosofsky Sedgwick and Adam Frank (Durham, NC: Duke University Press, 1995), 221.

19. Indeed, it is this contestation itself that might best characterize modernism—the moment when what "art" should or should not do becomes openly contested, when the role of art is no longer received knowledge or an institutionalized fact. As Adorno put it in the opening sentence of *Aesthetic Theory*, trans. Robert Hullot-Kentor (Minneapolis: University of Minnesota Press), "It is self-evident that nothing concerning art is self-evident anymore, not its inner life, not its relation to the world, not even its right to exist" (1).

20. Raymond Klibanksy, Erwin Panofsky, Fritz Saxl, *Saturn and Melancholy* (New York: Basic Books, 1964), 3.

21. Galen, "Function of Diseases of Brain and Spinal Cord," in *Diseases of the Black Bile*, from *On the Affected Parts*, trans. Rudolph E. Siegel (Basel: S. Karger, 1976), excerpted in *The Nature of Melancholy from Aristotle to Kristeva*, ed. Jennifer Radden (New York: Oxford University Press, 2000), 68.

22. For example, in his *Lincoln's Melancholy: How Depression Challenged a President and Fueled His Greatness* (New York: Houghton-Mifflin, 2005), Joshua Shenk describes the cure for melancholia that Lincoln seems likely to have sought during one of his most serious bouts of depression, in 1841. The treatment, drawing from the work of Benjamin Rush, was based still on the humoral theory, designed to purge the excess of black bile in one way or another with starvation, bleeding, and various purgatives. See 58–62; also Benjamin Rush, "Of Partial Intellectual Derangement, and Particularly of Hypochondriasis," in *Medical Inquiries and Observations upon the Diseases of the Mind* (Philadelphia: Kimball and Richardson, 1812), excerpted in Radden, *Melancholy*, 211–217.

23. Klibanksy et al., *Saturn and Melancholy*, 3.
24. *Hippocratic Writings*, ed. G. E. R. Lloyd (New York: Penguin Classics, 1983), 262.
25. See Klibansky et al., *Saturn and Melancholy*, 30.
26. For their discussion of the Aristotelian text see ibid., 15–41. The relevant Platonic text is the *Phaedrus*.
27. Cited by Stanley Jackson, *Melancholia and Depression: From Hippocratic Times to Modern Times* (New Haven: Yale University Press, 1986), 67. Cassian lived 360–435.
28. Translation from Greek meaning literally "noncaring state," and suggesting heedlessness, sluggishness, torpor. See ibid., 65. Also Cassian, *Of the Spirit of Accidie*, in *The Foundations of the Cenobitic Life and the Eight Capital Sins* (Grand Rapids, MI: Eerdmans, 1955), excerpted in Radden, *Melancholy*, 71–74.
29. Cited by Jackson, *Melancholia*, 67.
30. *Three Books on Life: A Critical Edition and Translation*, trans. and ed. Carol V. Kaske and John R. Clark (Binghamton, NY: Center for Medieval and Early Renaissance Studies, 1989). See discussion of Ficino in Klibanksy et al., *Saturn and Melancholy*, 254–274.
31. Klibanksy et al., *Saturn and Melancholy*.
32. See Radden's discussion of the debates about the singularity or multiplicity of melancholia, in introduction to Radden, *Melancholy*. In part, the multiplicity of types of melancholy owes something to the popularity of melancholy, its emergence as a mode of self-fashioning. For example, Shakespeare: "I have neither the scholar's melancholy, which is emulation; not the musicians, which is fantastical; not the courtier's, which is proud; not the soldier's, which is ambitious; nor the lawyer's, which is politic; nor the lady's, which is nice; nor the lover's, which is all of these; but it is a melancholy of mine own, compounded of many simples, extracted from many objects." *As You Like It*, act 4, scene 1.
33. Julia Kristeva, *Black Sun: Depression and Melancholia*, trans. Leon Roudiez (New York: Columbia University Press, 1989), 3.
34. Robert Burton, *Anatomy of Melancholia* (New York: Vintage Books, 1977), 20.
35. Kristeva, *Black Sun*, 3.
36. Burton develops the idea that the melancholic state of mind may be uniquely suited to intellectual pursuit, not only inasmuch as it helps one avoid melancholy, but in a more fundamentally constitutional way. However, at the same time, he acknowledges that the life of the mind may *make* one melancholy, in part because such a life tends to be both solitary and physically idle.
37. *The Origin of German Tragic Drama*, trans. John Osborne [*Ursprung des deutschen Trauerspiels*] New York: Verso 1977 (hereafter OGT), 140. Anselm Haverkamp, "Mourning Becomes Melancholia: The Leaves of Books," in

Leaves of Mourning: Holderlin's Late Work with an Essay on Keats and Melancholy, trans. Vernon Chadwick (Albany: State University of New York Press, 1996), 101–115, interestingly suggests that Benjamin's use of the term *Trauerspiel* or "mourning-play" references the "work of mourning" or *Trauer arbeiten* Freud describes in "Mourning and Melancholia."

38. Lawrence Babb, *The Elizabethan Malady: A Study of Melancholia in English Literature from 1580 to 1642* (East Lansing: Michigan State College Press, 1951), 184.

39. Ibid., 184–185.

40. There is not as much work on melancholy in Romanticism as one might think. See Guinn Batten, *The Orphaned Imagination* (Durham, NC: Duke University Press, 1998); Thomas Pfau, *Romantic Moods: Paranoia, Trauma and Melancholy, 1790–1840* (Baltimore: Johns Hopkins University Press, 2005); Haverkamp, *Leaves of Mourning.* Eleanor Sickels, *The Gloomy Egoist: Moods and Themes of Melancholy from Gray to Keats* (New York: Columbia University Press, 1932), remains a helpful survey. The English elegy from Gray to Yeats, for example, provides a rich terrain for study of this trend; on this see Peter M. Sacks, *The English Elegy: Studies in the Genre from Spenser to Yeats* (Baltimore: Johns Hopkins, 1957). On the modernist elegy, and its departure from the consolatory ethos of the earlier elegy, see Jahan Ramazani, *Poetry of Mourning: The Modern Elegy from Hardy to Heaney* (Chicago: University of Chicago Press, 1994).

41. Recent scholarship has made the case that here, too, the engagement with melancholy on the part of Keats or Wordsworth is also a way to reflect on the historicity of the moment. See Pfau, *Romantic Moods,* and Batten, *The Orphaned Imagination.*

42. See Radden, Introduction, 18–29, on the nineteenth-century medicalization of melancholy and the emergence of Kraepelin's view of depression. On the development of *depression* as a term, see Jackson, *Melancholia,* esp. 5–7. While "depression" became the dominant term in the psychological-medical context, it was used metaphorically much earlier, at least as early as Burton, who talks about "depressed moods."

43. See Kraepelin, "Manic-Depressive Insanity," in *Textbook of Psychiatry,* 8th ed. (1909–1915), excerpted in Radden, *Melancholy,* 260–279. Adolf Meyer is the other key figure here; on Kraepelin and Meyer see Jackson, *Melancholia,* 188–202.

44. In the 1950s Imiprimine was discovered to treat nonmanic depression, and to have a specific reaction on the physiological phenomenon that produced depression. Tricyclics and MAO inhibitors helped to isolate the chemicals in the brain that were involved in depression, which were the "biogenic amines," including norepenephrine and serotonin. Not until Prozac and the other SSRIs were these chemicals precisely targeted. A brief account of this history and summary of how the various antidepressants work is presented in Peter Kramer, *Listening to Prozac* (New York: Penguin, 1993), esp.

47–66, and Peter C. Whybrow, *A Mood Apart: Depression, Mania and the Other Afflictions of the Self* (New York: Basic Books, 1997), esp. 195–230. Also see Donald F. Klein and Paul Wender, *Understanding Depression: A Complete Guide to Its Diagnosis and Treatment* (New York: Oxford University Press, 1994).

45. *Listening to Prozac,* 55.

46. The term was coined by Donald Klein. See Klein and Wender, *Understanding Depression.*

47. One woman Kramer treated, for example, could be deeply affected by her boyfriend's short attention lapses, which threw her into moods in which she felt "disorganized, paralyzed, hopelessly sad, overtaken by unfocused feelings of urgency" (*Listening to Prozac,* 69).

48. Kramer finds himself coming to see rejection-sensitivity as a distinct disease because of the way Prozac is successful in treating these patients.

49. See foreword to *Living with Prozac and Other Selective Serotonin Reuptake Inhibitors (SSRIs),* ed. Debra Elfenbein (New York: HarperCollins, 1995), xiii.

50. He excluded manic depression from his argument, since it is a distinct clinical and physiological phenomenon, which, he concedes, may suit creative purposes. The classic defense of the manic-depressive as the creative type par excellence is Kay Redfield Jameson, *Touched by Fire.*

51. On this, see Jackson, *Melancholia and Depression,* 311–324.

52. Ibid., 317.

53. Ibid., 317–318.

54. A partial bibliography of this work would include: Melanie Klein, "A Contribution to the Psychogenesis of Manic-Depressive States (1935)," and "Mourning and Its Relation to Manic-Depressive States," in *The Selected Melanie Klein,* ed. Juliet Mitchell (New York: Penguin, 1991); for a Kleinian reading of modernism, see Esther Sanchez-Pardo, *Cultures of the Death Drive: Melanie Klein and Modernist Melancholia* (Durham, NC: Duke University Press, 2003); Nicolas Abraham and Maria Torok, *The Shell and The Kernel,* ed. and trans. Nicholas T. Rand (Chicago: University of Chicago Press, 1994); Edith Jacobsen, *Depression: Comparative Studies of Normal, Neurotic and Psychotic Conditions* (New York: International Universities Press, 1971); John Bowlby, *Loss: Sadness and Depression* (New York: Basic Books, 1980); Kristeva, *Black Sun;* Derrida, "*Fors:* The Anglish Words of Nicolas Abraham and Maria Torok," trans. Barbara Johnson, in *The Wolf Man's Magic Word,* ed. Nicolas Abraham and Maria Torok (Minneapolis: University of Minnesota Press, 1986), xi–xlviii, and Derrida, *Memoires for Paul de Man* (New York: Columbia University Press, 1988); Giorgio Agamben, *Stanzas: Word and Phantasm in Western Culture,* trans. Ronald L. Martinez (Minneapolis: University of Minnesota Press, 1993), esp. 3–35; Judith Butler, *Gender Trouble, Bodies That Matter,* and *The Psychic Life of Power;* the essays collected in David L. Eng and David Kazan-

jian, eds., *Loss: The Politics of Mourning* (Berkeley: University of California Press, 2003).

55. This also makes it different from a book such as Sanchez-Pardo, *Cultures of the Death Drive*, which examines Klein's theory of melancholia and uses it as a lens for the analysis of modernist practices.

56. "DRAFT G" (January 7, 1895), in Freud, *Standard Edition*, 1:200.

57. Karl Abraham, "Notes on the Psycho-Analytical Investigation and Treatment of Manic-Depressive Insanity and Allied Conditions" (1911), in *Selected Papers of Karl Abraham*, trans. Douglas Bryan and Alix Strachey (New York: Basic Books, 1927), 137–156. Abraham argues that "anxiety and depression are related to each other in the same way as are fear and grief" (137).

58. Freud, *Group Psychology and the Analysis of the Ego*, trans. and ed. James Strachey (New York: Norton, 1959), 29.

59. Freud writes: "We will try our fortune, then, with the supposition that love relationships (or, to use a more neutral expression, emotional ties) also constitute the essence of the group mind" (ibid., 31).

60. The original German here is more subtle: "Die Liebe hat sich so durch ihre Flucht ins Ich der Aufhebung entzogen," literally "The love has itself through its flight into the ego the sublation withdrawn." Freud here uses the Hegelian *Aufhebung*, sublation or canceling out. So it is not so much that it has "escaped extinction" as it has taken back into itself the possibility of canceling itself out and transforming itself into something else. Melancholia thus is precisely not a sublation, a stubbornness on the part of the emotion—or libido, Freud is not really clear which—to change.

61. In this, Freud is also alluding to an old image for melancholia, dating at least to Galen, who wrote: "As external darkness renders almost all persons fearful, with the exception of a few audacious ones or those who were specially trained, thus the color of the black humour induces fear when its darkness throws a shadow over the area of thought [in the brain]." Galen, *On the Affected Parts*, in Radden, *Melancholy*, 68.

62. I am thinking here of Lacan's discussion of the gaze, and his famous comparison of the effect of the gaze on the subject as a photo-graph, in *The Four Fundamental Concepts of Psychoanalysis*, 106. I discuss this metaphor-concept in Chapter 4.

63. On the interest and significance of this revision, especially regarding the logic of gender identification, see Butler, section entitled "Melancholy of Gender," in *Gender Trouble* (New York: Routledge, 1990), 57–65.

64. *The Ego and the Id* (1923), in *Standard Edition*, 19:29.

65. Ibid., 30.

66. This section's epigraph is from Andre Green, "Conceptions of Affect," in *On Private Madness* (London: Hogarth Press, 1972), 174.

67. One account of Freud's attempts to theorize affect can be found in Andre Green, *The Fabric of Affect in the Psychoanalytic Discourse*, trans. Alan

Sheridan (London: Routledge, 1999), first published in France in 1973 as *Le Discours Vivant*. Also relevant to my discussion here is Mikkel Borch-Jacobsen's examination of the concept of the "emotional tie" in Freud's work. He argues that the concept can be traced from Freud's early interest in hypnosis through to his writings on transference. See *The Emotional Tie: Psychoanalysis, Mimesis and Affect* (Stanford: Stanford University Press, 1992).

68. Freud, *An Outline of Psychoanalysis, Standard Edition*, 23:193.

69. Freud, *Group Psychology*, 46. For an analysis of the concept of identification in Freud and elsewhere see Diana Fuss, *Identification Papers* (New York: Routledge, 1995).

70. Borch-Jacobsen puts it as follows: "To affirm that 'the earliest emotional tie with another person' is identification is, in effect, to assert that that affect as such is identificatory, mimetic, and that there is no 'proper' affect except on the condition of a prior 'affection' of the ego by another. Another does not affect me because I feel such and such an affect in regard to him, nor even because he succeeds in communicating an affect to me by way of words. He affects me because 'I' *am* that 'other,' following an identification that is my affection, the strangest alteration of my proper autoaffection. My identity is a passion. And reciprocally, my passions are always identificatory" (*Emotional Tie*, 73).

71. Along these lines Butler has reread the Oedipal scenario, examining in particular the phenomenon of gender identification: by what process do we identify and mime our gender roles? Do we automatically imitate the parent who has the same gender as we do? How indeed do we become aware of this "sameness"? Perhaps, Butler suggests, gender identification is also a reaction to a loss. Hence (following the logic of Freud's own texts), Butler argues that before the little boy loses his mother or the little girl her father, the prohibition on same-sex desire mandates the foundational loss of the same-sex parent. The "sameness" on which we base our first moments of gender identification would be based first on our apprehension of a prohibition and the loss that stems from it. It is *that* loss that sets in motion our imitation of that same-sex object: the mother for the little girl or the father for the boy. Thus: the "melancholia of gender." See *Gender Trouble*, 57–72.

72. Butler, "Imitation and Gender Insubordination," in *Inside/Out*, ed. Diana Fuss (New York: Routledge, 1991), 27.

73. Derrida discusses melancholia in a few places, but, in my view, nowhere more relevantly than in *Memoires for Paul de Man* (New York: Columbia University Press, 1988), where he writes: "If death exists, that is to say, if it happens only once, to the other and to oneself, it is the moment when there is no longer any choice—could we think of any other—except that between memory and hallucination. If death comes to the other, and comes to us through the other, then the friend no longer exists except *in* us, *between* us. In himself, by himself, of himself, he is no more, nothing more. He lives

only in us. But *we* are never identical to *ourselves*, and between us, identical to us, a "self" is never in itself or identical to itself. The specular reflection never closes on itself; it does not appear *before* this *possibility* of mourning, before and outside this structure of allegory and prosopopoeia which constitutes in advance all "being-in-us," "in-me," between us, or between ourselves. The *selbst*, the *soi-même*, the self appears to itself only in this bereaved allegory, in this hallucinatory prosopopoeia—and even before the death of the other *actually* happens, as we say, in "reality." The strange situation I am describing here, for example that of my friendship with Paul de Man, would have allowed me to say all of this *before* his death. It suffices that I know him to be mortal, that he knows me to be mortal—there is no friendship without this knowledge of finitude" (28–29). He makes a similar point in *Fors*. I return to this Derridean formulation in my discussion of friendship in Platonov.

74. "Abreaction" is a neologism coined by Freud and Breuer to describe the process whereby the affect is disattached from the memory and the patient is "liberated" from the affect. See Jean Laplanche and J. B. Pontalis, "Abreaction," in *The Language of Psychoanalysis*, trans. Donald Nicholson-Smith (New York: Norton, 1973).

75. Josef Breuer and Sigmund Freud, *Studies on Hysteria*, trans. and ed. James Strachey (New York: Basic Books n.d.), 6 (their italics).

76. For a further discussion of the importance of the detail in Freud and Breuer's formulation here, see Naomi Schor's chapter on Freud, "Displacement: The Case of Sigmund Freud in Reading In Detail" (New York: Routledge, 1985).

77. Borch-Jacobsen, *Emotional Tie*, 46.

78. All the uncertainty about the relative value of repetition versus recollection recalls one of the oldest debates in literary theory—one that goes back to Aristotle and Plato—on the relative value of diegesis and mimesis. Mimesis, of course, is championed by Aristotle precisely for its close relation to emotion and is attacked by Plato for much the same reason. Aristotle thought that it was mimesis, in tragedy, that produced the highest kind of art, art that could produce the fear and pity necessary for catharsis. Plato, on the other hand, would forbid mimetic speech in the ideal Republic, since it encouraged imitation, and hence potentially dangerously inappropriate behavior. Mimesis was contagious; people were affected. For that reason, imitation, in those rare cases when it was allowed, should be only of that which is appropriate and ideal. See *Republic*, 392c–398b. On mimesis in Aristotle and Plato see Stephen Halliwell's excellent book *The Aesthetics of Mimesis: Ancient Texts and Modern Problems* (Princeton: Princeton University Press, 2002).

79. *Studies on Hysteria*, 17.

80. Borch-Jacobsen, *Emotional Tie*, 50.

81. The work of Daniel Stern is suggestive along these lines. In his study *The Interpersonal World of the Infant: A View from Psychoanalysis and Devel-*

opmental Psychology (New York: Basic Books, 1985), Stern examines the ways the capacity for infant relationality depends on the parent's ability to engage in what Stern calls "affective attunement" (138). Interestingly, he finds that parents accomplish this attunement by performing "some behavior that is not a strict imitation. . . . [W]hat is matched is not the other person's behavior per se, but rather some aspect of the behavior that reflects the person's feeling state." The path of least resistance here is to be experiencing an affective state *with* someone else. It is as if having affects at all depended on someone else sharing them. I return to this topic, and to Stern, in Chapter 5.

82. *Group Psychology,* 27.

83. From a transcribed recording of Lacan's talk at the "Kanzer Seminar," Yale University, November 24, 1975, trans. Barbara Johnson, cited in Shoshana Felman, "Turning the Screw of Interpretation," in *Literature and Psychoanalysis,* ed. Felman (Baltimore: Johns Hopkins University Press, 1977), 118.

84. Borch-Jacobsen gives a careful account of the development (and occasional return) of Freud's interest in hypnosis.

85. Sandor Ferenczi critiqued Freud on this point, arguing that it was in essence cruel to the patient to take such an emotional distance. On this, see especially *The Clinical Diary of Sandor Ferenczi* (Cambridge: Harvard University Press, 1988).

86. Freud, *An Autobiographical Study* in *Standard Edition,* 78–79.

87. From "Further Recommendations in the Technique of Psychoanalysis: Recollection, Repetition and Working-Through" (1914), in *Therapy and Technique,* ed. Philip Rieff (New York: Collier Books, 1963), 160.

88. Freud, "The Dynamics of the Transference" (1912), in Rieff, *Therapy and Technique,* 114.

89. This is Borch-Jacobsen's argument in *Emotional Tie.*

90. See Jacques Derrida, "That Dangerous Supplement," in *Of Grammatology,* Freud here is closer to Kant on the sublime in *The Critique of Judgment,* where, in similar fashion, the moment of affective experience, while a necessary component to the sublime, is ultimately valuable inasmuch as it is then contained by cognition and a recognition of the mind's powers of representation.

91. Freud, "Dynamics of the Transference," 114–115.

92. Freud, "The Unconscious," in *Standard Edition,* 14:177.

93. Lacan, *Four Fundamental Concepts of Psychoanalysis,* ed. Jacques-Alain Miller, trans. Alan Sheridan (New York: Norton, 1977), 217.

94. *The Interpretation of Dreams,* trans. and ed. James Strachey (New York: Avon, 1965), 601.

95. Christopher Bollas, *The Shadow of the Object* (New York: Columbia University Press, 1987), 27.

96. Along such lines Christopher Bollas writes, "the analysand compels the analyst to experience the patient's inner object world. He often does this by

means of projective identification: by inspiring in the analyst a feeling, thought or self-state that hitherto has only remained within himself" (*Shadow*, 5). What makes a good psychoanalyst is one who is open to being affected in this way, for this affectedness, and the ability of the patient to see that the analyst is affected, is crucial to the cure.

97. Freud, *Three Case Histories*, ed. Philip Rieff (Collier Books: New York, 1963), 27.

98. Borch-Jacobsen has suggested that the space of analysis is in some ways a public place, in the ancient Greek sense of a space of appearance and performance.

99. Benjamin, "Eduard Fuchs, Collector and Historian" is in SW3, 267.

100. Benjamin makes this remark in his "Agesilaus Santander," both versions of which are in *Walter Benjamin: Selected Writings*, vol. 2 (Cambridge: Harvard University Press, 1999) (hereafter SW2), 712–713, 714–715.

101. For the most thorough consideration of the significance of melancholy for Benjamin's thought, see Max Pensky, *Melancholy Dialectics: Walter Benjamin and the Play of Mourning* (Amherst: University of Massachusetts Press, 1993). Pensky's book is particularly strong in giving a philosophical explication of Benjamin's theories of tragedy and *Trauerspiel*, melancholia, allegory, and modernity. In some ways this is also the weakness of the book, as it turns Benjamin into more of a philosopher than I think he is. Pensky emphasizes the impossibility of a redemptive knowing, an epistemological blockage, as central to Benjamin's theory of melancholy. While this is a compelling theoretical rubric in its own right (and one well developed by Pensky) I do not think it is Benjamin's. Also, I differ from Pensky regarding his reliance on a Kristevan model of melancholia. In the Kristevan understanding, melancholia results from the failure to negate (a "denial of the negation") the loss of the maternal Thing with language. Kristeva argues that this is the transhistorical structure of melancholia, which varies in the forms it takes in different historical periods. Benjamin is, I think, far too interested in the historical specificity of loss and affective experience for Kristeva to be applicable here. I argue that melancholia for Benjamin not only is historically specific and not psychological in this manner but also is multiple.

Regarding the perception by others of Benjamin's melancholy character, Françoise Meltzer notes the implicitly moralizing tone—of Arendt and Adorno in particular—of much of the critical commentary on Benjamin's melancholy. "Acedia and Melancholia," in *Walter Benjamin and the Demands of History* (Ithaca, NY: Cornell University Press, 1996).

On the role and importance of affect in Benjamin's thinking about experience see Miriam Hansen (in my view, Benjamin's best contemporary critic), "Benjamin, Cinema and Experience: 'The Blue Flower in the Land of Technology,'" *New German Critique* 40 (Winter 1987): 179–224, and "Benjamin and Cinema: Not a One Way Street," *Critical Inquiry* (Winter 1999): vol. 25, Number 2, 306–343.

102. "Left-Wing Melancholy," in SW2, 425.
103. Ibid., 425. "The metamorphosis of political struggle from a compulsory decision into an object of pleasure, from a means of production into an article of consumption—this is literature's latest hit."
104. Ibid., 426. For a reading of this essay in relation to Benjamin's interest in historical methodology and the politics therein, see Wendy Brown, "Futures, Specters and Angels: Benjamin and Derrida," in *Politics out of History* (Princeton: Princeton University Press, 2001), 138–173, on "Left-Wing Melancholy" in particular, 168–172. Also see Pensky, *Melancholy Dialectics*, 6–12.
105. "Central Park" (hereafter CP), in SW4, 190.
106. On Benjamin's understanding of the anesthetizing effects of modernization and the aesthetic response to this, see Susan Buck-Morss, "Aesthetics and Anaesthetics: Walter Benjamin's Artwork Essay Reconsidered," *October* 62 (fall 1992): 3–41.
107. In *The Flowers of Evil*, trans. Anthony Hecht, ed. Marthiel and Jackson Mathews (New York: New Directions, 1955).
108. Hansen, "One Way Street," 311.
109. This is why hashish trances are also for Benjamin initiations into *Erfahrung*—they teach us to get lost in the object. "[E]vents took place in such a way that the appearance of things touched me with a magic wand, and I sank into a dream of them." "Hashish in Marseilles," in SW2, 678.
110. The past is situated "somewhere beyond the reach of the intellect and its field of operations, in some material object . . . though we have no idea which one it is. And whether we come upon this object before we die, or whether we never encounter it, depends entirely on chance." Cited by Benjamin, MB, 315.
111. "Experience is indeed a matter of tradition, in collective existence as well as private life. It is the product less of facts firmly anchored in memory [*Erinnerung*] than of accumulated and frequently unconscious data that flow together in memory [*Gedächtnis*]." MB, 314.
112. He discusses this decline in experience also in "The Storyteller."
113. See Benjamin's citation of Georg Simmel's "Metropolis and Mental Life" in MB, 191. Also on the shock experience, see Susan Buck-Morss, "Aesthetics and Anaesthetics."
114. This was also the source of the fascination with surrealism, of which he would say: "It was . . . precisely at the outset that Breton declared his intention of breaking with a praxis that presents the public with the literary precipitate of a certain form of existence while withholding that existence itself." "Surrealism," in SW2, 207–208. The term Benjamin provides for this "form of existence," the experience that surrealism promises, is "profane illumination." This would be an experience of intoxication that is not escapist but materialistic—that connects us to the world. For more on Benjamin's interest in and theory of surrealism, see Margaret Cohen, *Profane*

Illumination: Walter Benjamin and the Paris of Surrealist Revolution (Berkeley: University of California Press, 1993). Benjamin also remarks that the moment of revolutionary awakening would be "identical with the 'now of recognizability' in which things put on their true—surrealist— face." "N [On the Theory of Knowledge, Theory of Progress]," in *The Arcades Project*, trans. Howard Eiland and Kevin McLaughlin (Cambridge: Harvard University Press, 1999) (hereafter N), 464.

115. "On the Concept of History" (hereafter H), SW4, 391.

116. Baudelaire directly references the history of acedia and the monks who suffered it in his poem "The Wicked Monk" ("Le Mauvais Moine"), *Flowers of Evil*, p. 18. He writes:

> My soul's a tomb which, wicked cenobite,
> I wander in for all eternity;
> Nothing embellishes these odious walls.
> Oh slothful monk! When shall they learn to make
> Of the live pageant of my misery
> My hands their labor, my eyes their delight.

117. This is why "pure curiosity," he would also write, "arises from and deepens sorrow" ("N," 481).

118. The distinction between clock time and calendar time is another way to see the distinction. See thesis 15, H, 395. And elsewhere he writes, "The man who loses his capacity for experiencing feels as if he has been dropped from the calendar" (MB, 336).

119. "Omens, presentiments, signals pass day and night through our organism like wave impulses. To interpret them or to use them: that is the question. The two are irreconcilable. Cowardice and apathy counsel the former, lucidity and freedom the latter." "One Way Street," in *Walter Benjamin: Selected Writings* (Cambridge: Harvard University Press, 1996) (hereafter SW1), 483.

120. Freud and Breuer, *Studies on Hysteria*.

121. Thesis 2, H, 390. For a smart reading of this thesis, which connects it to an important exchange with Horkheimer, and a reading of the Theses as a whole see Michael Löwy, *Fire Alarm: Reading Walter Benjamin's "On the Concept of History,"* trans. Chris Turner (New York: Verso, 2005). Other readings of "Concept of History" I found helpful include: Rolf Tiedeman, "Historical Materialism or Political Messianism? An Interpretation of the Theses 'On the Concept of History,'" in *Benjamin: Philosophy, Aesthetics, History* ed. Gary Smith; Kia Lindross, *Now-Time/Image-Space: Temporalization of Politics* in *Walter Benjamin's Philosophy of History and Art* (Jyvaskyla, Finland: SoPhi, 1998).

122. "Franz Kafka," in SW2, 809.

123. Ibid., 810.

124. Karl Marx, *The Eighteenth Brumaire of Louis Bonaparte*, trans. Daniel De Leon (New York: International), 15.

125. Ibid., 18.
126. The complexity of Marx's fascination with specters and spectrality is the central topic of Derrida's *Specters of Marx.*
127. As Susan Buck-Morss writes, "if the social value (hence the meaning) of commodities is their price, this does not prevent them from being appropriated by consumers as wish images within the emblem book of their private dreamworld." *The Dialectics of Seeing: Walter Benjamin and the Arcades Project* (Cambridge: MIT Press, 1989), 180–181.
128. "The Meaning of Time in the Moral Universe," SW1, 286.

2. Affective Mapping

1. Kevin Lynch, *The Image of the City* (Cambridge: MIT Press, 1960).
2. "Cognitive Map and Spatial Behavior: Process and Products," in *Image and Environment,* ed. R. M. Downs and D. Stea (Chicago: Aldine, 1973), 2–26, cited by Robert M. Kitchin, "Cognitive Maps: What Are they and Why Study Them?" *Journal of Environmental Psychology* 14 (1994): 1. Kitchin's article, in addition to being an excellent survey and summary, also contains a full bibliography of work on cognitive mapping.
3. Lynch, *Image of the City,* 2.
4. "Cognitive Mapping," in *Marxism and The Interpretation of Culture,* ed. Lawrence Grossberg and Cary Nelson (Urbana: University of Illinois Press, 1988), reprinted in *The Jameson Reader,* ed. Michael Hardt and Kathi Weeks (New York: Blackwell, 2000), 277–287.
5. Jameson, *Postmodernism* (Durham, NC: Duke University Press, 1991), 51.
6. Louis Althusser, "Ideology and Ideological State Apparatuses," in *Lenin and Philosophy* (New York: Monthly Review Press, 1971).
7. "Cognitive Mapping," 283.
8. The key transition in this history for Jameson is the moment of colonialism, for it is then that "the truth of [daily] experience no longer coincides with the place in which it takes place. The truth of that limited experience of London lies, rather, in India or Hong Kong; it is bound up with the whole colonial system of the British Empire that determines the very quality of the individual's subjective life. Yet the structural coordinates are no longer accessible to immediate lived experience and are often not even conceptualizable for most people" (*Postmodernism,* 411). If colonialism meant that the truth of life in the metropolis was in some way determined in and by the colonies themselves (that is, quite far from a local context), then the intensification of globalization has meant that the systems that structure our lives and on which we rely in innumerable ways are even more diffuse, multiple, and distant. Accordingly, Jameson argues, the gap between the phenomenology of daily life and the totality of economic relations that shape that life has become even more unbridgeable. One of the worrisome things about postmodernism, in Jameson's view, is the abandonment of cognitive mapping as a project.

9. The aesthetic experimentation we see in modernism was, Jameson argues, in large part generated out of the desire to "square the circle," to produce formal devices for representing the structural system that was now no longer apprehensible from within the realm of everyday life. Like ancient Greek or medieval allegories of the divine, these experiments were attempts to articulate something across a gap, to represent something that was, strictly speaking, unrepresentable. These modernisms emerge in "forms that inscribe a new sense of the absent global system on the very syntax of poetic language itself, a new play of absence and present that at its most simplified will be haunted by the exotic and be tattooed with foreign place names, and at its most intense will involve the invention of remarkable new languages and forms" (*Postmodernism*, 411).

   In fact, sometimes defeat or the failure to produce a cognitive map, Jameson writes, can, "even more effectively, [cause] the whole architectonic of postmodern global space to rise up in ghostly profile behind itself, as some ultimate dialectical barrier or invisible limit" (415).

   See Jameson's reading of E. M. Forster's novel *Howard's End* and (more briefly) of Joyce's *Ulysses* along these lines: "Modernism and Imperialism," in *Nationalism, Colonialism and Literature*, ed. Terry Eagleton, Jameson and Edward W. Said (Minneapolis: University of Minnesota Press, 1990), 43–66.

10. *Postmodernism*, 54.

11. See, for example, Christopher Spencer, Mark Blades and Kim Morsley, *The Child in the Physical Environment* (Chichester, UK: Wiley, 1989), 108, cited in Kitchin, "Cognitive Maps." Also see Christopher Spencer and Jill Dixon, "Mapping the Development of Feelings about the City: A Longitudinal Study of New Residents' Affective Maps," *Transactions of the Institute of British Geographers*, n.s., 8 (1983): 373–383. The term *affective mapping* has also been used occasionally in political science; for example: Marc Swyngedouw, "The Subjective Cognitive and Affective Map of Extreme Right Voters: Using Open-Ended Questions in Exit Polls," *Electoral Studies* 20 (2001): 217–241, and Angus Campbell, *The American Voter* (New York: Wiley, 1960).

12. Gilles Deleuze and Felix Guattari, *A Thousand Plateaus*, trans. Brian Massumi (Minneapolis: University of Minnesota Press, 1987), 48–49.

13. To some degree, I am here glossing Adorno's ideas about the "aesthetic shudder"—some of Adorno's more Benjaminian moments, which are scattered throughout his *Aesthetic Theory*, trans. Robert Hullot-Kentor (Minneapolis: University of Minnesota Press, 1997) (hereafter AT). See esp. 244–245, 269, and 331.

14. *Moscow Diary*, trans. Richard Sieburth, ed. Gary Smith (Cambridge: Harvard University Press, 1986), 42. He was at the Pushkin Museum of Fine Arts; it has been deduced, on the basis of the museum's holdings and what was likely to have been on display at that time, that the painting was *Road to Pontoise*, although Benjamin says nothing specific about the painting in

question, as it is the quality of the experience and not the object as such he is concerned with here.

15. And, Adorno argues, the temporary negation of subjectivity at this moment rescues subjectivity. "The subject, convulsed by art, has real experiences; by the strength of insight into the artwork as artwork, these experiences are those in which the subject's petrification in his own subjectivity dissolves and the narrowness of his self-positedness is revealed" (AT, 269).

3. Reading into Henry James

1. See Leon Edel's account of the night in *Complete Plays of Henry James*, ed. Leon Edel (New York: Oxford University Press, 1990), 465–485.

2. The letter is to W. D. Howells, January 22, 1895, in *The Letters of Henry James*, sel. and ed. Percy Lubbock (New York: Scribner's, 1920), 1:231.

3. Letter to William Edward Norris, February 4, 1896, in *Henry James: Selected Letters*, ed. Leon Edel (Cambridge: Harvard University Press, 1974), 295.

4. In fact, as Richard Brodhead has noted, James was "an author peculiarly expressive of the institutional character [the *Atlantic*] wanted to maintain," even if he was not their best seller. Richard Brodhead, *The School of Hawthorne* (New York: Oxford University Press, 1986), 108. Brodhead sums up the conceptual scheme of the *Atlantic* in the following way. "It held at least the following elements in solution: an idea of literary discrimination, the sense that writing is and should be differentiated into mediocre and distinguishing classes; an idea of the moral or civic function of letters, the sense that the dissemination of distinguished writing can improve the tone of a culture and raise the level of its intelligence; an idea of entertainment, the sense that literature also has as a legitimate goal to interest and please a family-style audience" (110).

5. In his lucid and persuasive account of the origins of mass culture in the United States, *Selling Culture* (New York: Verso, 1996), Richard Ohmann places the date at 1893.

6. See Meredith McGill, "Commerce, Print Culture, and the Authority of the State in American Copyright Law," in *American Literature and the Culture of Reprinting, 1834–1853* (Philadelphia: University of Pennsylvania Press, 2003), 48.

7. *The Chap-Book* would be one such publication. See Brodhead's descriptions of *The Chap-Book* in *The School of Hawthorne* and in *Cultures of Letters: Scenes of Reading and Writing in Nineteenth Century America* (Chicago: University of Chicago Press, 1993), where he writes: "The announced intention of *The Chap-Book* was 'to be a distinctly literary periodical,' and the work this firm published includes a large portion of the late nineteenth-century writing since designated as literature. But here too we should note that this system published literature not in some absolute sense but in a particular understanding of the term: a sense that strongly dissev-

ers writing from the ethnically local and overtly political and conjoins it instead with careful craftedness, cosmopolitan internationalism, and the exercise of educated tastes" (7).

8. James to Howells, January 22, 1895.

9. See James's notebook entry for Saturday, January 12, 1895, in *The Notebooks of Henry James*, ed. F. O. Mathiessen and Kenneth B. Murcock (New York: Braziller, 1955), 178–179.

10. James to Fullerton, October 2, 1900, in James, *Selected Letters*, 326; for the other letters concerned see 322–328.

11. Leon Edel characterizes this classic element of James's style as his "*apparent unawareness* that he was using vivid libidinal language." *Henry James: A Life* (New York: Harper and Row, 1985), 83.

12. James to Fullerton, October 2, 1900, in *Selected Letters*.

13. James to Kipling, October 30, 1901, in *Selected Letters*, 334.

14. This was part of the attraction of the theater for James: having his plays performed would involve a literal stepping into the role he had created and reading of the words he had written.

15. On prosopopoiea see Paul de Man, "Autobiography as De-Facement," in *The Rhetoric of Romanticism* (New York: Columbia University Press, 1984), 67–81.

16. At the beginning of his career, Freud confronted these questions surrounding the role of affect, repetition, and recollection in therapy in *Studies on Hysteria* (1893–1895), wherein he and Josef Breuer held that the patient's recounting, with full affect, the traumatic event at the source of the hysteria was sufficient for the "cathartic" cure. Later, Freud realized that this was insufficient, that a more thoroughgoing making-conscious and narration was necessary. The term *transference* itself appears to have been first used in the *Interpretation of Dreams*, to refer not to the transference of an unconscious feeling from the past onto the person of the therapist but the general process whereby the unconscious manages to communicate with consciousness. *The Interpretation of Dreams*, trans. and ed. James Strachey (New York: Avon, 1965), 601. The infamous case of Dora was the occasion of Freud's first confrontation with the phenomenon of transference in therapy. See *Dora—An Analysis of a Case of Hysteria* (New York: Collier Books, 1963), esp. 138. See also "The Dynamics of the Transference" (1912) and "Further Recommendations in the Technique of Psychoanalysis: Recollection, Repetition and Working-Through" (1914), in *Therapy and Technique*, ed. Philip Rieff (New York: Collier Books, 1963). A helpful account of the history of the issues raised by affect and transference can be found in Mikkel Borch-Jacobsen, *The Emotional Tie: Psychoanalysis, Mimesis and Affect* (Stanford: Stanford University Press, 1992). He argues that the same basic problems can be traced from Freud's early interest in hypnosis through to his writings on transference. See Chapter 1 here for more on this.

17. He advocated that the analyst display in therapy a "calm quiet attentiveness," appear "impenetrable to the patient, and, like a mirror, reflect noth-

ing but what is shown to him." The two quotations are from "Recommendations for Physicians on the Psychoanalytic Method of Treatment (1912)," in *Therapy and Technique*, 118, 124.

18. Walter Benjamin, "One Way Street," in *Walter Benjamin: Selected Writings*, vol. 1, *1913–1926*, ed. Marcus Bullock and Michael Jennings (Cambridge: Harvard University Press, 1996), 466.

19. Henry James, *The Art of the Novel* (New York: Scribner's, 1934), 169.

20. James probably had in mind a book such as (if not precisely) *The Law of Psychic Phenomena* (New York: Weiser, 1968) by Thomson Jay Hudson, first published in 1892, which contains chapters entitled "Hypnotism and Crime," "A New System of Mental Therapeutics," "The Phenomena of Spiritism," and, most relevant here, "Phantasms of the Dead."

21. James, *Art of the Novel*, 172.

22. Ibid., 176.

23. Freud, "The Dynamics of the Transference," 114.

24. Henry James, *The Turn of the Screw* (New York: Norton, 1966), 2 (page references in parentheses hereafter).

25. For an important class-based reading of *The Turn of the Screw* that has influenced my own, see Bruce Robbins, *The Servant's Hand* (Durham, NC: Duke University Press, 1993). Also see Millicent Bell, *Meaning in Henry James* (Cambridge: Harvard University Press, 1991), for a reading in terms of desires and anxieties connected to the rules of class separation, 223–242. On the figure of Victorian governess more generally, see Mary Poovey, *Uneven Developments: The Ideological Work of Gender in Mid-Victorian England* (Chicago: University of Chicago Press, 1988), 126–163.

26. Niklas Luhmann, *The Differentiation of Society*, trans. Stephen Holmes and Charles Larmore (New York: Columbia University Press, 1982).

27. See Chapter 2 for more on systems.

28. Luhmann, *Differentiation of Society*, 249.

29. Ibid. The increased autonomy can produce a false sense of confidence in the efficaciousness of one's own operations. In fact, modernism could be seen as the recurring moment of misrecognition, whereby each system operates as if it can and should solve the world's problems. Modernist legal theory, economics, international relations (think of the League of Nations), linguistics (the invention of Esperanto) and, of course, literature and art are all colored with a strong redemptive strain.

30. Jochen Schulte-Sasse, "Afterword: Can the Imagination be Mimetic under Conditions of Modernity?" in Luiz Costa Lima, *Control of the Imaginary: Reason and Imagination in Modern Times* (Minneapolis: University of Minnesota Press, 1988), 215.

31. Jacques Derrida, *Specters of Marx* (New York: Routledge, 1994), 7.

32. The letter quoted in the epigraph is in James, *Selected Letters*, 293.

33. Bruce Robbins has pointed out that sex between servants and male children was widely practiced and known but rarely spoken about in late Victorian

England. He recounts the following anecdotal evidence. An officer in the Indian Medical Service wrote to Havelock Ellis as follows: "once at a club in Burma we were some twenty-six at a table and the subject of first intercourse came up. All had been led astray by servants save two, whom their sisters' governesses had initiated" (*Servant's Hand*, 197).

34. Shoshana Felman, "Turning the Screw of Interpretation," in *Literature and Psychoanalysis*, ed. Felman (Baltimore: Johns Hopkins University Press, 1977).

35. Edmund Wilson, "The Ambiguity of Henry James," in *The Triple Thinkers* (New York: Penguin, 1962).

36. "When the pronouncements of the various sides of the controversy are examined closely," Felman writes, "they are found to repeat unwittingly—with a spectacular regularity—all the main lexical motifs of the text" ("Turning the Screw," 98).

37. On April 6, 1895, Oscar Wilde was charged with "gross indecency" under section 11 of the criminal law enactment of 1885. Bail was refused. As James developed his idea for *The Turn of the Screw*, Wilde was in jail. James's apprehension of the Wilde trial must have been complicated by the fact that before Wilde's arrest, James's relation to him had been a competitive one. Wilde had been James's rival in the theater, successful where he had failed. Indeed James had gone to see Wilde's (successful) play *The Ideal Husband* the very night *Guy Domville* opened and bombed. To see Wilde, who it appeared had figured out how to be read by the "vulgar" theatergoing public that had stymied James, attacked by the public—one can imagine how this might have underscored for James the extraordinary difficulty and danger of dealing with the public at this moment. Publicity in the new mass public sphere was not only no protection, but it exposed one, left one's life open to all kinds of the wrong reading in. See James's letters of April 8, 1895, to Edmund Gosse, and April 28, 1895, also to Gosse, for his comment on the Wilde trials.

38. Michel Foucault, *History of Sexuality*, vol. 1, trans. Robert Hurley (New York: Vintage, 1978). See esp. chap. 2, "The Perverse Implantation," 36–49, on the shift from a discourse of acts (sodomy) to one of identity (homosexuality).

39. Eve Kosofsky Sedgwick, *Epistemology of the Closet* (Berkeley: University of California Press, 1990), 2.

40. It is regarding the historicity of "sexuality" that my reading differs most pointedly from Felman's. In her essay, Felman focuses on the Lacanian concept of desire and the way desire is structured by the displacement of the signifier. In a careful, close reading of the novella, she spotlights the tension between a continually displaced signifier that belongs to the order of *vision*—and here we find the ghosts—on the one hand, and on the other the governess's desire for knowledge, the desire to fix the signifier into a signified. Life, desire, reading, vision—these are on the side of the signifier, and

knowledge, death, fixity—these are on the order of the signified or "meaning." Miles's death illustrates the way "meaning itself thus unavoidably becomes the outcome of an act of violence" (164). While Felman's reading is correct strictly speaking, her analysis elides the historical conditions of possibility that make attractive a drama of knowability and secrecy regarding questions of illicit desire and sexuality. For Felman, the categories of sexuality and desire become oddly unhistorical. In her reading, repression, although an avowedly subtle and complex and *not* literal one, is still the universal constitutive factor in the creation of "sexuality." What we call sexuality, she argues, is what is produced out of the conflict between the libido and its repression. Felman cites Lacan: "all human structures, have as their essence, not as an accident, the restraint of pleasure—of fulfillment" (111). She continues: "It is indeed because sexuality is essentially the violence of its own non-simplicity, of its own inherent 'conflict between two forces,' the violence of its own division and self-contradiction, that it is experienced as anxiety and lived as terror" (111). To assert that sexuality is universally "experienced as anxiety and lived as terror" is to underestimate and undervalue the significance of a whole range of oppressions and violences that are based on sexuality and gender, usually to the benefit of one sexuality and one gender. Felman's approach to sexuality in this reading of James obscures the fact that sexuality functions as a *mechanism* of oppression. More to the point, regarding James, she excludes the possibility that James's evident preoccupation with sexuality might be motivated not by an interest in the universal fact of sexuality's constitution out of repression, but by a fearful interest in a historical drama unfolding before his eyes. Her rigorous disinterest, her position above the fray, seems to me to betray James's most earnest desire to produce interest, but it more seriously fails to take into account the local and historical aspects of a text's ability to affect an audience. We miss the way James had to read into his audience in order to get his audience to read into him.

41. Foucault, *History of Sexuality*, 48.
42. That James's cautionary allegory adheres particularly to the will to know as it concerns men, especially in their relations to other men, would seem to be underscored by the narrative's abandonment of Flora before the final climactic scene. The will to knowledge "dispossesses" Miles, but only makes Flora agitated and feverish. If Miles's demise is an allegory of the violence circulating around the possibility of male homosexuality, then perhaps Flora's illness suggests that the dangers attaching to the lesbian are different ones. The lesbian in the new discourse of sexuality is less likely to be murdered than to be left out of the narrative—invisible, abjected, shunted aside.

4. "What a Mourning"

1. The epigraph is from Du Bois, *Dusk of Dawn: An Essay toward an Autobiography of a Race Concept* (New Brunswick, NJ: Transaction, 1984) (orig. pub. 1968), 94.
2. Ibid., 59.
3. While we may see James's *Turn of the Screw*, as I argued in the previous chapter, for example, as providing an affective map of that structure of feeling called the will to know, it is not clear that readers desired or were able to pick up on the text's potential critical edge regarding the dangers inhering in the powers implicit in that will to know, and the fact that everyone to a certain extent is suffering the subjection and alienations that accompany it. I argue that it affected readers precisely because it was an affective map, but the nascent collective, political energies were not—at least as far we as we know—turned into an actual political movement. Someone else would have had to supply the political program that would make use of James's affective map. One might argue that such a political project has been articulated under the rubric of queer theory.
4. Johnson, *Along This Way* (New York: Viking, 1933), 203. For this citation, and well-known comments by Jessie Fauset, Langston Hughes, Williams James, and others, see Herbert Aptheker, *The Literary Legacy of W. E. B. Du Bois* (White Plains, NY: Kraus International, 1989), esp. 51–73, Johnson citation 72. On *Souls'* influence and reception see also David Levering Lewis, *W. E. B. Du Bois, Biography of a Race 1868–1919* (New York: Holt, 1993), esp. 291–296; Arnold Rampersad, *The Art and Imagination of W. E. B. Du Bois* (New York: Schocken Books, 1976), reprinted as introduction to *The Souls of Black Folk* (New York: Knopf, 1993) (references hereafter to *Souls* are to this edition, parenthetically within the text).
5. Henry Louis Gates Jr., introduction to *The Souls of Black Folk* (New York: Bantam Books, 1989), xxii.
6. Stuart Hall comments on his use of the term (which he borrows from Ernesto Laclau's *Politics and Ideology in Marxist Theory*) in "On Postmodernism and Articulation: An Interview with Stuart Hall," ed. Lawrence Grossberg, in *Stuart Hall: Critical Dialogues in Cultural Studies*, ed. David Morley and Kuan-Hsing Chen (New York: Routledge, 1996). See esp. 141–147. The relevant passages: "In England, the term has a nice double meaning because 'articulate' means to utter, to speak forth, to be articulate. . . . But we also speak of an 'articulated' lorry: a lorry where the front (cab) and back (trailer) can, but need not necessarily, be connected to one another. . . . An articulation is thus the form of the connection that *can* make a unity of two different elements, under certain circumstances" (141). He continues: "It is not the individual elements of a discourse that have political or ideological connotations, it is the way those elements are organized together in a new discursive formation. . . . So it is the articulation, the non-necessary link, between a social force which is making itself, and

the ideology or conceptions of the world which makes intelligible a process they are going through, which begins to bring onto the historical stage a new social position and political position, a new set of social and political subjects" (143–144). See also Jennifer Slack, "The Theory and Method of Articulation in Cultural Studies," in the same volume, 112–127.

7. Although how modest we think this assessment is depends on the meaning and value we give to the word "fugitive." On "fugitivity" see Fred Moten's "Knowledge of Freedom," *CR: The New Centennial Review* 4, no. 2, Fall 2004, 269–310, and "The Case of Blackness," *Criticism* 50, no. 2, Spring 2008.

8. The quotation in the epigraph is reported by Herbert Aptheker in his discussion of the autobiographical character of *Dark Princess,* introduction to *Dark Princess* (Millwood, NY: Kraus-Thomson, 1974), 17n17. Aptheker notes how a lynching in which the wife of the victim was not permitted to look upon the corpse because "he didn't have no face" produces the narrative observation "Something in Matthew died that day." Aptheker then goes on to recount the lynching of Sam Hose and writes in the footnote: "Dr. Du Bois once used these very words—'something died within me that day'—in describing this episode to the present writer." I was alerted to Aptheker's comment by a footnote in Paul Gilroy, *Black Atlantic: Modernity and Double Consciousness* (Cambridge: Harvard University Press, 1993), 240n12.

9. *Dusk of Dawn,* 58.

10. *The Philadelphia Negro* (New York: Schocken Books, 1967) (orig. pub. 1899), emphasized the relationship between the practices of everyday life and long historical processes at work in the African American community, with an eye toward producing the knowledge one would have to have of the African American situation as a totality in order to transform it. For more on *The Philadelphia Negro,* see David Lewis's description of the project in *Biography of a Race,* esp. 179–192; for an account of this book in the context of Du Bois's changing views about "science" and method, see Shamoon Zamir, *Dark Voices: W. E. B. Du Bois and American Thought 1888–1903* (Chicago: University of Chicago Press, 1995), esp. 89–92, and Adolph L. Reed, *W. E. B. Du Bois and American Political Thought; Fabianism and the Color Line* (New York: Oxford University Press, 1997), 27–41.

11. Cited by Du Bois in *Dusk of Dawn,* 63–64.

12. *Dusk of Dawn,* 67; also *The Autobiography* (New York: International, 1967), 221–222.

13. Ida B. Wells, *Lynch Law in Georgia,* chap. 2; Pamphlet, Chicago: This pamphlet circulated by Chicago Colored Citizens, 1899, and can be found at www.memory.loc.gov, and www.afroamhistory.about.com/library.

14. *Dusk of Dawn,* 67; *Autobiography,* 221–222.

15. *Stimmung* and *Gestimmstein* are both from same root, *Stimm,* "tune." See Chapter 3 here for more on Heidegger and *Stimmung.*

16. Heidegger, "Attunements are not *side-effects,* but are something which in advance determine our being with one another. It seems as though an attunement is in each case already there, so to speak, like an atmosphere in which we first immerse ourselves in each case and which then attunes us through and through." *The Fundamental Concepts of Metaphysics: World, Finitude, Solitude,* trans. William McNeill and Nicholas Walker (Bloomington: University of Indiana Press, 1995), 67.

17. Charles Guignon, "Moods in *Being and Time,*" in *What Is an Emotion? Classic Readings in Philosophical Psychology,* ed. Cheshire Calhoun and Robert C. Solomon (New York: Oxford University Press, 1984), 238.

18. This is also repeated without correction by David Levering Lewis in his biography. In fact, I nowhere found mention of Du Bois's alteration of the facts.

19. On the Sam Hose lynching see Philip Dray, *At the Hands of Persons Unknown: The Lynching of Black America* (New York: Modern Library, 2002), 3–16.

20. Jean Laplanche and J. B. Pontalis, *Dictionary of Psychoanalysis* (New York: Norton, 1973), 111.

21. See Du Bois's early Harvard essay "American Girl," in *Against Racism: Unpublished Essays, Papers, Addresses, 1887–1961,* ed. Herbert Aptheker (Amherst: University of Massachusetts Press, 1985), 19–20. Note also a story Du Bois recounts in *The Autobiography:* "On a Nashville street, 71 years ago, I quite accidentally jostled a white woman as I passed. She was not hurt in the slightest, nor even particularly inconvenienced. Immediately in accord with my New England upbringing, I raised my hat and begged her pardon. I acted quite instinctively and with genuine regret for a little mistake. The woman was furious; why I never knew; somehow, I cannot say how, I had transgressed the interracial mores of the South. Was it because I showed no submissiveness? Did I fail to debase myself utterly and eat spiritual dirt? Did I act as an equal among equals? I do not know. I only sensed scorn and hate; the kind of despising which a dog might incur" (121). See also discussion of relation to and incidents with white women in chap. 1 of Manning Marable, *W. E. B. Du Bois, Black Radical Democrat* (Boston: Hall, 1986), 1–20.

22. Du Bois acknowledged in his eulogy for his wife that "something in her died" when their son died. For a reading of this scene, and of *Souls* more generally in the context of nineteenth-century concerns about and theories of sympathy, see Susan Mizruchi, "Neighbors, Strangers, Corpses: Death and Sympathy in the Early Writings of W. E. B. Du Bois," in *Centuries Ends, Narrative Means,* ed. Robert Newman (Stanford: Stanford University Press, 1996), 191–211, reprinted in Du Bois *The Souls of Black Folk,* ed. Henry Louis Gates Jr. and Terri Hume Oliver, Norton critical ed. (New York: Norton, 1999), 272–295, and revised and expanded in Mizruchi, *The Science of Sacrifice: American Literature and Modern Social Theory* (Princeton: Princeton University Press, 1998), 269–366.

23. It is worth remembering here that in *Souls,* Du Bois's narration of the "passing of the first born" serves the specific rhetorical function of dramatizing the persistent threat of despair facing African American persons, showing that Du Bois is familiar with that despair.

24. This acceptance of depression in the instance of his son's death may also help explain why Du Bois appeared to direct his emotional resources toward the death of Hose, as it was a death for which he had found an emotional strategy. Perhaps Du Bois's melancholic recommitment to a new kind of political practice in response to Hose's death is also a way to deal with the loss of his son. Like an open wound, loss held unresolved can draw excess cathectic energy to itself.

25. Cited in Lewis, *Biography,* 226, from Du Bois interview, Columbia University Oral History Project, 146–147.

26. *Dusk of Dawn,* 94.

27. *Being and Time,* trans. John Macquarie and Edward Robinson (San Francisco: Harper and Row, 1962), 178, from the German edition *Sein und Zeit* (Tübingen: Niemeyer, 1979), 138–139.

28. Ibid., 178, German ed. 138.

29. "The Political Uses of Alienation: W. E. B. Du Bois on Politics, Race and Culture, 1903–1940," *American Quarterly* 42, no. 2 (June 1990): 303.

30. Benjamin, "Eduard Fuchs, Collector and Historian," in *Walter Benjamin: Selected Writings,* vol. 3 (Cambridge: Harvard University Press, 2002) (hereafter SW3), 267.

31. Nahum Chandler, "Between," *Assemblage* 20 (1994): 26–27.

32. Langston Hughes, "Border Line" in *Selected Poems of Langston Hughes* (New York: Knopf, 1959), 81.

33. See Eve Sedgwick on this: "It is the interlocutor who has or pretends to have the less broadly knowledgeable understanding of interpretive practice who will define the terms of the exchange" (*Epistemology of the Closet,* 4).

34. This is one of several comments on sympathy in the book. See also for example: "the future of the south depends on the ability of the representatives of these opposing views to see and appreciate and sympathize with each others position" (*Souls,* 148). Also: "The nineteenth was the first century of human sympathy,—the age when half wonderingly we began to descry in others that transfigured spark of divinity which we call Myself; when clodhoppers and peasants, and tramps and thieves, and millionaires and—sometimes—Negroes, became throbbing souls whose warm pulsing life touched us so nearly that we have cried with surprise, crying, 'Thou Too! Hast thou seen sorrow and the dull waters of hopelessness? Has Thou known life?' And then all helplessly we peered into those Other worlds, and wailed, 'O World of Worlds. How shall man make you one?'" (172). Here, as elsewhere, Du Bois sees the experience of sorrow and hopelessness, depression itself, as a significant point of sympathy across the color line.

35. See Chandler on the problem in Du Bois in *The Problem of the Negro as Problem for Thought* (forthcoming), esp. chap. 1, "Of Exorbitance: The

Problem of the Negro as a Problem for Thought." Also see Chandler, "The Economy of Desedimentation: W. E. B. Du Bois and the Discourses of the Negro," *Callaloo* 19, no. 1 (1996): 78–93.

36. The idea of sympathy in nineteenth-century literature and philosophy is a large area of scholarly interest. For the classic positions on *Uncle Tom's Cabin,* see Ann Douglas in *The Feminization of American Culture* (New York: Knopf, 1977), and Jane Tompkins, "Sentimental Power: *Uncle Tom's Cabin* and the politics of Literary History," in *Sensational Designs: The Cultural Work of American Fiction, 1790–1860* (New York: Oxford University Press, 1985), 122–146. Also James Baldwin, "Everybody's Protest Novel," in *The Price of the Ticket* (New York: St. Martin's Press, 1985). On sympathy in Du Bois, in addition to Mizruchi see Zamir on sympathy, *Dark Voices,* esp. pp. 42–45, and Robert Gooding-Williams, "Du Bois's Counter-Sublime," *Massachusetts Review* 35, no. 2 (Summer 1994): 202–224, reprinted in *Souls,* Gates and Oliver ed., 245–262, in which, in my estimation, the strongest case is made for the centrality of sympathy to Du Bois's project in *Souls.*

37. Jean-Luc Nancy, *Being Singular Plural,* trans. Robert D. Richardson and Anne E. O'Byrne (Stanford, CA: Stanford University Press, 2000), xiii.

38. On the autobiographical in Du Bois see Nahum Chandler, "The Figure of the X: An Elaboration of the Du Boisian Autobiographical Example," in *Displacement, Diaspora and Geographies of Identity,* ed. Smadar Lavie and Ted Swedenburg (Durham, NC: Duke University Press, 1996), 235–272.

39. In an unpublished paper, Robert Gooding-Williams cites, on this practice of card exchange, Mrs. Longstreet, *Good Form: Cards, Their Significance, and Proper Uses* (New York, 1889). A brief search on eBay revealed that Victorian calling cards such as the ones Du Bois probably purchased are frequently referred to as "gorgeous," suggesting that this word was part of the original marketing discourse surrounding the cards.

40. The connotative field outlined by the word "peremptorily" deserves brief commentary here, as the word bears a great deal of significatory weight in Du Bois's description. From the Latin "perimere," which means "to take away or cut off," or "to destroy," it made its way into English via Roman jurisprudence, where it indicated *putting an end to* or *final,* as in "peremptory decree," *Oxford English Dictionary.* These violent, legal associations linger in Du Bois's use, where an imperious and dictatorial manner is conveyed, as well as (as one dictionary has it) an "offensive self-assurance" (*American Heritage Dictionary*).

41. On the picturesque in *Souls* see Sheila Lloyd, "Du Bois and the Production of the Racial Picturesque," in *100 Years of the Souls of Black Folk: A Celebration of W. E. B. Du Bois,* ed. Robert Gooding-Williams and Dwight A. McBride, special issue, *Public Culture* 17, no. 2 (Spring 2005): 277–297.

42. See Zamir, *Dark Voices,* 113–168, esp. 116–117, 153–155: Reed, *Du Bois,* esp. 91–125; Dickson Bruce, "W. E. B. Du Bois and the Idea of Double Consciousness," *American Literature* 64, no. 2 (June 1992): 299–309,

reprinted in *Souls*, Gates and Oliver ed., 236–244 (parenthetical page references to this essay hereafter are to this reprint).

43. Reed is most explicit in this sense, writing: "I argue that Du Bois's double consciousness was embedded most significantly in the neo-Lamarckian thinking about race, evolution and social hierarchy that prevailed in a strain of reform-oriented, fin-de-siecle American social science. To that extent, I demonstrate that, in appropriating the notion, sundry intellectuals misread Du Bois ahistorically and instead project their own thinking on him" (*Du Bois*, 91–92). While Reed is quite helpful, not only in making a compelling connection to that social scientific context but also in tracing out a history of varied readings of double consciousness, my point, contra Reed, is that what is most interesting and indeed politically effective about the notion of double consciousness is its multivalence, its demand to be read into, and that moreover, this is not an accidental element of Du Bois's textual practice but indeed a central component of his rhetorical strategy to "use and make mood."

44. A brief look at some of the criticism gives us a feel for the varied investments in readings of *Souls*. Zamir, for example, claims that "the account of double consciousness in the first chapter of *Souls* represents the black middle class elite facing the failure of its own progressive ideals in the late nineteenth century" (*Dark Voices*, 116). Dickson Bruce, alternately, writes that "although in the essay Du Bois used double consciousness to refer to at least three different issues—including first the real power of white stereotypes in black life and thought and second the double consciousness created by the practical racism that excluded every black American from the mainstream of the society, the double consciousness of being both an American and not an American—by double consciousness Du Bois referred most importantly to an internal conflict in the African American individual between what was 'African' and what was 'American.'" ("Du Bois," 238). Gilroy, moving in yet another direction, avers that while "double consciousness was initially used to convey the special difficulties arising from a black internalization of an American identity," he wishes to "suggest that Du Bois produced this concept at the junction point of his philosophical and psychological interests not just to express the distinctive standpoint of black Americans but also to illuminate the experience of post-slave populations in general. Beyond this, he uses it to animate a dream of global cooperation among peoples of color which came to full fruition only in his later work" (*Black Atlantic*, 126).

45. Thus, where Reed differentiates the psychological from the historical, asserting that "James saw the divided self as alternately a psycho-physiological and a spiritual or mystical phenomenon; for Du Bois the idea was sociological and historical" (*Du Bois*, 105), I am interested precisely in the connection between the psychological and the historical/sociological that double consciousness facilitates.

46. Hegel is also a relevant point of comparison here. In making the connection between a social relation and the internal "warring" he calls double consciousness, Du Bois echoes, as Shamoon Zamir has shown, the moment in Hegel's *Phenomenology* when the master-slave dialectic is internalized as unhappy consciousness, also figured as an experience of division (*Dark Voices*, 114). "In using Hegel as a resource," Zamir writes, "Du Bois neither psychologizes history nor reproduces a progressive and optimistic teleology of enlightenment. He moves instead toward a complex historicization of psychology" (115). I basically agree with Zamir here, and my concern is precisely this historicization of psychology, which, however, Zamir does not fully develop. But the conflict that Du Bois internalizes here is different from and more specific than the master-slave dialectic; that is, Du Bois experiences a rejection, one redolent with particular social and affective significances. As I am suggesting, if we see double consciousness as the internalization of a severed emotional tie, then another parallel emerges, and that is the one with Freud's theory of melancholia, itself also a response to and revision of the master-slave dialectic.

47. This special agency Freud first refers to as the "ego ideal," later the "super-ego." While the distinction is never definitively resolved by Freud, the ego ideal suggests a model to be copied, whereas with the term *super-ego*, the critical, judging function is emphasized. See Laplanche and Pontalis, entries in *Dictionary*, for helpful glosses and relevant references.

48. Freud, *Group Psychology and the Analysis of the Ego*, trans. and ed. James Strachey (New York: Norton, 1959), 52.

49. Freud, "Mourning and Melancholia," *The Standard Edition of the Complete Psychological Works of Sigmund Freud*, 14, trans. and ed. James Strachey (London: Hogarth Press, 1957), 248.

50. Freud noted that in that kind of situation the ego ideal serves a kind of compensatory function, taking into the ego ideal all the demands or qualities the environment makes of the ego that the ego cannot live up to. "When he cannot be satisfied with his ego itself, he may nevertheless be able to find satisfaction in the ego ideal which has been differentiated out of the ego" (*Group Psychology*, 52).

51. Richard Wright, "The Psychological Reactions of Oppressed People," in *White Man, Listen!* (New York: HarperCollins, 1995), cited in Gilroy, *Black Atlantic*, (161).

52. On this, see especially *Group Psychology*.

53. Lacan, *Four Fundamental Concepts of Psycho-Analysis*, ed. Jacques-Alain Miller, trans. Alan Sheridan (New York: Norton, 1977), 106.

54. Thus Lacan's many versions of "I am unable to see myself from the place where the other is looking at me" (*Four*, 167). The gaze has a "pulsatile, dazzling and spread out function" (89).

55. Lacan argues that the fact of our visibility, the gaze, how we imagine ourselves being seen, is always in relation to a felt lack, a desire to be seen in a

totalizing, complete way: as "really me." In the mirror the child sees a whole body, a gestalt that seems coherent, and that the child identifies with. But we are never as whole as our bodily outline might suggest, and the desire for a coherent, unified self remains a fantasy, which is never fulfilled but which we persistently seek in the look of the other. "The identity that seems to be that of the subject is in fact a mirage arising when the subject forms an image of itself by identifying with others' perception of it" (Juliet Mitchell, introduction to *Feminine Sexuality: Jacques Lacan and the école freudienne*, ed. Juliet Mitchell and Jacqueline Rose, trans. Jacqueline Rose, 5).

56. Also: "the waste of double aims, this seeking to satisfy two unreconciled ideals, has wrought sad havoc with the courage and faith and deeds of ten thousand thousand people,—has sent them often wooing false gods and invoking false means of salvation, and at times has even seemed about to make them ashamed of themselves" (*Souls*, 10).

57. In *Shame and Its Sisters: A Silvan Tomkins Reader*, ed. Eve Kosofsky Sedgwick and Adam Frank (Durham, NC: Duke University Press, 1995), 133.

58. Tomkins, *Affect, Imagery, Consciousness* (New York: Springer, 1991), 3:325.

59. See discussion of affect in Freud in Chapter 1.

60. Tomkins: "This is because the contempt of the other constitutes a total rejection. When the other shows contempt, there is a presumption that the self which so offends the other is disgusting and should be just as disgusting to the one who offends as to the other" (in *Shame and Its Sisters*, 158).

61. Tomkins writes: "As soon as the infant learns to differentiate the face of the mother from the face of a stranger (approximately seven months) he is vulnerable to the shame response" (ibid., 140). Shame emerges as a response to an interruption of this most vital relationship, at the same time that it serves as a way to withdraw from interaction with a stranger, communicating nonetheless the desire for relationality with someone familiar. Michael Franz Basch adds: "shame-humiliation throughout life can be thought of as an inability to effectively arouse the other person's positive reactions to one's communications. The exquisite painfulness of that reaction in later life harks back to the earliest period when such a condition is not simply uncomfortable but threatens life itself." "The Concept of Affect: A Re-Examination," *Journal of the American Psychoanalytic Association* 24 (1976): 765–766, cited in Eve Sedgwick, "Shame, Theatricality and Queer Performativity: Henry James's *Art of the Novel*" (Durham, NC: Duke University Press, 2003), in *Touching Feeling: Affect, Pedagogy, Performativity* 37–8.

62. *Shame and Its Sisters*, 137.

63. Sedgwick "Shame," 36.

64. Shame operates, as Tomkins writes, "ordinarily only after interest or enjoyment has been activated, and inhibits one of the other or both" (*Shame and Its Sisters*, 134).

65. Tomkins: "Insofar as one responds to the contempt of the other with shame, one has not entirely accepted the disgust of the other. . . . Contempt . . . is a powerful instrument of discrimination and segregation. By

means of contempt, the other can be kept in his place. If however, the response to contempt is shame, this characteristic consequence of distancing is much attenuated" (*Shame*, 158). Also: "in a democratically organized society . . . when one man expresses contempt for another, the other is more likely to experience shame than self-contempt insofar as the democratic ideal has been internalized. This is because he assumes that ultimately he will wish to commune with this one who is expressing contempt and that this wish is mutual" (139).

66. Darwin, for example, writing about shame and the blush, in *Expression of the Emotions in Man and Animals* (New York: Philosophical Library) (orig. pub. 1872), cites a comparison between the blush and the veil: "According to Macrobius, who lived in the fifth century ('Saturnalia' B. vii. c. 11), 'Natural philosophers assert that nature being moved by shame spreads the blood before herself as a veil, as we see anyone blushing puts his hands before his face'" (321–322).

67. Lacan, *Four*, 112.

68. Later in "Of the Training of Black Men," Du Bois thematizes this history, referring ironically to freed slaves as "the things themselves" (*Souls*, 74), and, commenting on capital's ready rhyme with a racist logic after slavery had been abolished: "the tendency is here, born of slavery and quickened to renewed life by the crazy imperialism of the day, to regard human beings as among the material resources of a land to be trained with an eye single to future dividends" (77).

69. One can see such cards quickly through a Google image search, or a search on eBay, as many of these now "collectible" cards are for sale as souvenirs.

70. Adrian Piper has brilliantly reread and transformed the visiting card, creating her own "calling card" to be given out at social events. Reproduced in Piper, *Out of Order, Out of Sight* (Cambridge: MIT Press, 1999), 1: 220. Text as follows:

> Dear Friend,
>
> I am black.
>
> I am sure you did not realize this when you made/laughed at/agreed with that racist remark. In the past, I have attempted to alert white people to my racial identity in advance. Unfortunately, this invariably causes them to react to me as pushy, manipulative, or socially inappropriate. Therefore, my policy is to assume that white people do not make these remarks, even when they believe that there are no black people present, and to distribute this card when they do.
>
> I regret any discomfort my presence is causing you, just as I am sure you regret the discomfort your racism is causing me.
>
> Sincerely yours,
> *Adrian Margaret Smith Piper*

71. See Michael Warner, "The Mass Public and the Mass Subject," in *The Phantom Public Sphere*, ed. Bruce Robbins (Minneapolis: University of Minnesota Press, 1993), 252.

72. As Lauren Berlant put it, "the power to suppress the body, to cover its tracks and its traces, is the sign of real authority." "National Brands/National Bodies: *Imitation of Life*," in Robbins, *Phantom*, 176.

73. I am borrowing here from my essay "Warhol Gives Good Face: Prosopopoiea and the Politics of Publicity," in *Pop Out: Queer Warhol* (Durham, NC: Duke University Press, 1996), 105. The relevant passage there reads: "The disembodied public self is attractive for what it enables one to see that one is not: to be public is to transcend particularity, embodiment and domesticity, the spaces where the disenfranchised have historically been made to dwell. For those who have not been able to transcend their specific corporeality in the abstract realm of citizen, their hyperembodiment serves as a continual obstacle to power and pleasure." See also Warner, "Mass Public," 239.

74. This second self, a public self, is, both prosthetic—an extension of one's self—and prophylactic—it can stand in for you, and to a certain extent protect you. A public self can be criticized, attacked, say, in the press, while a "private" self remains behind a veil, as it were.

75. "The Fact of Blackness," in *Black Skin, White Masks* (New York: Grove Press, 1967), 109.

76. It is important to note here that this is particularly or only true for the African American subject who wishes to gain access to the privileges available in the white world, or, more precisely, who wishes to succeed in a sphere so far prohibited to black persons—as an intellectual who might publish and get a job teaching philosophy in a university, for example, or a writer, a doctor, or other professional. The subjects of Zora Neale Hurston's Eatonville, Florida, for example, do not really seek such recognition, nor are they especially aware of the white world.

77. Ellison, *Invisible Man* (New York: Signet, 1947), 438.

78. De Certeau, *The Practice of Everyday Life* (Berkeley: University of California Press, 1984), 37.

79. Du Bois, *Darkwater: Voices from Within the Veil* (New York: Schocken, 1969) (first published 1920), 29.

80. As the editors of one edition of *Souls* tell us, "in African American folklore, seventh sons as well as those children born with a caul, a membrane that sometimes covers the head at birth, are reported to have special abilities, such as predicting the future and seeing ghosts" (*Souls*, Gates and Oliver ed., 10).

81. *In the Break: The Aesthetics of the Black Radical Tradition* (Minneapolis: University of Minnesota Press, 2003), 1.

82. Regarding this aspect of Du Bois's argument, Zamir's argument is in some ways at its most persuasive. Zamir notes how for Hegel national culture, *Sittlichkeit,* is the only way to respond to the unhappy consciousness. Although here, too, the specificity of how culture functions for Du Bois, and

235 · Notes to Pages 132–133 · 235

how it functions in relation to a very specific historical situation, reverses in some ways the Hegelian program.

83. As I discuss in the next section, the songs are, first of all, based in African American experience, not only in the sense that they are "the articulate message of the slave to the world" but also in the way that, in the age of postwar neoslavery, they articulate the ghostly survival of that past in the present. Furthermore, they do this work of articulation by appropriating and intensifying elements of the African musical tradition. Finally, although white people are sometimes deeply affected by hearing the songs, and while they *should* respect the songs, more often than not this music "has been neglected, it has been, and is, half despised, and above all it has been persistently mistaken and misunderstood" (*Souls*, 198). This music is a culture not only made within the veil but also mostly experienced there.

84. Posnock, *Color and Culture: Black Writers and the Making of the Modern Intellectual* (Cambridge: Harvard University Press, 1998), 10 and elsewhere. See also Eric Sundquist, who asserts that "without question, Du Bois sought an ideal of culture beyond the color line." *To Wake the Nations* (Cambridge: Harvard University Press, 1993), 468.

85. Sundquist: "As it enacts the theory of double consciousness, the code of the spirituals epitomizes the paradox upon which Du Bois founded his career— that cultures could be learned, shared, and made universal, but that the hierarchy of racism left the dominant culture ignorant of the singular spiritual heritage that the institution of slavery had embedded within its own nation" (ibid., 538). I would add to Sundquist's observation that the paradox is not only that racism left the dominant culture ignorant of the sorrow songs but that the sorrow songs themselves only came into being *because* of racism. Their origin lies in slavery. The two cannot be separated. Their end can only be understood as participation in the kingdom of culture if that culture itself were to be radically transformed.

86. Raymond Williams, *Keywords* (New York: Oxford University Press, 1976).

87. "Criteria of Negro Art" (1926), reprinted in *W. E. B. Du Bois: A Reader*, ed. David Levering Lewis (New York: Holt, 1995), 514, 515. Du Bois's strategy is one that with remarkable consistency had been obligatory for the African American cultural worker since Phillis Wheatley. The achievements of black persons must bear the burden of representing "the race," demonstrating that black people are equal in intelligence (and thus in humanness) to white people.

88. In the paralipomena to "On the Concept of History," Benjamin writes: "the existence of the classless society cannot be thought at the same time that the struggle for it is thought," in *Walter Benjamin: Selected Writings*, vol. 4 (Cambridge: Harvard University Press, 2003), (hereafter SW4), 407.

89. Although even here, I would add, the ideal is complicated by Du Bois's suggestion that America might be better of if it *replaced* "her vulgar music with the soul of the Sorrow Songs." If this is the kind of cowork Du Bois has in mind, all the better, but the replacement of (bad) white culture with (much

better) black seems not to be a transcendence of the veil but the destruction of it.

90. Marcuse, "The Affirmative Character of Culture," in *Negations: Essays in Critical Theory* with translations from German by Jeremy J. Shapiro (Boston: Beacon Press, 1968), 120.

91. Ibid., 118–119.

92. Ibid., 109.

93. *Lohengrin,* one of the most frequently performed operas of the late nineteenth and early twentieth centuries, was first performed in 1850; its first performance at the Metropolitan Opera was in 1883.

94. Anne E. Carroll, "Du Bois and Art Theory: *The Souls of Black Folk* as a 'Total Work of Art,'" argues that Wagner's ideal of the *Gesamtkunstwerk,* or "total work of art" serves as a model for Du Bois's *Souls of Black Folk;* in Gooding-Williams and McBride, "100 Years," 235–254. It will become clear how and why I disagree with this argument.

95. In his "Queering the Souls of Black Folk," Charles I. Nero emphasizes the importance of this moment, along with John's earlier citation of Queen Esther ("If I perish, I perish") in an interesting reading of "Of the Coming of John" as a drama of homosocial desire and homosexual panic. In Gooding-Williams and McBride, "100 Years," 255–276.

96. A reading along such lines is suggested, for example, by Houston Baker, *Long Black Song* (Charlottesville, Virginia: University of Virginia Press, 1990) and Eric Sundquist, *To Wake,* 522–524.

97. In making this case, I am in sharp disagreement with Russell A. Berman's reading of the story in "Du Bois and Wagner: Race, Nation, and Culture between the United States and Germany," *German Quarterly* 70, no. 2 (Spring 1997): 123–135. Berman essentially argues that the story is pro-Wagnerian, indeed a rewriting in many ways of *Lohengrin,* and that "Wagner and Lohengrin stand in as a site of a life without prejudice" (128). Berman goes so far as to assert that "it would be too facile" to see the juxtaposition of lynching and Wagner's music as a moment of critique. "There is," he avers, "no textual evidence that Du Bois might be distancing himself from the music."

98. Theodor W. Adorno and Max Horkheimer, "The Concept of Enlightenment," in *The Dialectic of Enlightenment,* trans. Edmund Jephcott, ed. Gunzelin Schmid Noerr (Stanford: Stanford University Press, 2002), 25.

99. Ibid., 26.

100. Ibid.; here I borrow the translation from Fredric Jameson, *Late Marxism: Adorno, or, The Persistence of the Dialectic* (New York: Verso, 1990) 129–130.

101. Ibid.

102. Adorno and Horkheimer, "The Concept," Jephcott trans., 25.

103. The epigraph to this section is from William Francis Allen, Charles Pickard Ware, and Lucy McKim Garrison, *Slave Songs of the United States* (1867; reprint, Bedford, MA: Applewood Books, n.d.), iv.

104. Sundquist, *To Wake*, 533.

105. In the most sustained engagement with the implications of the musical epigraphs for a reading of *Souls*, Sundquist has argued that Du Bois's epigraphs serve the function that epigraphs often do: they offer a commentary on the text. In the case of *Souls*, this commentary is "half-veiled," not immediately apparent to the reader. One would have to know music, and know the songs, so as to recover the words, and to have a sense of what those songs signified in other contexts in order to bring them into antiphonic conversation with the chapters themselves. Sundquist writes: "Hidden within the veil of black life, the music and words of the sorrow songs form a hidden, coded, language in *The Souls of Black Folk*, one that recapitulates the original cultural function of the spirituals themselves. In a more comprehensive sense, therefore, the music functions antiphonally with respect to Du Bois's written text, such that one must hear sounds that are not on the page" (ibid., 470).

106. See, for example, comments made by William Francis Allen: "The voices of the colored people have a peculiar quality that nothing can imitate; and the intonations and delicate variations of even one singer cannot be reproduced on paper. And I despair of conveying any notion of the effect of a number singing together" (in Allen, Ware, and Garrison, *Slave Songs*, iv). He later cites now famous comments by his collaborator Miss McKim: "It is difficult to express the entire character of these Negro ballads by mere musical notes and signs. The odd turns made in the throat, and the curious rhythmic effect produced by single voices chiming in at different irregular intervals, seem almost as impossible to place on the score as the singing of birds or the tones of an Aeolian Harp." Among many others, see also: James Weldon Johnson, preface to *The Book of American Negro Spirituals* (New York: Viking Press, 1925), esp. 30; Zora Neal Hurston's famous inveighing against the transcribed spirituals in "Spirituals and Neo-Spirituals," in *The Negro*, ed. Nancy Cunard (New York: Continuum International Publishing Group, 1996). For a consideration of the social and ideological circumstances of the northern U.S. interest in the songs and their transcription see Ronald Radano, "Magical Writing: The Iconic Wonders of the Slave Spiritual" in *Lying Up a Nation: Race and Black Music* (Chicago: University of Chicago Press, 2003), 164–229.

107. Gerard Genette, *Paratexts: Thresholds of Interpretation*, trans. Jane E. Lewin (Cambridge, UK: Cambridge University Press, 1997), 1.

108. Ibid.

109. Stepto, *From Behind the Veil: A Study of Afro-American Narrative*, 2nd ed. (Urbana: University of Illinois Press, 1991). See especially chap. 1, "I Rose and Found My Voice: Narration, Authentication, and Authorial Control in Four Slave Narratives," 3–31, on the authenticating framing device written by white persons. See chap 3 on Du Bois's use of framing devices. Also see Brent Edwards, *The Practice of Diaspora: Literature, Translation, and the*

Rise of Black Internationalism (Cambridge: Harvard University Press, 2003), 38–40, on politics and poetics of framing "blackness" in African American texts, Du Bois in particular.

110. One can find a facsimile of Wheatley's first book of poetry, published in 1773, on several websites, including http://darkwing.uoregon.edu/~rbear/wheatley.html. On Wheatley in particular see H. L. Gates, "Writing 'Race' and the Difference It Makes," in *"Race," Writing and Difference*, ed. Gates (Chicago: University of Chicago Press, 1986).

111. Thus, for example, Frederick Douglass's *Narrative* contains a "Preface" by William Lloyd Garrison, a "Letter from Wendell Phillips, Esq.," and a short "Appendix" by Douglass himself, clarifying certain remarks he makes criticizing slave religion.

112. On this, see Alan Durant: "Notation marks an ordering of bodily movements of musical performance in addition to immediate verbal directives, and provided historically the possibility for pieces of music of a specialized, if restricted, kind of permanence." *Conditions of Music* (Albany: State University of New York Press, 1984), 98, cited by Alexander Weheliye in "The Grooves of Temporality" in Gooding-Williams and McBride, "100 Years," 319–338), 320.

113. Weheliye (in ibid.) pursues a reading of *Souls* along such lines, provocatively examining Du Bois's "mixology" of various kinds of texts, arguing that this mix produces a "phono-graph" that echoes the sounds of the songs, even if, or inasmuch as, it cannot itself *be* sound. Weheliye makes use of Benjamin's essay "On the Concept of History" to read Du Bois's fragmented text in a fashion with which I am in great sympathy, as will become clear.

114. For this photo, see David Levering Lewis and Deborah Willis, *A Small Nation of People: W. E. B. Du Bois and African American Portraits of Progress* (Washington, DC: HarperCollins, 2003), frontispiece.

115. Jon Cruz, *Culture on the Margins: The Black Spiritual and the Rise of American Cultural Interpretation* (New York: Princeton University Press, 1999). Cruz helpfully details the context in which the songs were transcribed, and the use to which they were put, arguing that they were used toward the project of producing "ethnosympathy" for African Americans, a task that was especially important to the abolitionist project. This seems helpful and right, especially regarding the aims of the early transcribers, and their semianthropological sense of their project. However, the argument underplays the multiple uses the songs were put to, not just as sources of knowledge but as sources of pleasure, for example, or as I have suggested, as a site for feelings of opposition, dissatisfaction, and struggle to reside.

116. See note 103 here; Higginson, *Army Life in a Black Regiment* (New York: Norton Press, 1984).

117. Mrs. M. F. Armstrong, Helen W. Ludlow, and Tomas P. Fenner, *Hampton and Its Students, With Fifty Cabin and Plantation Songs* (New York: Put-

nam's, 1874). *The Story of the Jubilee Singers with Their Songs*, ed. J. B. T. Marsh (Boston: Houghton Mifflin, 1880).

118. See Sundquist, *To Wake*, 492. Paul Gilroy makes the interesting suggestion that the "unusual combination of communicative modes and genres" we see in the Hampton and Fisk songbooks "is especially important for anyone seeking to locate the origins of the polyphonic montage technique developed by Du Bois in *The Souls of Black Folk*" (*Black Atlantic*, 89).

119. About this, James Weldon Johnson writes: "These songs passed through a period when the front ranks of the Negro race would have been willing to let them die. Immediately following Emancipation those ranks revolted against everything connected with slavery, and among those things were the Spirituals. It became a sign of not being progressive or educated to sing them." (preface, *Spirituals*), 49.

120. See Ronald Radano, *Lying Up a Nation*, esp. "Magical Writing," 164–229, on transcription and transcribability.

121. Benjamin, "On the Concept of History," 391.

122. On this, see Moten, *In the Break*, in particular 1–14.

123. The epigraph from Benjamin is in "On the Concept of History," 390.

124. In a suggestive parallel, Charles Baudelaire made a similar observation after hearing Wagner, in 1860. "At first it seemed to me that I knew this music already, and later, in thinking it over, I understood what had caused this illusion. It seemed to me that the music was my own, and I recognized it as any man recognizes those things he is destined to love." *Selected Letters of Charles Baudelaire*, trans. and ed. Rosemary Lloyd (Chicago: University of Chicago Press, 1986), 145–146, cited in Philippe Lacoue-Labarthe, *Musica Ficta (Figures of Wagner)*, trans. Felicia McCarren (Stanford: Stanford University Press, 1994), 2.

125. See Sundquist on this, *To Wake*, 465–466.

126. Levine, *Black Culture and Black Consciousness* (New York: Oxford University Press, 1977), 6. On West African origins of African American music see also Johnson, preface, *Spirituals;* John Lovell Jr., *Black Song: The Forge and the Flame, The Story of How the Afro-American Spiritual Was Hammered Out* (New York: Paragon House, 1972), esp. 24–70; Eileen Southern, *The Music of Black Americans, A History* (New York: Norton, 1971), esp. 3–24.

127. Levine, *Black Culture*, 6 and 20.

128. And although he notes that "he knows little of music and can say nothing in technical phrase," he makes the direct connection between a song such as "You may bury me in the east" and "do bana coba."

129. Sundquist, *To Wake*, 528.

130. Steven Feld suggests that this is true of music more generally. "The significant feature of musical communication is not that it is untranslatable and irreducible to the verbal mode but that its generality and multiplicity of possible messages and interpretations brings out a special kind of 'feeling-

ful' activity and engagement on the part of the listener, a form of pleasure that unites the material and mental dimensions of music experienced as fully embodied." "Communication, Music, and Speech about Music," in *Music Grooves,* ed. Charles Keil and Steven Feld (Chicago: University of Chicago Press, 1994), 91, cited by Radano, *Lying Up a Nation,* 22. Along similar lines, Mladen Dolar argues that singing is "bad communication," preventing a clear understanding of the text, which is precisely why it is such a rich site for imaginative reading in. *The Voice and Nothing More* (Cambridge: MIT Press, 2006), 30.

131. Derrida, *Specters of Marx* (New York: Routledge, 1994), xix.

132. See Johnson, *Along This Way,* 203; and Sundquist, *To Wake,* esp. 470, on black middle-class refusal to sing the sorrow songs (he cites Newman White), and 560, on Crummell's arguments for leaving the slave past behind and instead going back to Africa for a usable past. The key difference with Crummell concerns the place of slave culture. Where Crummell wishes to leave the past behind, Du Bois, quite clearly, wishes to base a model of African American culture in the culture of slavery. I agree with Sundquist's observation that it is not the actual content of Crummell's thinking that is important to Du Bois, and also with Robert Gooding-Williams ("Du Bois's Counter-Sublime"), who reads Du Bois's rhetorical strategy in relation to Crummell as a "masterpiece of indirection," at once appropriating and replacing key elements of Crummell's thinking. My only addition to this scholarship would be the observation that Du Bois also admires Crummell's skill, resourcefulness, and tenacity in avoiding despair. Du Bois sees in Crummell someone else for whom mood was central to any consideration of African American political resistance and survival.

133. Douglass: "every tone was a testimony against slavery, and a prayer to God for deliverance from chains." *Narrative of the Life of Frederick Douglass, An American Slave* (New York: Penguin Books, 1982), 58.

134. Claims for the beauty of the songs and their collective nature are likewise shared. In addition, Douglass discusses their capacity for expressing the dehumanizing nature of slavery and soliciting sympathy, not only from whites but from himself, as a free man.

135. Douglass, *Narrative,* 57.

136. Ibid., 57.

137. Ibid., 58.

138. The influence of this view extended far beyond Douglass; see for example, Levine, *Black Culture,* esp. 5–19.

139. Frank Kirkland, "Modernity and Intellectual Life in Black," *Philosophical Forum* 34, nos. 1–3 (1992–1993), 140. Kirkland also reads Du Bois in relation to Benjamin's ideas about melancholia and allegory, citing *The Origin of German Tragic Drama.*

140. This is in some ways analogous to the way Baudelaire presents what just happened as if it were antiquity. See Benjamin section of Chapter 1 here.

141. Benjamin, "On the Concept of History."

142. Benjamin, "N [On the Theory of Knowledge, Theory of Progress]," in *The Arcades Project*, trans. Howard Eiland and Kevin McLaughlin (Cambridge, Harvard University Press, 1999), 479.

143. The full last sentence of King's speech reads: "When we let freedom ring, when we let it ring from every village and every hamlet, from every state and every city, we will be able to speed up that day when all of God's children, black men and white men, Jews and Gentiles, Protestants and Catholics, will be able to join hands and sing in the words of the old Negro spiritual, 'Free at last! free at last! thank God Almighty, we are free at last!'"

144. "N," 479.

145. Levine, among others, also emphasizes the flexible, mobile nature of the songs.

146. Jackson also writes: "The 'Freedom Songs' began back during the Montogomery boycott when the Negroes began singing in the churches to keep up their courage. . . . Using songs as a way of expressing protest and gaining strength and hope runs way back deep in the American Negro's past. When the colored slaves on the plantations sang, 'Steal Away to Jesus, I ain't got long to stay here,' they weren't talking just about Heaven; they were expressing their secret hope that they, too, would have their chance to escape up North to freedom." *Movin' on Up* (1968), excerpted in *Readings in Black American Music*, ed. Eileen Southern (New York: Norton, 1971), 266. Most famous of these songs of course was "We Shall Overcome," composed later than but based on slave songs.

147. Also see Zamir on the mobility and openness of the songs. I am borrowing from Benjamin's "The Storyteller" here. He argues that the trace of the storyteller clings to the story "the way the handprints of the potter cling to the clay vessel." "The Storyteller: Observations on the Works of Nikolai Leskov," in SW3, 149.

148. Benjamin, "On Some Motifs in Baudelaire," in SW4, 316. For Benjamin, the past is never solely our own anyway: "what has been forgotten . . . is never something purely individual," he remarks in another context. "Franz Kafka," in *Walter Benjamin: Selected Writings*, vol. 2 (Cambridge: Harvard University Press, 1999), 809.

149. This is the function Benjamin suggested "the story" once served, and he argues that the novel arises in part in order to internalize this relational memento mori function as the storyteller disappears into the historical past.

150. Gilroy also emphasizes this distinction, writing that "the moment of jubilee . . . has the upper hand over the pursuit of utopia by rational means" (*Black Atlantic*, 68).

151. The unexpectedness of this moment of future revolution is foreseen in Du Bois's experience of the songs. Just as "concerning the *memoire involontaire* . . . its images [are ones] we have never seen before we remember them" (Benjamin, "A Short Speech on Proust," 1932; not available in English, cited in Miriam Hansen "Benjamin, Cinema and Experience: The Blue Flower in the Land of Technology," New German *Critique* 40, Winter

1987, 179) so too we can say that the paradoxality of Du Bois's encounter with the sorrow songs is that he has recognized something he never heard before. He has awakened to something completely new to him, something that discloses a world, which is at the same time a spectral return of the past.

152. See Derrida, *Specters of Marx*, 65.

153. As Moten writes, "if the sensual dominant of the performance is aural (if you're at home, in your room, with the recording), then the visual emerges as that which is given its fullest possibility by the aural" (*In the Break*, 172).

5. Andrei Platonov's Revolutionary Melancholia

1. Translations are my own unless otherwise noted. I have learned from and drawn on Anthony Olcott's translation (*Chevengur* [Ann Arbor, MI: Ardis, 1978]), and Robert Chandler's translation of sections of *Chevengur*, in *Glas: New Russian Writing*, ed. Natasha Perova and Joanne Turnbull, vol. 20, *The Portable Platonov* (Moscow: Glas, n.d.). Gene Kuperman's translation of small sections of *Chevengur* has also proved a valuable reference, in Valery Podoroga, "The Eunuch of the Soul: Positions of Reading and the World of Platonov," trans. Gene Kuperman, South Atlantic Quarterly 90, no. 2 (1991): 357–408. Hereafter I give page references in the text to the Olcott English version and the Russian: *Chevengur: Roman i Pov'esti* (Moscow: Sovetskii Pisatel', 1989) (the epigraph is from 96/109).

2. While each of these terms has a very differently suggestive meaning in Russian, as in English, I would not say that Platonov obeys a consistent rule in distinguishing the two, though he does not entirely collapse them either. For example, the same relationships are alternatively described as *druzhba* (friendship) and then *tovarishchestvo* (comradeship). Platonov appears to be suggesting the ways the new official discourse of *tovarishchestvo* clears an institutional space for *druzhba*, and at the same time expands the affective force and complexity of *tovarishchestvo*.

3. A tradition going back at least to Robert Burton's *Anatomy of Melancholia*, which, we may recall, contained the first utopia to be written in English. Also see Wolf Lepenies, *Melancholy and Society*, trans. Jeremy Gaines and Doris Jones (Cambridge: Harvard University Press, 1992), on the relationship between utopia and melancholy.

4. On Platonov's life see Mikhail Geller, *Andrei Platonov v Poiskakh Schast'ya* [Andrei Platonov in the Pursuit of Happiness] (Moscow: MIK, 1999), which is of the "life and works" genre and remains the most thorough book-length study of Platonov. The only such study in English is Thomas Seifrid, *Andrei Platonov: Uncertainties of Spirit* (Cambridge, UK: Cambridge University Press, 1992); see 1–32 for a helpful introduction to Platonov's work, and 99–131 for a reading of *Chevengur* in particular. For an excellent general introduction to Platonov, see Tony Wood, "Annals of Utopia," *New Left Review* 33 (May–June 2005): 118–132. Other general

considerations of Platonov include Joseph Brodsky, "Catastrophes in Air," and Tatyana Tolstaya, "Andrei Platonov's Unusual World," in *Pushkin's Children: Writings on Russia and Russians* (New York: Houghton Mifflin, 2003), 218–226.

5. *Portable Platonov,* 11.

6. Vladimir Nabokov, *Eugene Onegin, a Novel in Verse,* vol. 2, Alexander Pushkin, trans. Vladimir Nabokov (Princeton, NJ: Princeton University Press, 1991), 141. On the use of the word *toska* in the 1930s, see Sheila Fitzpatrick, "Happiness and *Toska:* An Essay in the History of Emotions in Pre-war Soviet Russia," *Australian Journal of Politics and History* 50, no. 3 (2004): 357–371.

7. Related is Benjamin's use of the verb *grübeln,* to brood, and *Grübler,* the brooder. On Benjamin's use of this word see Max Pensky, *Melancholy Dialectics: Walter Benjamin and the Play of Mourning* (Amherst: University of Massachusetts Press, 1993).

8. See my Introduction here.

9. On Fyodorov's influence on Platonov see: Ayleen Teskey, *Platonov and Fyodorov: The Influence of Christian Philosophy on a Soviet Writer* (Amersham, UK: Avebury, 1982); Geller, *Platonov,* 28–53; Seifrid, *Platonov,* 20–24; David M. Bethea, "Chevengur: On the Road with the Bolshevik Utopia," in *The Shape of Apocalypse in Modern Russian Fiction* (Princeton, NJ: Princeton University Press, 1989), 145–185. Elena Tolstaia-Segal, "Ideologicheskie Konteksty Platonova" (1982), reprinted in *Andrei Platonov: Mir Tvorchestva* (Moscow: Sovremenyi Pisatel', 1994), 47–83, considers other influences, including Bogdanov, Proletcult, and the Futurists. For relevant discussion of Fyodorov in particular see Irene Masing-Delic, *Abolishing Death: A Salvation Myth of Twentieth-Century Russian Literature* (Stanford: Stanford University Press, 1992), 76–104, and Eliot Borenstein, *Men without Women: Masculinity and Revolution in Russian Fiction 1917–1929* (Durham, NC: Duke University Press, 2000), 26–28. On Fyodorov see Svetlana Semyonova, *Nikolai Fyodorov: Tvorchestvo Zhizni* (Moscow: Sovetskii Pisatel', 1990), and Gacheva and Semyonova, eds., *H. F. Fyodorov: Pro e contra* (Saint Petersburg: Izdatel'stvo Russkogo Khristianskogo Gumanitarnogo Instituta, 2004).

10. Fyodorov was praised, for example, by, among others, Leo Tolstoy and Konstantin Tsiolkovsky, the founder of Soviet rocket science.

11. "The mass of mankind will be transformed from a crowd, a jostling and struggling throng, into a harmonious power when the rural mass of common people [*narod*] become a union of sons for the resurrection of their fathers, when they become a relatedness, 'a psychocracy.'" From *Philosophy of the Common Task,* "The Question of Brotherhood or Relatedness and of the Reasons for the Unbrotherly, Dis-Related or Unpeaceful State of the World, and of the Means for the Restoration of Relatedness," trans. Ashleigh E. Moorhouse and George L. Kline, excerpted in *Russian Philosophy,*

vol. 3 (Chicago: Quadrangle Books, 1965), 26, in Russian, *N. F. Fyodorov, Sobranie Sochineniy V Chetyryokh Tomakh*, vol. 1 (Moscow: Izdatel'skaya Gruppa "Progress," 1995), 44 (page references to both editions hereafter).

12. See Borenstein in particular on the patriarchal nature of Fyodorov's vision.

13. "The question of the force which compels the two sexes to unite in one flesh as a transition to the being of a third by means of childbearing is the question of death: a man's exclusive adherence to his wife forces him to forget his forefathers and brings political and civil enmity into the world" (Fyodorov, *Philosophy of the Common Task*, 24/43).

14. Other relevant aspects of Fyodorov's project include the critique of progress: "Progress," Fyodorov writes, "consists in the sense of superiority, first, of a whole generation (the living) over their forefathers (the dead), and second, of the younger over the older generation" (37/51); and the emphasis on the importance of emotion: "Knowledge deprived of feeling will be knowledge only of causes in general, and not the study of the causes of disrelatedness . . . disrelatedness is a consequence of the lack of feeling, a forgetting of the fathers, a falling out of the sons. But as soon as the intellect arrives at feeling there is remembrance of the dead fathers (in museums), together with the union of the sons with those dead fathers and of the fathers who are still living (the religious community) for the education of their sons (the school)" (28/45).

15. This is because, to begin with, the English version of *Chevengur* has been out of print for several years. But even in Russian the novel was not published in the Soviet Union until 1988. The book was censored on the very eve of its publication in 1929. Not until the mid-1930s, after the standardization of socialist realism as a doctrine, did Platonov gain reentry into the publishing world, mainly with rather modest and realistic portraits of Soviet life. On the novel's nonpublication and the exchange with Gorky afterward, see Geller, *Platonov*, 180–187.

16. Seifrid, *Platonov*, 100.

17. Geller suggests that *Chevengur* is what Mikhail Bakhtin calls a "mennipean satire," the "universal genre of final questions. Actions in it occur not just 'here' and 'now,' but in the whole world and in eternity: on earth, the underworld, and the heavens" (*Platonov*, 189). On plot and temporality in *Chevengur* see 188–189 and 187–254. Also see Bethea, *The Shape of Apocalypse*, 34–46, 145–185; Angela Livingstone, "Time in *Chevengur*," *Slavonic and East European Review* 82, no. 4 (October 2004): 801–819, esp. 816–819; Hallie A. White, "Time out of Line: Sequence and Plot in Platonov's *Chevengur*," *Slavic and East European Journal* 42, no. 19 (Spring 1998): 102–117; Thomas Seifrid, "Forms of Belatedness in Platonov's Prose," in "A Hundred Years of Andrei Platonov," ed. Angela Livingstone, special issue, *Poetics: The Journal of the British Neo-formalist Circle* 26 (autumn 2001): 38–48. White's essay includes a helpful chart of events in the novel as they occur in chronological time (and which events are too temporally vague to be included) as compared to their appearance in the narrative.

18. Lukacs makes the case for a realism in which a social system and its key class positions are mapped out in several places. See in particular the essays in *Realism in Our Time: Literature and the Class Struggle* (New York: Harper and Row, 1964).

19. For a careful close reading of this paragraph as exemplary of Platonov's stylistic particularities, see Angela Livingstone, "Danger and Deliverance: Reading Andrei Platonov," *Slavic and East European Review*, 80, no. 3 (July 2002): 401–416.

20. Often the word *izdeliye* is used alongside the word for the thing it was made out of ("made of leather"), or by what means it was made ("handmade" or "factory made"). The two examples in the Ozhyogov Russian dictionary are "product of hand-made *izdeliye*" and "repair of metal *izdeliye*." In other words, the word itself contains the suggestion of a relationship between the object and a process. It is not the word used to describe a work of art (this is *proizvedenie*).

21. Changing the human relation to the object world was of course a major concern and area of debate in the early Soviet period. On Rodchenko's notion of the "object as comrade" see Christina Kaier, *Imagine No Possessions* (Cambridge: MIT Press, 2006). A more thorough inquiry here would also consider the long philosophical tradition concerned with making and madeness, in particular around the concept of praxis in Hegel, Marx, Sartre, and others.

22. Derrida, *Specters of Marx*, trans. Peggy Kamuf (New York: Routledge, 1994), 65.

23. On this: "Zakhar Pavlovich's *toska* was stronger than his awareness of the uselessness of labor and he continued to cut stakes until full nocturnal exhaustion. Without a craft [*remesla*], Zakhar Pavlovich's blood flowed from his hands to into his head, and he began to think so deeply about everything at once that only nonsense came out, while in his heart arose a melancholy fear [*toskliviy strakh*]. . . . He was tortured by various kinds of feelings that never appeared when he worked" (11/14–15).

24. Podoroga, "Eunuch," 361. On Platonov's "style" see also Fredric Jameson on Platonov's peculiar irony, in "Utopia, Modernism and Death," in *Seeds of Time* (New York: Columbia University Press, 1994), 88–92, 113–122.

25. Podoroga, "Eunuch," 360.

26. On this, Adorno: "Artworks are alive in that they speak in a fashion that is denied to natural objects and the subjects who make them. They speak by virtue of the communication of everything particular in them. Thus they come into contact with the arbitrariness of what simply exists. Yet it is precisely as artifacts, as products of social labor, that they also communicate with the empirical experience that they reject and from which they draw their content." *Aesthetic Theory*, trans. Robert Hullot-Kentor (Minneapolis: University of Minnesota Press, 1997), 5.

27. The idea, as Michel Blanchot eloquently puts it, is that "if someone becomes his own master even in death, master of himself through death, he

will be master also of that omnipotence which makes it felt by us through death, and he will reduce it to a dead impotence. Kirilov's suicide thus becomes the death of God. Hence his strange conviction that this suicide will inaugurate a new era, that it will mark the turning point in the history of humanity, and that, precisely, after him men will no longer need to kill themselves. His death, by making death possible, will have liberated life and rendered it wholly human. "The Work and Death's Space," in *The Space of Literature* (Lincoln: University of Nebraska Press, 1982), 97.

28. Ibid., 103.

29. Derrida, *The Politics of Friendship*, trans. George Collins (New York: Verso, 1997), 288.

30. The epigraph to this section is from *Walter Benjamin: Selected Writings*, vol. 2 (Cambridge: Harvard University Press, 1999) (hereafter SW2), 694.

31. Jean Luc Nancy (*The Inoperative Community*, trans. Peter Connor, Lisa Garbons, Michael Holland and Simona Sawnhey (Minneapolis: University of Minnesota Press, 1991), 33.

32. Daniel Stern, *The Interpersonal World of the Infant: A View from Psychoanalysis and Developmental Psychology* (New York: Basic Books, 1985), 138.

33. Ibid., 139.

34. Ibid., 141.

35. Ibid., 156.

36. The Russian *skuchat'* can indicate not only boredom in the English sense but also feeling depressed or, as in *skuchat' po komu-to*, missing someone.

37. Derrida, *Memoires for Paul de Man* (New York: Columbia University Press, 1988), 33.

38. Ibid., 29.

39. Podoroga, "Eunuch," 362.

40. Fredric Jameson makes this point in "Utopia, Modernism and Death," 97.

41. More specifically, the word is used to describe the state of obliviousness or forgetfulness that we all are in in relation to our ancestors: we have forgotten them, we ignore them, and in this sense it is as if we are all in a state of sleepwalking insofar as we do not pay attention to this basic reality, that is, not just human mortality, but the death of our parents, and their parents before them, as the very origins and condition of possibility of our own existence.

42. This is a long list, but, see, for example, Derrida on Rousseau, ". . . That Dangerous . . . Supplement," in *Of Grammatology*, trans. Gayatri Spivak (Baltimore: Johns Hopkins University Press, 1974), or Benjamin, "The Storyteller: Observations on the Works of Nikolai Leskov," in *Walter Benjamin: Selected Writings*, vol. 3 (Cambridge: Harvard University Press, 2002), 143–166.

43. From the well-known definition of "structure of feeling," Raymond Williams, *Marxism and Literature* (New York: Oxford University Press, 1977). See Glossary.

44. Podoroga, "Eunuch," 361.

45. On the *skoptsy,* see Laura Engelstein, "From Heresy to Harm: Self-Castrators in the Civic Discourse of Late Czarist Russia," in *Empire and Society: New Approaches to Russian History,* ed. Tereyuki Hara and Kimitaka Matsuzato (Sapporo: Slavic Research Center, November 2005), 1–22. See also Eric Naiman, "The Discourse of Castration," in *Sex in Public: The Incarnation of Early Soviet Ideology* (Princeton: Princeton University Press, 1997), 124–147; and on desire in Platonov more specifically, Naiman, "Andrej Platonov and the Inadmissibility of Desire," *Russian Literature* 23 (1988): 319–367.

46. Another notable moment would be the one where Chepurny lies down to sleep for the night with a traveling blacksmith, who accuses him of being an "activist" in bed (198–199/220–221). See *Men without Women,* Borenstein, 231–232.

47. Paramanov, "Chevengur I okrestnosti," *Kontinent* 54 (1987): 333–375, cited in Borenstein, *Men without Women,* 236 (his italics).

48. Igor Kon, *The Sexual Revolution in Russia: From the Age of the Czars to Today,* trans. James Riordan (New York: Free Press, 1995), 51.

49. Cited by Naiman, *Sex in Public,* 130.

50. Even if, as Laura Engelstein argues, there is something of a pre-Soviet development of institutional discourses of sexuality: *The Keys to Happiness: Sex and the Search for Modernity in Fin-de-Siècle Russia* (Princeton: Princeton University Press, 1992).

51. Lenin, for example, in his famous discussions with Klara Zetkin, argued that Freudian theories of sexuality "arise from the personal need to justify personal abnormality or hypertrophy in sexual life before bourgeois morality." *Reminiscences of Lenin, Dealing with Lenin's Views on the Position of Women and Other Questions* (London: Modern Books, 1929), 52.

52. Seeing a landscape where "poor people lived alone and without movement, dying like firewood set upon the bonfire," Dvanov remarks "There you go—the raw material of socialism! . . . Not even a single building, just the *toska* of nature—orphans!" (121/135). Or, when a local party official sends Dvanov off to look for socialism in the countryside, the official seems to think that "probably the poor had already gathered together on its own accord and organized itself according to socialism," since ". . . they don't have any protection, except for comradeship" (63/73).

53. Benjamin, "Doctrine of Similarity," 695.

54. Ibid., 698.

55. Paolo Virno, *Grammar of the Multitude* (New York: Semiotext(e), 2004), 21. See also Michael Hardt and Antonio Negri, *Empire* (Cambridge: Harvard University Press, 2000), and Hardt and Negri, *Multitude: War and Democracy in the Age* (New York: Penguin Empire Press, 2004). Virno has proposed the "multitude" as a way to conceptualize the forms of collectivity that have arisen in our post-Fordist moment. He finds the multitude a useful concept because it moves beyond the opposition between the "indi-

vidual" and "the people," indicating a potentially agential political grouping in which members retain their singularity but which also does not become fused into a singular "people."

56. See Benjamin, "Unpacking My Library," in SW2, 486–493.
57. See Aristotle on friendship and use in *Nicomachean Ethics,* trans. J. A. K. Thomson (New York: Penguin, 1956), 262, 265. He also notes the necessity for similarity between friends, 267, 272.
58. "Friendship as a Way of Life," in *Foucault Live!* trans. John Johnston (New York: Semiotext(e), 1989), 205.

Acknowledgments

No doubt, in the very long time it has taken me to write it, this book has been the object of my own melancholic clinging. One of the primary pleasures this has afforded me is the number of teachers, colleagues, and friends I have been able to engage in its name.

I have all along been quite lucky in the area of teachers, nowhere more than in graduate school in the Program in Literature at Duke University, where many of the ideas and arguments herein found their origin. My dissertation committee offered an embarrassing wealth of assistance, encouragement, and counsel. I owe a great deal to the friendly and generous support of Fredric Jameson, whose voracious interest in everything, keen and attentive guidance, and general good mood provided what I found to be an exceptionally generative context in which to think and work. Eve Kosofsky Sedgwick's intellectual courage and audacity, the sheer force of her powerful mind, and her relentless insistence against moralizing was a frequent inspiration for me. Before anyone else she understood the interest of this book project, and the knowledge of her support sustained me through many moments of doubt. Conversations with Jan Radway changed my thinking about relationality and the emotional tie in ways that have affected the tone and trajectory of this book's arguments in basic ways. She was also a stunningly helpful reader of chapters; her gift for lucidity remains a model for me to this day. Nahum Chandler, who came to my committee toward the end of my graduate career, offered an intellectual hospitality without rival; many a conversation with Nahum left a deep impression on my thinking, not least the one in which he encouraged me to write about Du Bois. Thomas Lahusen never had a doubt about the interest of *toska* or of Platonov and I am grateful for his advice and assistance.

A few other teachers deserve mention here. At Duke, Michael Moon's brilliant teaching, helpful counsel, and frequently hilarious conversation was a regular aid. I also learned a great deal from Naomi Schor, whose engagement on the theme of melancholia and aesthetics were a welcome boost. Earlier, at Amherst College, Tom Dumm, Nathaniel Berman, and most of all Dana Villa stimulated and sustained my intellect with great generosity and care.

Nobody has taught me more about how to think and be in the world than my graduate school colleagues and friends. Brian Selsky, whom we all miss greatly, showed me many things about teaching and thinking, and few did more to create an intellectual community during my time in Durham. From the very beginning, José Estéban Muñoz was a great friend, sharing his considerable knowledge and intelligence with great charity; he continues to teach me a great deal about the nature of friendship, and the complex interwinings of emotional, intellectual, and political commitments. Mandy Berry's charisma, humor, and camaraderie was a frequent inspiration; few understood the usefulness of antidepressive aesthetic practices better than she. I remember many a meal with Katie Kent, whose warm conversation, humor, and acuity was an indispensable resource. Any number of discussions (on topics ranging from Hegel to gardening) with Marcus Embry, whose friendship has been a revelation of generosity, remain fundamental touchstones for me. I was sustained as well by Eleanor Kaufman's idiosyncratic ways and regularly surprising insights and intellect, and the numerous kindnesses she has directed my way. Jennifer Doyle was a frequent first reader of essays and early audience for much of my writing, and I benefited greatly from her critical attention and smart advice. Gus Stadler offered a sympathetic understanding of the emotional power of aesthetic experience and much else besides. Thomas Sherratt's lessons in antidepressive living are still with me. I am thankful also for Mary Moessinger's kindnesses and guidance, Gene Kuperman's brilliance and intense conversation, Hank Okazaki's enthusiasm and encyclopedic televisual and filmic knowledge, the erudition of Joe Karaganis and his willingness to argue and debate, Kate Baldwin's encouragement around our common interest in the relationships between the African American and Russian literary-cultural traditions, and Xudong Zhang's shared concern with alternative modernities.

Time spent in Moscow since my first trip there in 1988 has affected my thinking fundamentally in a number of ways. It has been a site for research and a place where one could see history unfolding in surprisingly and instructively dramatic fashion. Most significant, however, are the friends there who have nourished and inspired me intellectually and emotionally with extraordinary kindness and generosity. Lena Petrovskaya read several different drafts of various chapters, and offered persistent, exacting, enthusiastic, and enabling feedback and encouragement, as well as sage advice. Conversations with Sasha Ivanov about *toska*, Benjamin, and Moscow and much else have affected my thinking about just about everything. I do not know if I have ever met anyone smarter than Oleg Aronson, and I only hope that little bits of his intelligence have rubbed off on me from time to time; conversations with Oleg are frequently revelatory. Valery Podoroga's thinking in several arenas and the example and the originality of his thought have been crucial reference points. I am also grateful for the abundance of concrete advice and insight he has offered over the years, as well as the bounty of his hospitality. Conversations about affect and Benjamin and Russia with Susan Buck-Morss, at least one of them in Moscow, were also important to my thinking about this book.

The University of Virginia proved to be a fine place to think and get work done, and I profited from the intelligence of my colleagues and students there. The friendship of Tan Lin was essential to surviving Charlottesville, and he has continued to be my most reliable adviser on aesthetic matters of many sorts. Eric Lott has been a kind and incisive reader of parts of the book and an indispensably willing ear for complaints and conspirings of all kinds. Conversations about modernism with Howard Singerman while coteaching, and after, were energizing and transformative; many thanks to him also for his comments on different parts of the book. Susan Fraiman has been a sharp, lucid, sensitive reader and a good friend. Ted Siedlecki offered valuable counsel and encouragement at several key moments. Tom Scanlan, Tejumola Olaniyan, Deborah McDowell, Marion Rust, Frannie Nudelman, and Rita Felski also offered valuable feedback, advice, and support.

I also benefited from exchanges with students, including Sarah Blackwell, Matt Chayt, Joon Lee, James Mulholland, Brad Rogers, Kristin Romberg, and Matt Sandler. Conversations with and feedback and support from Heather K. Love and Ben Lee affected my thinking and writing most directly.

At Wayne State University I have found a superbly supportive intellectual environment. One could not imagine a more helpful or intellectually engaged chair than Richard Grusin, whose counsel has aided me on a number of occasions and whose conversation is a frequent source of pleasure and stimulation. Kathryne Lindberg's humor, intellect, and erudition have been a regular and incomparable resource, her aesthetic enthusiasms a delight; her comments on the Du Bois chapter in particular were enormously helpful. I am grateful too for Donna Landry's engaged and energizing feedback, for her willingness to become interested in Platonov, and for her and Gerald MacLean's various hospitalities and kindnesses. The presence of Cannon Schmitt and Dana Seitler, while it lasted, was a boon; they each read parts of the manuscript and gave useful feedback. Sarika Chandra has been a regular adviser on matters intellectual and pedagogical; she is a great colleague and even better friend. In Barrett Watten I have found an enthusiastic interlocutor on a number of issues central to the book. Steven Shaviro, Sheila Lloyd, Carla Harryman, Robert Aguirre, Ross Pudaloff and Ken Jackson have also been sources of friendly encouragement and collegial good will. Charles Kronengold generously read the Du Bois chapter and offered crucial advice and encouragement. He and Carol Vernallis made Detroit a much more interesting and hospitable place than it otherwise would have been. I have been fortunate enough here to also benefit from the presence of a smart and engaged group of graduate students, including Kristine Danielson, Ryan Dillaha, Sarah Ruddy, Michael Schmidt, and Joel Shapiro. Special thanks to Michael Schmidt for his help with the book's indexing.

Sabbatical leaves from the University of Virginia and Wayne State provided me with essential time in which to write, as did a Wayne State University Research Grant and a Humanities Center Grant. Thanks also to Hilary Ratner, the Vice President for Research, and Robert Thomas, Dean of the College of Liberal Arts and Sciences, at Wayne State University, for help financing the preparation of the index.

Earlier versions of portions of the present work appeared as follows: "Reading into Henry James," *Criticism* 46, no. 1, published by Wayne State University Press; and "Moscow and Melancholia," *Social Text* 66 (Spring 2001), published by Duke University Press. Thanks to the original publishers of these two articles.

In addition to those already mentioned, several friends deserve special thanks. Over the last several years, Douglas Crimp's emotional, intellectual, and professional support and generosity have lifted and supported me time and again. I have profited a great deal from his positively beneficent presence, his aesthetic companionship, and the example of his scholarship and friendship both. The company of Phil Harper has provided any number of pleasures over the years; his advice has been invaluable, his intellectual engagement a gift. I have no kinder audience, no more rewarding interlocutor than Nicholas Baume, and he has provided enthusiastic encouragement and a sympathetic ear at many crucial moments. The most regular and essential assistance has been provided by Danielle Aubert, whose desire for the completion of this book likely exceeded my own, and whose company played a central role in keeping me sane while that completion occurred.

Of course, it all begins with one's family, and I feel quite lucky to have been encouraged and advised and pushed and supported in so many ways by mine. Marcia Dean has offered a boundless source of encouragement, understanding, counsel, and comfort, as well as, on occasion, crucial financial assistance. Joe Flatley has helped materially as well, in more ways than one, and his attention, conversation, and companionship have provided a precious and sustaining pleasure. My brother, Jason Flatley, my first and most fundamental ally, has inspired me in more ways than he knows. Despite—or because of—their differences from each other and from myself, Marcia, Joe, and Jason have shaped my concerns and interests in foundational ways. My grandparents, Agnes Flatley, whose absence is felt most acutely, and Andy and Betty Holmes, provided vital support at various stages in this book's composition.

At Harvard University Press, kind anonymous readers gave helpful advice and encouragement. Phoebe Kosman has been a patient and attentive shepherd of the manuscript through its various stages. Thanks also to Tonnya Norwood for her expert management of the book's production process. At the Press, I owe the most gratitude to Lindsay Waters, who has been a remarkably smart, supportive, understanding editor. Long and exciting conversations with Lindsay about affect, aesthetics, and Walter Benjamin gave me the very valuable feeling that the book had as its destination an understanding reader. I consider his publication of the works of Walter Benjamin to be an intellectual event of the highest value, and I am delighted that this book is coming into the world by way of his stewardship.

Index

Abraham, Karl, 43, 211n57
Abraham, Nicholas T., and Maria Torok, 210n54
Acedia, 1, 35–36, 70–72, 193, 215n2, 217n116
Adorno, Theodor, 8, 135, 166, 207n19, 245n26; on "aesthetic shudder," 8, 80–84, 166, 219n13; and Horkheimer on culture, 86, 140; on subjectivity, 220n15
Aesthetic experience, 18, 136, 138, 149; and affective mapping, 6–7, 80–84; as mood, 24; Adorno on, 80–84; and historicity, 81–84; solicited by Platonov, 169, 179–185
Aesthetic practice, 2, 3, 5, 19, 43, 90, 149, 219n9; affective mapping as, 4–8, 80–84, 92, 189; and melancholia, 4–10, 24, 33, 36, 38, 41, 107, 169–171, 173; and mood, 5, 23–24, 27; as self-estrangement, 6, 24, 80–84, 92, 189; as anti-depressive, 41; James and transference, 90–93. *See also* Adorno, Theodor; *Izdeliye*; Marcuse, Herbert
Affect: Nietzsche on, 3; and modernism, 4; and history, 4, 81; definition of, 11–19; Aristotle on, 12; as distinct from drives, 12; relational aspects, 12, 15–19, 56, 175–176, 202–203n23; autonomy of, 12–13; as distinct from emotion, 12–16, 199n3; Tomkins on, 12–16, 201n14; cognitive approach, 13–14, 200–201n9; universality of, 14–15, 201n16; and

cybernetics, 15–16; materiality of, 16–19; Benjamin on, 17–19, 68–75; in Marxism, 27; and Freud, 50–64; in psychoanalysis, 50–64; and transference, 55–64, 89; and mimesis, 52–56, 62; and temporality, 54, 60, 73. *See also* Emotion; Mood; Structure of feeling
Affective mapping: definition, 2, 4–8, 76–84; and collectivity, 4, 79, 90, 92, 106; as aesthetic practice, 4–7, 80–84, 92, 189; as anti-depressive, 4–6, 106; self-estrangement in, 6–7, 80, 83; and cognitive mapping, 8, 76–77; and political agency, 78–79; historicity, 84, 105–106; and reading in, 103–104; as term in geography and political science, 219n11. *See also* Aesthetic practice
Agamben, Giorgio, 210n54
Ahmed, Sara, 198n1, 200n2
Alienation, 6, 36, 37, 67–68, 76, 115, 122–126, 137, 139, 161, 165, 166, 188, 197n16, 225n3. *See also* Self-estrangement
Allegory, 2, 6, 7, 37, 38, 65, 67, 83, 102, 118, 123, 128, 135, 166, 177, 181, 189, 213n73, 215n101, 240n139; ending of *The Turn of the Screw* as, 7, 102, 224n22; and melancholia, 37, 38, 65, 67; sorrow songs and, 147, and Platonov's characters, 163, 172, 178. *See also* Benjamin, Walter

Harvard University Press is a member of Green Press Initiative (greenpressinitiative.org), a nonprofit organization working to help publishers and printers increase their use of recycled paper and decrease their use of fiber derived from endangered forests. This book was printed on 100% recycled paper containing 50% post-consumer waste and processed chlorine free.